Welcome to this collection of essential reads for the modern lawyer – a collection of 24 articles curated from the first 30 issues of Globe Law and Business' law firm management journal.

Modern Lawyer is known for helping professionals navigate the changing legal services landscape, featuring insights from in-house counsel, legal tech specialists, lawyers, law firms, and business leaders, who all bring a fresh perspective to legal services delivery.

Essential Reads for the Modern Lawyer draws on the journal's wealth of opinion pieces, interviews, and thought leadership, which together comprise an invaluable and wide-ranging analysis of the topics that really matter to those working throughout the legal ecosystem. The book is divided into six key areas:

- Leadership;
- Culture, diversity, and ESG;
- Talent;
- Business development;
- Finance; and
- Technology.

Readers may be struck by the evolving nature of the journal as they dip into the book, and notice how the design and format has changed since the first issue back in 2017. What hasn't changed is the deep insight and reflection that has gone into every single article, making them all just as relevant today as they were when first hot off the press. As such, the pieces are presented unchanged, with the caveat that each article is of its time.

Bringing together the journal's most popular and impactful articles, this collection is valuable to any professional working in legal services looking to develop their career. We hope you enjoy these essential reads.

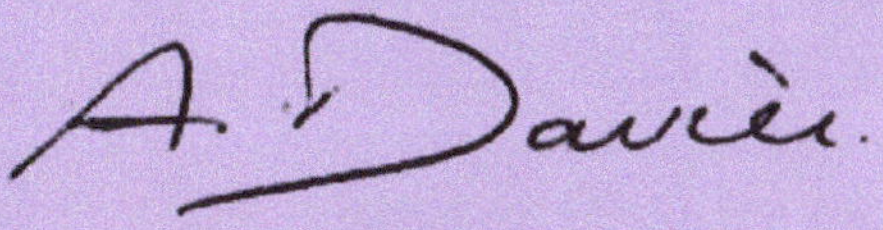

Alex Davies
Editor, Modern Lawyer

Contents

Leadership

Finding a new way through difficult conversations

Alison Nolan

No one enjoys being the bearer of bad news. Alison Nolan explains how to give difficult feedback the right way to foster stronger working relationships.

"We need to talk." Why does that statement cause such a frisson when we hear it? What do we mean by "having a difficult conversation"? We can probably all think of a conversation we know we need to have, but we would really rather avoid. Maybe it's a conversation in which we have a high stake, and we fear we will not be in control of the outcome. Or we are assuming that we know what the other person will think or say in reply – and it's not good!

Typical examples in law firms might include:

- someone's behaviour or performance is not meeting expectations;
- you need to give a client bad news;
- there is deep disagreement among a group who need to make a joint decision;
- you need to get a colleague, over whom you have no authority, to do something they do not want to do.

What do all these have in common? Most difficult conversations are simply those where we expect others to disagree, and do not have the authority or power to ensure we get the outcome we want. What are we assuming that makes us expect the conversations to be difficult? There may be many assumptions:

- we may get angry or upset;
- the other person may get angry or upset;
- our request may be denied;
- we may not be understood;
- we may make ourselves vulnerable;
- we may make matters worse;
- we may be proved wrong.

The list is probably endless, and there is usually some negative emotion attached to these assumptions – fear, anger, shame. And our discomfort with these emotions can make us abandon all the good communication skills we know how to practise when things are going well: listening, open-mindedness, curiosity, respect, ease, humour, tolerance, encouragement, even love. So why would we let the best principles of conversation go, just when we need them most?

Advice about difficult conversations tends to be rather formulaic, prescriptive, even controlling or manipulative. There is a clear end in sight and the framework or model is designed to manhandle the other person to your end. They can seem like a lifeline in treacherous waters – and there are some, such as the BEERS model, which can certainly help us navigate through the difficulties of giving critical feedback (see table on the following page).

But I would like to explore a different approach, based on the work of Nancy Kline, who has developed the concept of the Thinking Environment.[1] Creating a 'thinking environment' means that we establish and sustain the conditions that enable people to think well for themselves, in any situation. This is incredibly important when we are in conflict, and opposite to what we so often try to do, which is to shut down the thinking of the person we see as our 'opponent'. In working life, where relationships are paramount and need to be maintained, there is no genuinely good outcome to this. As Nancy Kline writes, in the context of conflict mediation: "Thinking is not the first word that comes to mind when you consider conflict. Thinking usually, in fact, makes a quick exit when battles begin."[2]

How to prepare for a difficult conversation

Before we take a look at how the Thinking Environment can help support good outcomes in difficult situations, it's worth looking at the role of Emotional Intelligence for leaders. A prerequisite of a successful outcome in a difficult conversation is to ask ourselves some honest questions about our purpose for the conversation, and to be prepared to do some work on ourselves before we

Behaviour	Describe the action or behaviour (eg, Last week I heard you tell an associate that it wasn't that important to get her timesheets in on time) Avoid commenting on aspects of personality or making judgments (eg, you are constantly undermining my authority with the associates)
Effect	What happened, or is likely to happen, as a result? (eg, As a result, she has spread this around the rest of the team, and I am now having to chase them to get their timesheets in, so we can bill the client)
Expectation	What do you want the other person to do, or stop doing? (eg, As a fellow partner, I need you to support me in my management role, including making sure we stick to basic business disciplines)
Result	Make the consequences clear (eg, If you do, we will all earn more respect from the associates, and our group figures will be in much better shape. If you don't, it will make us all look disorganised, and undermine the team)
Solution	Ask for the other person's views (eg, What do you think?) This question forms a great segue into establishing a thinking environment to support dialogue and come to a mutual solution that is more than just grudging compliance.

tackle it. Sometimes in difficult conversations we actually want to cut off the real independent thinking of the other, because we fear it will not be in our best interest. We enter the conversation already in battle dress.

So what are some good and not so good purposes for a difficult conversation?

Good purposes

- understand why something is happening, or not happening;
- improve performance or working relationships;
- help move towards an existing agreed goal;
- reach a new agreed goal.

Not so good purposes

- prove myself right;
- coerce another to change or to do what I want;
- make myself feel better;
- discharge my negative feelings.

Some of Daniel Goleman components of emotional intelligence are particularly helpful here when thinking about how to prepare for a difficult conversation.[3]

Self-awareness

- Take time to sit down and feel what you are feeling about the situation, and about the conversation. Recognise and acknowledge how you feel.
- Work out for yourself how you might be contributing to the situation. Accurate self-assessment and openness to feedback are key here.

Self-management

- Be prepared to manage your own difficult emotions or impulses – to talk about how you feel, without acting it out.
- Use whatever works for you to connect you with your values and integrity.
- Mindfulness practice can help ground you in who you are and where you are.
- Be willing to admit your own mistakes.

Social awareness

Practising empathy as part of your everyday leadership forms the basis for being able to empathise even when things get tough. Forming the habit of looking at everyday situations from other perspectives helps develop an increasing ability to deal with complexity, ambiguity and conflict. Ask and listen every day.

Exploring assumptions

I would add one more crucial preparation before you go into a difficult conversation (adapted from the Thinking Session® by Nancy Kline). That is to ask yourself the question: What am I assuming that is making me think this is going to be a difficult conversation? Take your time with this, as there may be more than one answer. So each time you come up with an answer, ask yourself: What else am I assuming that is making me think this is going to be difficult? Continue asking the question until you really have run out of answers. And finally ask: Of all these assumptions, and any others that spring to mind, what is most making me think this is going to be difficult? And is it true?

Of course it may be true. A simple example would be – I'm assuming that when I give this feedback to James, he will not recognise it. This could be true, in which case you might ask yourself: And what am I assuming that causes that to make me think this is going to be difficult? If you keep going on this track, you are likely to find an untrue limiting assumption that is making you think the conversation will be difficult. You then have a choice – what could you assume instead that would change the situation for you?

This kind of question is a powerful tool for loosening the hold of assumptions we make that we may not be aware of and that limit us. A very effective question to ask yourself in those situations where you persistently do not have the conversation you need to have is: What am I assuming that is stopping me having this conversation?

You can take yourself through this process by spending 10 minutes in a quiet place with a pen and a piece of paper. Even more effective is to have someone else ask you the question – a coach or a trusted colleague – who will commit to listening to you and giving you full attention while you think for yourself, without interruption, comment or giving advice. They are your assumptions, and only you will know what they are.

Case study: Difficult feedback

Sylvie's world view

It's 6:00pm and Sylvie is expecting her recently recruited associate, Simon, to get back from Dubai at any moment – the last leg of his journey home following a two-week project in Indonesia. She knows she has a difficult conversation ahead of her and is feeling uncomfortable. Yesterday, Sylvie met with the client, who had some feedback about Simon. The client was already quite short-tempered about a bill that had turned out to be higher than expected, and Sylvie had had to use all her skills to manage the client's annoyance and come to an agreement about the bill. Towards the end of the meeting, the client let Sylvie know that Simon was getting a reputation for being over-legalistic in his advice and they suspected he was taking more time than was warranted on some aspects of the deal, just to exercise his legal muscle. Added to that, a client meeting that had been scheduled for next week was now brought forward to tomorrow, and the client wants assurance that Simon will not use that occasion to go into unnecessary legal detail.

As Sylvie waits for Simon, she reflects on how to handle the conversation with him. She knows that as the meeting has been brought forward there will be several hours of additional work, which Simon will be best placed to do as he is familiar with the papers. No doubt he will be like her previous associate and have some social meeting lined up or other excuse for not staying late. She is also annoyed that he has clearly ignored her previous advice to keep his communications with the client succinct and commercial. She plans to get tough with him and insist that he stays and completes this work so she can review it in the morning before the client meeting. She is working on another matter with an urgent deadline, which will keep her in the office for another four hours at least.

Simon's world view

As the plane starts its descent, Simon's mind turns to the evening ahead. He knows he really has this one chance to salvage his relationship with his partner of three years, and he does not want to blow it. He has had to let her down so many times because of client commitments and unexpected additional workloads and she has told him in no uncertain terms that she needs to be able to rely on him more. She was having a difficult time herself with her father being so ill, and he wants to be there for her. The amount of travel he has had to do in this current project is not helping. Simon has been away for four out of the last six weeks so tonight he has planned a special meal and some quality time with Anne.

The last two weeks have been tough. The client is

Practising empathy as part of your everyday leadership forms the basis for being able to empathise even when things get tough.

To listen to someone else, particularly where there is conflict, is deeply challenging.

constantly changing his mind. First he wants to see every detail of the advice he has drafted, and then he complains that it is all legal mumbo jumbo and why can't he just have the answer? Simon is trying really hard to get the balance right, and he thinks he is just about getting there. He is relishing the opportunities he is getting in this new job to really stretch himself. Sylvie seems to trust him to just get on with it. She has helped him a lot in learning to judge how to handle a difficult client and he has a huge respect for her knowledge and expertise. Simon is really proud of the latest piece of work he has done for the client, which was particularly complex, and has potentially saved the client from running into serious regulatory difficulties.

As the plane lands, although Simon feels tired he is satisfied with a job well done. He is looking forward to a quick debrief with Sylvie, and then to spending some quality time with Anne.

How do you expect this conversation will go?

Unless Sylvie finds a way to surface her assumptions and then park them, and enter the conversation with an open mind, the answer will be 'not well'.

What assumptions are Sylvie and Simon both making, and are they true?

How to hold a conversation that generates the best independent thinking from everyone present

Nancy Kline has written extensively about the principles and behaviours that need to be in place for people to think well together – they are called the "Ten Components of a Thinking Environment®". Here we focus on four of them, in the context of difficult conversations.

Attention – *Listening with palpable respect and interest, and without interruption*[4]

To listen to someone else, particularly where there is conflict, is deeply challenging. It means trusting yourself to know what to say when it comes your turn to speak, without preparing it while the other person is having their turn. But it is the only real basis for any conversation that has creative value. Everything else is just repetition. And I would argue that where there is apparent conflict of interest, there has to be creation. Either we need to create a new understanding, which will show us that our assumptions are false, or we need to create a new action, which both of us can sign up to. Without real attention and listening – which are inseparable – there will be no fresh thinking on either side.

So you could start by asking a question and assuring the person that you are really, really going to listen to their answer, and you are not going to stop listening until they tell you they have finished. You may think this could take a very long time, but usually people take and keep the floor because they are protecting it from being stolen by someone else. Given the opportunity, they will say what they have to say, and then they will stop.

Equality – *Treating each other as thinking peers*[5]

We are not talking here about hierarchical equality. Nor are we talking about who is smarter or more experienced or more senior. We're talking about inherent equality of value as thinking human beings. Treating others as equal thinkers generates mutual respect, which opens up the way for dialogue.

Treating each other as thinking peers enables us to start to step away from our entrenched position, to consider the thoughts of the other as a valid alternative perspective, whether you agree with them or not. The hallmarks of this are to give equal turns to speak, with full attention, and to keep agreements and boundaries.

Ease – *Offering freedom from internal rush and urgency*[6]

To do this requires that, on the practical side, you set aside the right amount of time to have the conversation. Thinking about when to initiate a difficult conversation, how to introduce it, allowing the other person time to hear and process what you are saying.

And on the emotional side, it means managing your own feelings so that they do not spill over. This does not mean repressing them, and there may be times when you need to be willing to acknowledge both your difficult feelings and those of the other person. Ease is not easy in the crush of pressure we all tend to work under, and becomes even harder as we enter into a conversation we perceive as difficult, but even an awareness of the need to be centred, present and with a positive intent, will help.

Appreciation – *Offering genuine acknowledgement of a person's qualities*[7]

Can you find something in the situation or the person which you genuinely can appreciate? If so, say it. If you can't, look again. It can even be something as simple as "I appreciate you finding the time to have this conversation". The more you practise appreciation in the rest of your life, the easier it becomes to see something positive, however small, in the person in front of you. Saying it out loud helps people to think more clearly. They do not think well under a barrage of criticism, even if that criticism is not spoken.

The key is to keep your appreciation specific, sincere and succinct.[8]

Case study: A deep disagreement

Charles is chairing the practice group leadership team meeting this afternoon. He has half-an-hour set aside to plan for the meeting. He's not looking forward to it. At last month's meeting they started to talk about the strategic direction of the group and there were some widely different and entrenched views around the table. The conversation ended up with a heated argument between two of the partners. The two newly promoted partners did not say a word, and looked as though they wished they were somewhere else. From the side conversations he has had, and heard about, over the last few weeks, factions are beginning to form.

At a leadership programme he attended recently, they had introduced a way of running a meeting that seemed to engage everyone and allow different perspectives to be considered with equal attention. Charles decides he will give it a try. Not much to lose after all – things could not get any worse than they already were. This is how he planned to run it:

- He would circulate a question ahead of the meeting, to focus the minds of those attending.
- He would ask everyone to have a turn at speaking briefly at the beginning of the meeting, to make sure everyone felt able to contribute.
- In that 'round' he would ask them to say what they felt was going well in the practice right now.
- He would acknowledge that they had had a difficult discussion last time, and that there were clearly some very divergent views.
- He would say that he wanted to make sure everyone's views were heard and respected, that he believed the best way forward was to create the conditions where all members of the group could think well for themselves. That way the group's decision would benefit from everyone's best thinking.
  - To achieve that, he would ask the group to agree to some 'ground rules' for the meeting:
  - We will put our devices on silent, and out of sight.
  - We will listen with respect to one another, and we will not interrupt, ever.
  - In return for not being interrupted, we will agree to be succinct when it's our turn to speak.
- He would then have another 'round', where each partner could give his or her current view on the topic.
- He would remind the group about the ground rules, and then invite open discussion.
- At the end, he would have a final round, with the question "What is your freshest thinking on this topic?"

He really did not know how this was going to go, but at least it could not be any worse than it was last time.

How to improve the quality of every meeting

I hope it will be apparent from the case study above and the descriptions of the components that make up an environment where everyone can contribute their best thinking, that these ideas are not just applicable to difficult conversations, but to every meeting we have. It's easy to begin by applying just one or two of these principles to your conversations, and even that will have a palpable effect on the quality of thinking that takes place in your working world. The case study above sets out a framework you can use to create better meetings.

Over many years of coaching, I would estimate that 70% of the issues brought to me by clients come down to a conversation that needs to take place, and hasn't. Often the need for the conversation only emerges as the client thinks through his or her goal, challenge or conundrum. Unspoken conversations account for a

Over many years of coaching, I would estimate that 70% of the issues brought to me by clients come down to a conversation that needs to take place, and hasn't.

mass of misunderstanding and inertia in organisations, and unsatisfactory conversations can create further frustration, anger and disappointment.

In today's complex world, it has never been more important that we learn to listen to one another, especially to those with whom we seem to disagree, or whose voice expresses something different from the cultural norms in which we find ourselves. In our own teams and organisations, we have the opportunity to change the way we relate to one another for the better, one conversation at a time, so as to build better, more effective and more sustainable organisations.

Alison Nolan is an independent consultant, working mainly with professional service firms. She specializes in organizational and personal change, working with leaders and their teams to improve performance. She is also an executive coach. Alison can be contacted via her website, www.theplacetothink.com or at alisonhnolan@gmail.com.

1 N Kline, *Time to Think: Listening to Ignite the Human Mind* (Cassell, 2014).
2 N Kline, *More Time to Think: The Power of Independent Thinking* (Cassell, 2015).
3 D Goleman, R Boyatzis and A McKee, *The New Leaders* (Time Warner, 2003).
4 See http://www.timetothink.com.
5 *Id.*
6 *Id.*
7 *Id.*
8 *Id.*

We need to have a serious talk about culture

Peter Alfandary

Law firms ignore cross-cultural intelligence at their peril. Peter Alfandary explains why more need to take note when working at an international level.

Most lawyers have heard the expressions 'audit' or 'due diligence'. That is hardly surprising.

What is surprising is how few have heard of the terms 'cultural due diligence' or 'cultural audit'. Even more surprising is how few firms operating internationally, actually undertake a *cultural audit* or a *cultural due diligence exercise* as part of their cross-border work.

Surprising, because we are in a profession where lawyers and law firms are increasingly being judged as much on the *How* they provide their services as on the *What* they provide in the sense of their brainpower and technical ability.

However, when working on any matter that has an international dimension to it, it should be blindingly obvious that getting the cultural aspect right is absolutely crucial to client service and to client satisfaction.

It is really very simple. You can win and lose clients because of a failure to understand the national cultural context in which they operate. Incidentally, the same thing applies, of course, to fellow lawyers. You can win or lose the trust and respect of fellow lawyers in other jurisdictions (including in countries where your firm may even have an office) for the same reason.

Understanding cultural differences is both an art and science. It is also a skill. Understanding about the impact of culture in business is called 'cultural intelligence' (CQ).

As the legal market becomes increasingly homogenous and increasingly difficult to navigate, CQ is becoming more and more important. Defined by two leading researchers and academics, Ang and Earley, as "an individual's capacity to function effectively across cultures", CQ is now a crucial skill for any lawyer seeking to work in an international context.

Lawyers and law firms which profess to understand about culture should be systematically carrying out cultural audits both as part of new matter intake and when managing their projects.

In simple terms this means that they need to ask themselves, up front, a series of key questions so as to ensure that they get the *How* right and give top-quality service to their clients. Questions, such as, 'culturally speaking':

- What is the client's preferred style of communication?
- How do they manage time?
- How is trust built?
- What is their preference in terms of reasoning and thinking patterns?
- What do I need to know about their hierarchy or appetite for risk?

Most firms do not do this.

CQ and culture

In the 1990s the business world began to focus on 'emotional intelligence' (EQ), which in essence is an individual's ability to combine thinking with emotions so as to understand and empathise with others. EQ, following the work done by Daniel Goleman, is seen as a crucially important tool for successful leadership.

CQ focuses not on our intellect or our emotions but more on our ability to work effectively and efficiency across cultural and national boundaries.

Culture is basically the *Who*, the *What*, the *Why* and the *How* we behave when viewed collectively as a group by others with whom we interact as well as by ourselves as part of the group to which we consider that we belong. It is as Hofstede, one of the gurus of the subject has said: "the collective programming of the mind which distinguishes the members of one group from another".

Indeed, every reader of this article has been programmed for and by their culture. We are not born

French, British, German, American, Chinese, Brazilian or Russian – we become British, French, Russian, Saudi – culture is learned behaviour.

One of the best ways to think about culture is to visualise an iceberg.

When we first land in another country, the cultural differences hit us at their most simplistic level, and without any noticeable effort on our part. We immediately notice differences in language, dress, smells, signs, climate and food – the visible part of the iceberg that is above the water line.

The invisible part of the iceberg, the mass below the water, is much bigger and much more significant than its tip.

Dwelling just below the surface are marked distinctions in how we communicate, deal with conflict, manage our time and approach problems. There are deep-rooted differences in perceptions of professionalism, etiquette, right and wrong and acceptable behaviour.

Lawyers who want to succeed in international markets must constantly ask themselves important questions, such as:

- What makes individuals in this particular culture different to those I normally interact with?
- What style of communication to do they prefer?
- How do they make decisions, manage their time, analyse problems and deal with conflict?

The answers are less obvious than you might think.

The culturally intelligent businessperson and lawyer must spend time addressing these questions, and must strive to become an expert at functioning effectively across cultures. By looking under the water line, he or she can deepen professional and business relationships with both colleagues and clients.

Lawyers are like other people

Every client and every lawyer walks into a conference room (or gets on to a conference call) carrying his or her unique cultural baggage. In that sense lawyers are normal.

Or, to put it in other terms, we all walk in with our iPods containing our unique and very specific choices of music. Culturally, we assume that because we all own iPods, we all have the same music on them. The reality is that some lawyers have jazz and opera on their iPods while others listen only to hip-hop and metal.

Similarly, a Mac and a PC may be used for performing the same tasks but inherently they are in fact built, designed and programmed entirely differently. The trap of similarity in this case is the assumption that because the Mac and PC are both computers, they can talk to and understand each other immediately and intuitively. The truth is that communication is possible, but only with additional software.

Some lawyers and some clients are Macs whereas some are PCs. Macs and PCs can talk to each other but they need additional software.

CQ is the software that all lawyers now need if they are going to excel at the *How*. One of the tools for getting better at CQ is the cultural audit.

The cultural audit

In its most basic form, the cultural due diligence audit looks at the way different cultures look at time, run meetings, negotiate, communicate, reason and make decisions, trust and build relationships and attach importance to hierarchy.

Here are just some of the questions that the diligent lawyer working for a non-national client or on a cross-border deal should be asking.

How does this client manage time?

In some cultures, such as Germany, the United Kingdom and the United States, time is thought of as highly linear. Diaries are respected religiously, meeting times are rigorously adhered to, and interruptions are disliked. People concentrate on one activity or relationship at a time and deadlines are observed. These monochronic cultures are diametrically opposed to their polychronic equivalents.

In South America, most of Southern Europe, Africa and much of the Middle East, time can be viewed differently, and may be seen as more of a guideline than a rule. People may well multitask and can focus simultaneously on multiple relationships. Timetables and deadlines may well change if new circumstances arise, and do so without incident.

Some lawyers and some clients are Macs whereas some are PCs. Macs and PCs can talk to each other but they need additional software.

The British use of understatement, of humour and of self-deprecation is a source of much confusion and misunderstanding.

Italians or Brazilians do not believe there is much of a problem if a meeting or the conference call starts 15 minutes late. By this time, of course, the American or German will have interpreted this lateness as either disrespect, or lack of seriousness or professionalism.

What is the client's dominant style of communication?

In 'direct communication' cultures such as the United States, Israel and the Netherlands, communication will tend to be very direct and unambiguous. Indeed, it may be so direct that it is sometimes misinterpreted as rudeness. In other 'indirect' cultures, for example Japan or the United Kingdom, the unsaid may well be as important as the said. The Dutch or American listener will need to learn the skills and acquire the patience to successfully decode the message.

The British, in particular, need to learn that they are often nigh incomprehensible to the rest of the world. Their use of indirectness and metaphor is not only hard for foreigners to read, but is also often interpreted as hypocrisy. The British use of understatement, of humour and of self-deprecation is a source of much confusion and misunderstanding. This is hardly surprising where being "a little bit disappointed" means very angry, where "I am not certain that I completely agree" means I do not agree, or where the remark "that is a courageous proposal" means that the suggestion is ridiculous.

How does this client reason and make decisions?

Influenced by the great empirical philosophers – Bacon, Locke and Hume – Brits and Americans tend to reason inductively. Theirs is a facts-first/bottom-up approach – observe first, look for patterns, come up with an initial hypothesis and then devise a theory for the next time something similar occurs. The bias here is towards pragmatism.

Much of the rest of Europe reasons deductively – Cartesian logic dominates thinking. The approach is therefore more top-down and principles-led. The approach here is theory, hypothesis, observation and then conclusion.

Inductive thinkers tend to want short executive summaries and up-front answers – can I do it or can't I? Deductive thinkers will want to understand how the answer was obtained – they will want to see the proof and the background analysis.

Take a typical PowerPoint presentation. What for the British audience are too many slides and too much analysis leading invariably to the comment "we have been sitting here for 40 minutes, when are we going to hear something practical and useful?", for the German, Italian or French audience may be normal. Conversely, a short punchy British or US-style presentation going straight to the answer or recommendation, may lead to a suspicion by the deductive thinker that the speaker is an amateur, cannot be taken seriously and has failed to do any proper analysis.

Finally what better example of these diametrically opposed ways of reasoning than the common and civil legal systems. The common law, inductive, and at its origin, created from case law; and the civil law system, deductive, with its roots in codification.

How to I build trust with this client?

In a relationship business like the law, trust is paramount. Trust also has a cultural dimension to it.

In some cultures, the United States for example, trust is often facts-based. Trust is mainly built through a mental process especially in the early stages of a business relationship. The buying process will be based on product, track record, deeds, experience and price. The emotional and the practical are separated; relationships are changeable; loyalty can change. The deal is paramount.

In many other cultures, for example the Middle East, China or India, trust is not facts-based but 'earned' through relationship building. Trust is personal and individual. Trust is emotional; it is affective; it will be built in social interaction such as meals; relationships grow slowly; "I want to see if I like you and trust you before I give you work"; loyalty is strong and durable. The relationship is paramount.

These differences have an immense effect on every lawyer's life. It goes to the core of 'lawyering' as a business, everything from the way a firm will have to flex its business development efforts in different countries to the skills its lawyers will require to successfully nurture and maintain client relationships. How trust is built also goes to the core of every cross-border negotiation.

Other questions

The above are a few of the basics.

A full cultural audit will go deeper. It will ask questions about formality versus informality in relationships. It will consider very carefully the style and purpose of meetings. It will look at the client's preference for either short-term or long-term planning in strategy formulation. It will look at the relative importance of hierarchy in different cultures and how this affects decision-making and getting proper instructions.

An even fuller audit will also ask about the client's relative preference for stability versus change, about their desire for harmony versus confrontation. In the area of negotiations it will analyse whether a discussion-based negotiation with an emphasis on a verbally direct but emotionally restrained approach should be used, or conversely whether engagement-based negotiations (where the emphasis will be more confrontational and emotionally expressive) are a preferable tactic. The deeper audit will even look at different cultures' appetites for risk, the need for certainty, as well as on how a country's political environment and in some cases its religious culture impacts on business.

What can go wrong without CQ?

Undertaking a cultural audit is a *sine qua non* for lawyers operating at any international level.

Technical ability is only the starting point in our increasingly competitive market. The *What* is a given. The *How* is the key to continued prosperity. Commoditisation of legal services has become an unstoppable force in our homogeneous world. Differentiation, while still achievable, is ever more elusive.

Without CQ, the 21st-century lawyer cannot excel. Without CQ, expectations between in-house legal departments within the same group but in different countries or between the different country offices of international law firms, may fail to be met.

Without CQ, local legislation or local procedures may not be properly understood, time and deadlines may be mismanaged, styles of legal advice between lawyers or with clients may become confusing, advice may be misinterpreted and misunderstood, legal concepts will become lost in translation and nuances will be missed or misconstrued.

Stress levels between offices in international firms, and between lawyer and client generally, will increase and will compound misunderstanding. Time will be wasted, legal costs will increase, write-offs will escalate, and clients will be dissatisfied.

If we accept that the *How* is a critical part of the service equation, then we can no longer risk having our lack of CQ jeopardise client service, or lead to mistakes.

A word of caution

This is directed to all the native English-speakers reading this article.

Paul Watzlawick, the Austrian-American psychologist, once stated: 'What is true is not what I say but what the other person understands'.

English, as we know, has become the *lingua franca* of the business world and as a result of lawyers working internationally.

But language is full of nuances, mistranslations or 'false friends'. Even between native English speakers confusion can reign. 'Quite good' to an American means very good. To the British, it implies that something is just okay. When Americans table an idea they postpone discussing it. The British, on the other hand, put it on the immediate agenda.

Words such as 'eventually' (*finally*, as opposed to *possible* or *maybe*), 'benefits' (*advantages* as opposed to *profits*), 'director' (*board member* as opposed to *manager*), 'agenda' (*list of meeting points* as opposed to *diary*), and 'realise' (*become aware of* as opposed to *achieve*) may mean different things to the native and non-native English speaker.

Native English speakers must avoid the over-use of colloquialisms. In one recent presentation, in English, to an audience of European lawyers, the following expressions were used by eminent speakers – *recoil, gutted, cram in, crib sheet, chipper, soak up, clinch, bandwidth, air time, straight from the off* and *bee's knees*. For some listeners, each of these words or expressions acted as a distraction and each distraction detracted from the overall message. Their use was at best culturally insensitive and at worst damaging to the speaker's credibility.

Idiomatic expressions, used extensively by British or Americans, confuse and are counterproductive. We should avoid throwing 'curve balls' to non-native English speakers or asking them to 'step up to the plate'

'Quite good' to an American means very good. To the British, it implies that something is just okay.

and we should all stop 'beating around the bush' if we are going to 'hit the ground running' as CQ lawyers.

An extremely bright and able French executive with a good command of English recently admitted to me that he 'missed' about 30% to 40% of every conference call which either involved Brits or Americans. So as the old adage goes: 'Watch your language'.

Conclusion

The modern lawyer and modern law firm must embrace CQ.

Some multinational companies now consider the subject so important that CQ training has become a mandatory part of the induction process of all new hires at every level of the organisation.

CQ is already on the curriculum of some major international law firms and is taught in a number of leading business schools. It is not, however, just a skill to be embraced by major firms or global in-house legal departments. It affects every lawyer working in an international environment.

CQ is an integral part of excellence. It is not a *soft* skill but a critical *hard* skill that we all need to acquire.

Lawyers from every jurisdiction need to become cultural experts and cultural guides if they are to become better lawyers.

So permit me a call to arms.

Ignore culture at your peril. If you really care about client relationships make culture part of the service you provide to your clients. Live it, breathe it and teach it in your firms. CQ is a legal skill that is not optional. It is one that is absolutely essential to success.

Peter Alfandary is a former English solicitor who has spent over 30 years as a partner in private practice advising international clients. He now lectures and trains executives in both corporations and professional service firms worldwide on CQ. His TEDx on CQ entitled "The Myth of Globalisation" can be found on YouTube and the TEDx website. Peter can be contacted on LinkedIn at https://www.linkedin.com/in/peter-alfandary/

How leadership challenges evolve over the career of a lawyer

Christopher Bockmann

There is a lot more to the career of a lawyer than the typical step changes of qualifying as an associate and then becoming a partner. This article explores the more informal step changes and what personal development needs they can create for a lawyer. Recognising, understanding and addressing those needs not only impacts performance and therefore career progression but also a sense of personal fulfilment in the job.

Introduction

Helping individual lawyers diagnose the nature of their needs is a key step in identifying the type of support they might benefit from. The intention of this article is to provide a greater perspective on the needs of lawyers as they evolve during their career. Career phases will alternate between stable and transitional periods. Career and professional development support in law firms has traditionally been concentrated at associate level rather than at partner level – the peak of achievement in the profession. The need for coaching and mentoring is being increasingly felt at partner level with the broadening range of contributions being expected notably in business development and firm management. Partner succession is also becoming an increasingly new area of attention and will be addressed when talking about the needs of senior partners.

Career stages are influenced by professional factors such as changes in formal roles and in seniority. There are also numerous informal career changes that matter. During those stages a lawyer may face a number of professional or even personal challenges such as having to renegotiate relationships, coping with anxieties linked to acquiring new skills and greater responsibilities. These challenges will surface irrespective of the size of firm as they are inherent to a lawyer's career progression. Careers are also impacted by less identifiable personal factors. These will typically affect levels of career motivation, ambition and choices. Both professional and personal factors will be explored in this article.

Addressing these needs, with coaching, is essential as they influence behaviours that will help a lawyer become a better professional and may therefore enhance career satisfaction and progression.

Associate career stages

The career of an associate will be shaped by the nature of the work, requiring an ever-broadening range of skills. Some law firms decide to formalise these stages to provide a sense of career path and progression, and may apply a selection process to move from one step to another. Professional development needs are at their most pressing in the run-up to a potential promotion and in the first months following promotion. This is therefore an effective moment to resort to coaching.

In the career of an associate there is a gradual shift from an early emphasis on developing a broad legal grounding to a wider range of skills, primarily client- and people-related. The technical development is naturally maintained throughout the career of the lawyer, but from a developmental perspective it will diminish in importance over time.

When looking at possible coaching and mentoring needs, stages of development (needs) of an associate can be broadly grouped under the following categories:

- individual contributor/junior associate;
- case/matter manager/senior associate; and
- counsel/partner candidate.

Junior associate

I need to fit in and get up to speed as quickly as possible

The first years of an associate are principally about developing legal, research and drafting skills applied to a business environment. The priority is to enable the associate to become operational as a business lawyer as efficiently and swiftly as possible. The emphasis is primarily on the acquisition and fine-tuning of professional and technical skills. This development process is achieved through practice and is often referred to as the apprentice model. In many ways informal mentoring characterises this apprentice model in which there is a virtuous loop of practice-feedback-learning-application. The custom of a more junior lawyer sharing an office with a more senior one

The senior associate's development needs will revolve around how to provide feedback, reflecting on and understanding different motivational drivers in a team and linking those to setting targets.

is in many ways also a form of informal mentoring – helping the younger associate move up the learning curve. This helps the junior associate gain exposure to how legal expertise is applied in practical client work. The reflective dialogue created in mentoring will help the young associate in reframing, probing, generating hypotheses and designing new approaches to adopt in applying legal expertise to client matters. Many junior associates regularly share how much they learn by just listening to a more senior lawyer working on the phone.

There is also a parallel exercise of integration into the workplace environment, where mentoring can play an important role. This may even take the form of buddying. The objective of such an integration exercise is to help the individual lawyer understand the values of the firm they joined, standards of behaviour and work ethics – all critical to ensure a long-term future
for the new recruit.

Senior associate

I will only be able to take on more responsibility if I let go of my urge to control and therefore delegate more.

The key evolution as a lawyer moves from junior to senior associate is a wider scope in responsibilities in managing matters, the teams involved and dealing with clients. These are gradual changes and formal promotion, when in place, confirms a potential that has already emerged with the associate. A senior associate will also start to feel pressure from both below (juniors) and above (partners) and will be expected to know everything on a matter.

This is the first significant career transition for a lawyer because it requires a shift towards greater management-type of activity and represents a departure from what has been one of the main sources of professional progression so far – technical competence. It will engage the lawyer in a regular exercise of self-awareness. This exercise in self-awareness and consequent fine-tuning will remain a vital ability throughout the rest of the lawyer's career.

People management

The senior associate needs to balance supervising and taking responsibility for work done by more juniors without an excessive form of micro-management. This process means to shift from a position of individual to a team contributor.

It is important to stress the sense of loss of control for the senior associate in the exercise of delegation. Being prepared to let go of tasks in order to engage in new ones represents a significant challenge and will remain with the lawyer as they grow into the career and in responsibilities. In an environment where setting ambitious targets for billable hours is often the norm, delegation may pose a dual threat – fewer recorded hours for the senior associate and possibly a budget overspend of recorded hours for the junior associate trying to get to grips with stretching tasks.

The senior associate's development needs will revolve around how to provide feedback, reflecting on and understanding different motivational drivers in a team and linking those to setting targets. All of which requires the senior associate to develop greater emotional intelligence – an ability to recognise and guide one's emotions and those of others. These are areas where coaching can really provide value.

Client management

How can I pay more attention to what my client really needs?

At senior associate stage (or at times earlier), lawyers need to develop an understanding of how to manage and meet clients' expectations and gradually learn how to grow a relationship with a client. Such an ability requires the lawyer to be able to form – through excellent listening and questioning skills – a highly individualised picture of what a client needs and how the legal service should be provided to meet that client's needs most effectively. In other words, it implies developing a greater commercial awareness of the client's situation. Lawyers will also need to handle challenging client conversations. As such, client management relies on similar aptitudes of emotional intelligence used in managing people.

Developing the relationship beyond the (regular) transactions requires developing a greater commercial understanding of the client's business drivers beyond the provision of a technical/legal solution.

Partner candidate

As discussed earlier, coaching needs can be more pronounced in preparation for and just after important career stages. Preparing for partnership, the most significant career stage in a lawyer's career, is one of those critical moments. This moment is defined from the stage when partners believe that a senior associate is on track and therefore needs further support to provide him or her with the best chance of success. This could, therefore, cover several years. Ideally, the earlier this is engaged, the better the results from a development point of view.

First is the need to reaffirm the expectations outlined above for senior associates around people and client management skills as well as a greater sense of commercial awareness. The possible reward of partnership can also be a real incentive to address a need that might have been put aside for a while.

Partner career stages[1]

Partners' careers are not structured in the same way as that of associates, yet phases of development can be identified over the whole career of a partner. These phases are influenced by the nature of contributions and level of responsibilities in client relationships and in firm management, whether formal or informal. These phases will engage primarily the leadership and entrepreneurial qualities of the lawyer.

On-boarding

As a new partner I feel the clock has been reset and because I am now a partner I am expected to deal with the situation on my own.

On-boarding for recently elected partners can represent a challenging transition.

The essential challenge met by a recently promoted partner is a paradoxical combination. The partner will feel tremendous personal satisfaction at having achieved the highest form of recognition at their firm – joining the partnership – yet it is also a form of professional 'reset'. The newly elected partner will also rapidly realise that what has been a major contributor to their professional success so far may be insufficient to grow and meet the new expectations as a partner. Many partners have shared the challenges of having the clocks put back to zero again, going from a high-performing senior associate held in high regard by partners, to becoming the most inexperienced member of the partner group who needs to demonstrate the validity of the decision in making him or her a partner.

At this particular stage, the need revolves principally around reassurance on the normality of the ambiguous feelings of satisfaction and anxiety. Mentors can respond well to such needs.

Junior partner

Junior partners are primarily concerned with being on track and meeting their firm's expectation of being a partner. Legal expertise, transactional skills, client management skills and hard work have already become part of the assets of the lawyer and have contributed to making it to partner.

One of the difficulties for a junior partner lies in the fact that firms seldom express explicitly what is expected of their young partners. The culture of law firms is characterised by a socialised process whereby expectations are not formulated explicitly, rather they get revealed over time, a process that is faithful to the apprentice-model of learning. As a senior associate, some leadership and entrepreneurial qualities may have been developed but the need becomes much more acute as a junior partner. At this stage of their career, junior partners face several professional challenges that can be grouped as follows.

Business generation

There are two elements to business generation: developing clients and increasing market visibility by developing new services and products.

A partner needs to grow legitimacy with clients, developing further commercial sense, moving from being a key contact in a client relationship managed by a partner to developing a partner badge and becoming the principal client contact on his or her own account.

One of the difficulties for a junior partner lies in the fact that firms seldom express explicitly what is expected of their young partners.

This is in fact key to the partner's future.

Raising market visibility requires increasing investment time, placing pressure on effective billing time (see more under 'Balancing producing and managing' below). The challenge resides in balancing the short-term need to generate billable hours and the long-term goal to raise overall level (rate) of billable hours through greater added value, visibility and innovation in legal advice. Peer pressure may force
the relative inexperienced partner to go either way. Resisting this peer pressure may provoke misunderstandings or trigger unhealthy reactions.

The changing nature of relationships

The junior partner goes through a phase in which relationships need to be re-contracted with former peers – senior associates – with whom a new form of legitimacy and authority needs to be established. Credibility also needs to be built with the new peers – partners. As the balance of those relationships shifts, the new partner needs to demonstrate greater empathy to understand the possible reactions of others and exercise greater assertiveness with subtlety. One of the more complex relationships to manage is with the partner(s) that sponsored the senior associate for partnership. These partners were more than likely the most important source of work for the senior associate. The junior partner may still depend in the early years on this work referral but some of the sponsoring partners will want to see the new partner start to develop their own book of business. Some of those sponsoring partners may even start refraining from passing on work because of the implicit fear of competition. This last point matters because it can be a source of confusion.

The nature of the relationship with clients is also changing. The young partners will realise that as a partner they have ultimate responsibility for the client relationship and will need to address any performance or communication issues that may originate in the team. Clients go to partners for advice but also for criticism on the performance on a matter. The most stressful times in a young partner's early career are likely to be around coping with this challenging responsibility and the fear of losing a client.

Balancing producing and managing

I have now five jobs but only one is billable, please help!

In addition to building up one's practice, the junior partner will be exposed to a number of new areas of responsibility and will need to balance producing and billing matters with carefully managing the investment time (business development, team and financial management). As Lorsch and Mathias pointed out in the *Harvard Business Review* (1987), this balance is skewed towards producing by the identity of a lawyer – advising clients and applying legal expertise is what initially drew the individual to the profession. Depending on the opportunities provided as a senior associate, a partner may be more or less familiar with some of those areas of responsibility. Although the junior partner will have learnt to delegate at an earlier stage, becoming partner places renewed emphasis on the ability to free up time (delegate and prioritise) for investment-type activities. So from a professional point of view this means further letting go of control yet containing the risk of negligence. It becomes even more important for the partner to accept and strengthen the ability to succeed through others.

The complexity for the young partner is that all the three needs set out above are interlinked – it is only by freeing up more time (delegating) that the partner will be able to engage in greater business development, which in turn will help generate a pipeline of work for their team and reinforce/validate the changes in relationships. Re-positioning oneself is what will contribute to greater support from associates and fellow partners who might be more predisposed to share clients and matters/cases.

Seasoned partner

At this stage, which is probably the longest phase of all, partners will have developed a personal reputation in the market but also within the firm. Professional developmental challenges will mainly arise from a role change such as taking on management responsibilities.

Management roles

In a management role, the challenge is to be both part of the partnership and 'above' it, in order to steer it.

A possible significant evolution for a seasoned partner is when taking on executive responsibilities (practice,

Professional developmental challenges will mainly arise from a role change such as taking on management responsibilities.

Partnerships sometimes have difficulties in evaluating and appreciating the different types of contribution involved in taking a management role.

office level or wider geographic ones). This tends to be more complex in a partnership than in other types of organisation by virtue of the nature of partnerships. These roles yield limited formal powers and are not always held in high regard by peers/fellow owners of the business. As a consequence, partners taking these roles need to make a particular effort to use and further develop leadership qualities – an ability to articulate, embody and realise a story of possibilities that connects meaningfully with those over whom influence is exercised. It is above all an informal method of authority.

From a development need point of view, a seasoned partner may find the challenge of management roles particularly difficult as it calls upon a different skill set from being a successful lawyer. It is true that having an impressive portfolio of clients and deals/cases will often be a prerequisite for getting into management roles, but it is more about legitimacy for getting the role than necessarily a reflection of competence for the role. Such success in the practice and the confidence that comes with it may also reduce a partner's ability to listen, a key ability in a management role. Partners are particularly prone to such behaviour because they have a status that equates with professional achievement, and as partners they are likely to be more isolated from external feedback that may provide perspective.

Partners taking management roles are likely to face two imperatives in extending their informal authority:

- Manage a different time frame. The cycles of strategy formulation, execution and impact which are key in any executive role tend to be much longer than legal practice related. This can be a source of frustration and even impatience in how the executive role is lived. Timeframes change from the practice – partners craving short-term results in order to feel satisfied and fulfilled are likely to be frustrated.
- Enlarge one's network of people. This requires working with a broad range of people of different personalities, values and ambition. This ability to overcome personal differences for the sake of a greater goal can also be described as developing political skills.

Another significant change in taking a management role is the shift in the source of professional satisfaction from an external one, clients who show their appreciation through the fees they pay and the feedback, to an internal one where the prime source of appreciation is from the peer group of partners. In taking those roles, partners move away from the day-to-day activity and the frequency of client contact is likely to change and possibly diminish. Partnerships sometimes have difficulties in evaluating and appreciating the different types of contribution involved in taking a management role. Coaching may provide support insofar as taking management roles may affect a partner's self-image and therefore confidence.

Senior partner

Senior partners are those who have reached full professional maturity. Their role is likely to concentrate on managing senior client relationships, enhancing the firm's reputation in the market, enriching the partnership, and mentoring other partners. As very experienced professionals, none of these challenges are likely to provoke a need for support.

Where a need may arise is in relation to stepping down from a management role or passing down over other major responsibilities, for example client relationship, in other words preparing for one's own succession. The challenge lies in the fact that these changes mean that the partner may start contemplating the concluding years of their career at the firm. This career phase may occur at the same time as the personal transition into late adulthood (addressed below). This transition is further accentuated where the partner is a founder of the firm or has played a significant role in its development.

The nature of the challenge in this career stage is two-fold:

- Stepping down and the prospect of leaving behind a role and all that comes with it (eg, status, identification with a role of power). There is a real issue for partners stepping down from a management role, as the challenges of rebuilding a practice after several years of having concentrated a significant time on management

The mid-life transition, sometimes several months long, will have an impact on the mental presence, relationships and ultimately the performance of the lawyer.

are numerous. In the future, as working life extends for health and financial reasons and firms need to explore ways to capitalise on the experience of their most senior partners, the 'of counsel' type of role may become a more regular feature at law firms. This role may have an important part to play in the transmission of expertise, networks and client relationships.

- Stepping out. This relates to options for continued professional fulfilment beyond the firm. In the past decade, stepping out for senior partners was primarily towards retirement, in itself anxiety provoking. Increasingly, this will change towards continued professional activity albeit at a lesser rhythm and maybe in the form of a portfolio of activities. This could be seen as a post-career.

The two are intrinsically linked: the more attractive the options in stepping out, the easier it will be to step down. Many factors facilitate the transition: a sense of having left a legacy and completed a lifetime's work, having been a good steward – leaving one's firm better than it was found – and having found a trusted heir.

At this stage of their career, it is helpful for senior partners to consider a number of elements:

- Coming to terms with the transition. For a partner taking an of counsel type of role, it is accepting a (reduced) role which has a different status and recognition in the firm, reconciling oneself with the need to work longer than planned. For some partners this transition may be more clearly associated with the final years at their firm.
- Gaining clarity on the key and possibly evolving personal ambition that will continue beyond the role and being a partner at that firm. Reconnecting with one's personal aspiration may facilitate developing a range of options for moving beyond one's firm.
- Seeking a better understanding of any awkward dynamics and changing patterns in power relationships that may take place in a succession process between an incumbent leader and potential successor.

Personal life cycles in a career

It is important to review other triggers for making use of coaching. These triggers are not linked to formal changes in roles but rather originate in personal life cycles and individual drivers, yet have a clear spill-over effect onto the professional realm.

The nature of the triggers for these cycles will vary. These can be associated with the various development cycles of adulthood, while others will find their origins in the high-pressured environment or be associated with some traits linked to the profession. Those development needs may not necessarily be age-related and therefore may affect a lawyer at any time in their career. These cycles may differ in cause but may have common characteristics, for example feelings of doubt, anxiety, sadness or weakened motivation. The effects can be felt professionally, affecting performance, but also in private life by disrupting relationships.

Although some of these cycles and syndromes may occur at any time in a lawyer's career, they are more likely to affect partners because of greater pressure, a longer career as a partner (as opposed to an associate). Moreover, as there are no real formal career stages, some of those cycles may feel more pronounced in the absence of career milestones.

The mid-life transition

I have had a successful career as a partner, but what now?

In the words of L Mainiero and S Sullivan, "the first half of life is about compulsion, second half is about choices". Many professionals will pass through one or more mid-life transitions. Those transitions can be gradual or abrupt and a professional may be more or less conscious of the transition. In some cases, transition may be provoked by the individual (loss of professional fulfilment, confidence) or induced by external factors (eg, absence of promotion to partner, market slow down). This period highlights the importance of engaging in meaningful activity for a professional, whether in relationship to society (making a contribution), clients (adding value), one's team (sense of belonging), but also to oneself (feeling empowered). David Maister highlighted the importance in engaging in meaningful work for professionals like lawyers.

Mid-life transitions are characterised by a feeling of a reduced congruence between chosen professional goals and ambition (eg, wanting to be a lawyer, a partner or a litigator) and achieved goals. There can be several possible sources of disappointment – maybe the lawyer has not been able to achieve the goal, or maybe not to sufficient satisfaction. The lawyer may have succeeded in achieving the ambition but realises it does not bring the hoped-for personal fulfilment and therefore is characterised by a certain form of disillusionment.

The mid-life transition, sometimes several months long, will have an impact on the mental presence, relationships and ultimately the performance of the lawyer. It will typically lead to two outcomes: either recommit to initially chosen professional goals and ambition, maybe with some fine-tuning (eg, taking a management role in one's firm, or developing a new line of business) or a reassessment leading to more profound choices (changing type of organisation or changing profession). US psychologist, Bob Kegan, calls this the stage when adults move into self-authoring mode in which an adult will develop an internal compass, be able to formulate their own sets of judgement rather than being dependent on an inherited frame of mind and ambitions (eg, family, professional peers, significant others, or pressure of a perceived role such as partner).[2]

It is important to stress that it is normal for all professionals to have these periods at various times in their career. It may be that in some cases it is helpful to bring these questions to light with the help of a coach to gain perspective on underlying causes rather than just understanding symptoms at the surface. Clarity can then support building strategies that bring greater alignment between personal drivers and professional context.

Late adulthood transition

Professionals reaching the concluding phase of their careers may feel the need for a broader contribution, having achieved their set goals to a certain level of satisfaction. The developmental psychologist, Erik Erikson, refers to this period as one of generativity[3]: striving to make a mark and create something that will outlast them, whether at their firm or in society more generally as a source of motivation and reward. This desire to contribute is what leads lawyers at this stage to take on greater mentoring roles, and to encourage their firms to take an active role in corporate social responsibility.

The prelude to this second transition may manifest itself through similar symptoms (motivational or behavioural) as the earlier midlife transition.

Other professional crises and syndromes

Disillusionment with partnership

A partner may become disillusioned by the evolution of the profession and/or the role of partner. He or she may feel alienated by an increasing detachment from key decisions in the firm or loss of control over client relationships, a weakening sense of entrepreneurialism. This could also simply be caused by a too large a gap between perception and reality of what is associated with partnership. It is likely that such disillusions will be combined with one of the mid-life or late-adulthood transitions.

Bathsheba syndrome

With professional success can come a certain amount of complacency, partially reinforced by status, level of financial reward and access to information, people and resources. A secondary effect identified by Ludwig and Longenecker[4] is a temptation of thrill-seeking activities and possible transgression of firm values and even ethical norms. "Power corrupts" goes the popular saying. The Bathsheba syndrome is named after the wife of King David of Israel (1000 BC). The king was a visionary, highly appreciated by his people and wealthy. He could not resist seeking the forbidden – having an affair with the wife of his best army officer. He ordered his commander to send this officer unsupported to a lethal battlefield. The officer was killed, the king lost his best soldier, his commander rebelled against him, and internal strife in his kingdom grew when this was discovered. He lost the child he had with Bathsheba. It is as if some form providential punishment for his actions had fallen upon him. The authors suggest a number of lessons against such self-destructive behaviour:

- it can happen to anyone – King David was not unethical at the outset;
- a balanced life (including private/professional) reduces the likelihood of such slippage;
- avoid complacency by maintaining focus on the primary task; and
- surround oneself with people at work and in private that can either challenge or comfort when either is needed.

This last point is particularly important for senior partners who may feel alone in handling the challenges of their roles.

Coaching can provide a safe space for a partner to be both supported and guided in their reflections and yet be challenged on some assumptions that may be the source of dissatisfaction.

The summit syndrome

This syndrome is linked to the notion of reaching a plateau in one's career. For Pascale and Parsons,[5] this is a "vulnerable time for over-achievers ... after the novel demands of the current position have been conquered and before the next job begins". Some partners may experience after many years a feeling of boredom in keeping on with the same type of work, even if the law evolves and new client relationships are developed. The negative impact on performance, health and private life can be significant. The authors suggest a number of symptoms as one approaches, reaches and descends from the plateau. Internal symptoms will include discontent, doubt about personal impact and cynicism. From the outside, the person is likely to see a dip in performance, and, worse, may start hiding this dip from the organisation. Distractions may start to dilute focus through various coping mechanisms such as engaging in obsessive behaviours (eg, hobbies, food), in dangerous sports or in substance abuse, and others not so different from the Bathsheba syndrome.

Burnout

The pressure of the legal profession is high and periods of physical and mental tiredness are common. Lawyers learn how to manage these pressures – there is in fact a form of natural selection in which endurance grows over time. However, in some cases, the challenges may be more profound and lead to a burnout. A burnout is characterised by a number of signs both physical (loss of/excessive appetite, sleep, fitness) and mental (mood swings, helplessness, feeling alone).

Coaching will help by:

- breaking down the challenges;
- reality checking;
- reconnecting with personal desires; and
- regaining control over one's life.

Impostor syndrome

The term 'insecure over-achievers' (in fact the two are linked) is sometimes used to describe lawyers. A partner working for a large firm once said that a lawyer, and especially a partner, may feel insecure when considering the hourly fees 'objectively'. Were the partner to provide the same legal service outside their firm, would the same rate be accepted? In other words, is there real value for the fees charged? The impostor syndrome is more about perceptions and fear than an effective weakness in professional capability. The impostor lives in fear of being discovered one day and that their role and success is seen as a fraud. As a consequence, these individuals can be particularly reluctant to receive feedback on performance and sensitive to criticism, which in some cases is necessary to continue progressing professionally.

Conclusion

Development needs have multiple origins and feed lifelong learning. There are also real opportunities in personal growth. Growing self-awareness over time is key to the ability to recognise those needs and how they affect professional and private behaviour. Such an ability is also critical in understanding the sources of professional satisfaction and growth, an essential ingredient for the high performance that the law firm environment requires. When there is no role change, any development needs are likely to have their origins in a gap in alignment between one's sense of purpose and fulfilment and the professional activity one engages in. The meaning of being a partner is also evolving, with the increase in the size of firms, market changes and demands of the role.

The practice of self-awareness supports the lawyer in becoming more autonomous and better prepared to face future challenges. Above all, it helps to bring greater coherence between the professional and the private, an essential foundation for the overall personal wellbeing and therefore improved and sustainable performance.

Christopher Bockmann works extensively with lawyers helping them to become more effective professionals and aligned both as individuals and as teams. He speaks regularly at conferences and law firm events on leadership challenges, leadership succession, career life cycles, teamwork and decision-making. He worked for many years for Clifford Chance and Linklaters in post-merger integration work.

1 This section draws on a Europe-wide study conducted in law firms on partners' careers highlighting new trends in partners' careers and identifying key phases of career transitions of partners. The study was conducted by Christopher Bockmann between July and December 2013 across international law firms with a combined revenue of €2.5 billion. The study included a survey of more than 270 partners on career aspirations and challenges, as well as some 60 interviews of partners across Europe.

2 See Robert Kegan, *In Over Our Heads: The Mental Demands of Modern Life* (Harvard University Press, 1994).

3 See Erik Erikson, *Childhood and Society* (WW Norton & Co, 1950).

4 Ludwig and Longenecker, "The Bathsheba Syndrome", *Journal of Business Ethics* (1994).

5 Pascale and Parsons, "Crisis at the Summit", *Harvard Business Review* (2007).

Does your personality influence your potential for partnership?

Edward Walker

While it is trite to point out that the legal sector is undergoing a number of significant changes, law firms remain fundamentally people businesses. Having the right people in the right roles at the right time is consequently a key challenge. Firms that make best use of their talent gain a competitive edge, while those that fail to utilize their lawyers effectively can see their performance deteriorate and staff turnover rise.

The majority of law firms continue to be owned and led by groups of partners. While the size and complexity of many firms necessitates partners delegating certain management powers to an executive board, the distinctive organizational culture within which law firm leaders operate frequently leads to what Empson characterizes as "a clumsy combination of reluctant leaders and autonomous followers."[1]

This means the leadership capacity of a law firm is reflected in the combined abilities of the whole partnership, not just the incumbents of nominal leadership positions, such as senior or managing partner. Identifying lawyers with the potential to become effective partners is, therefore, crucial to ensuring the long-term success of a firm.

Firms that make best use of their talent gain a competitive edge, while those that fail to utilize their lawyers effectively can see their performance deteriorate and staff turnover rise.

Do I have the potential to become a successful law firm partner?

This is a question that almost every lawyer asks themselves at some point in their career. Sometimes the self-doubt continues after partnership has been achieved, a pattern of thinking that is referred to as imposter syndrome.[2] In reality, very few lawyers become partners at the firm they originally train with; this is especially true at elite US and City of London firms, where
the percentage achieving partnership is typically low single-figures. On reflection, this is perhaps unsurprising when we consider the broad range of attributes that are required to be an effective law firm partner:

- *Personality.* Effective partners possess a combination of personality traits that help them positively resolve complex situations, despite the presence of ambiguity and risk.
- *Cognitive ability.* An effective partner has the capacity to learn from experience, adapt to new situations and make use of information and opportunities.
- *Skills.* Effective partners possess both the legal and non-legal skills necessary to perform their current role. These skills will be dictated by the precise demands of the role and the overall structure of the firm.
- *Knowledge.* An effective partner must understand the legal sector, the workings of their own firm and their clients. They must also recognize when it is necessary to consult the expertise of others.
- *Experience.* Effective partners have a breadth of experience to draw upon. This is not limited to legal expertise but also experience gained from secondments (both geographical and organizational), managing people, budgets and processes, and involvement in ad hoc project work. These experiences can be gained from working in one or more organizations and sectors.
- *Values.* An effective partner has a consistent, constructive set of values congruent with the strategic goals and operating procedures of their firm.

Notwithstanding the arithmetic, most lawyers begin their career with the goal of becoming a partner. They subsequently go on to make significant personal sacrifices in trying to achieve this goal. Despite knowing the odds are stacked against them, many lawyers are left disillusioned when it eventually becomes clear that they will not become a partner. Predictably, it is at this key juncture that significant numbers of lawyers leave their firm (and sometimes the profession), often unclear precisely what it was that they were perceived to lack.

From the law firm's perspective, junior lawyers are recruited for many reasons, only one of which is creating a pipeline of future partners. This means the firm needs to balance short-term goals – for example, filling fee-earner vacancies – against longer-term goals, such as developing the future leaders of the firm. These multifarious objectives require individuals with different capabilities and experience. Even more problematic, in some instances the attributes that make an individual well-suited for one role can be at variance with another.

The ability to define and identify that elusive variable known as potential is for that reason of significant importance to law firm strategy.

The ability to define and identify that elusive variable known as potential is for that reason of significant importance to law firm strategy. Potential takes time to develop; it is also influenced by experiences. The sooner an individual's potential is identified, the sooner a firm can start to expose that individual to experiences that will enhance their development and maximize their future success.

Potential for what?

This is a necessary question for a firm to answer before identifying which individuals possess potential. In a workplace context, potential suggests that an individual has the requisite qualities to successfully perform other (usually more complex) roles at some point in the future. Success and potential thus refer to common outcomes at different points in time; success referring to past achievements or demonstrations of ability, whereas potential focuses on an individual's future capacity to succeed.

Historically, workplace references to an individual's potential implicitly meant their leadership potential. Within law firms this was understood to entail a lawyer's potential to become a partner at the firm. More sophisticated approaches to talent management have emerged that recognize different categories of potential. Pendleton & Furnham,[3] for example, identified three broad types of role – technical, supervisory, and strategic. Each places different demands on the individual meaning different capabilities and experience are required in order to perform the role successfully. Allowing for different categories of potential increases the number of people who will be identified as having potential. It also enables the development of "talent pools" containing those individuals identified as being likely to succeed in certain roles.

Law firms that adopt this approach to managing talent are likely to retain the category of leadership potential as part of their strategy for developing partners. This is often in conjunction with adding further categories that support other strategic goals – for example, introducing new technology or pursuing technical excellence. As this approach to talent management becomes more commonplace, lawyers should start to recognize that their future success is strongly linked to pursuing a career path that makes the most of their potential, and that trying to pursue alternative paths increases the likelihood of career derailment.

The use of potential in graduate recruitment

Lawyers who are recruited immediately following the completion of their legal studies are primarily selected on the basis of their potential. This makes sense as most have limited legal work experience through which they can demonstrate a track record of success. It is important to recognize, however, that they are typically selected for their potential to be a successful associate, not a successful partner. This is a pragmatic response from firms who need their new hires to start contributing as quickly as possible. From a lawyer's perspective this approach is also beneficial, as it maximizes the likelihood that they will be successful in their initial role on joining the firm.

Unfortunately, because the work of an associate and partner is very different, the selection process for junior lawyers tells us relatively little about an individual's suitability for the role of partner. A model of leadership potential that can be used early in a lawyer's career to identify those who in the future will possess all the attributes of a successful partner (as listed above) would, therefore, be highly valuable.

Identifying potential partners – a model and measure of leadership potential

Silzer & Church's[4] 2009 model of potential has heavily influenced organizational approaches to leadership and potential. Developed with specific reference to the workplace, the model identifies three dimensions of potential.

The temporal link between success and potential means they should be underpinned by common characteristics that remain relatively stable over time. While all three dimensions of potential are linked to success, their degrees of stability differ from one another, with career potential the least stable and foundational potential the most stable. As a result, foundational dimensions of potential are the first markers of future success to emerge. Identifying and measuring these markers is consequently the best way to assess an individual's suitability for partnership early in their career.

Research has shown cognitive ability[5] and (certain) personality traits[6] are foundational dimensions of leadership success. This means they are reliable predictors of effective partners even in the early stage of an individual's career. This makes them both essential elements in a model of partnership potential, with cognitive ability the natural starting point. Elite law firms are already very selective about recruiting individuals with high levels of cognitive ability. This is because cognitive ability is linked to success in many roles, especially those that involve complex problem-solving; this makes it a useful marker of potential for both associates and partners. It also means that associates will tend to have the cognitive ability necessary to be a successful partner, meaning cognitive ability is unlikely to prove useful when identifying potential partners, as, broadly speaking, all lawyers are quite similar in respect of this attribute.

Research has shown cognitive ability and (certain) personality traits are foundational dimensions of leadership success.

This leaves personality traits as the most likely indicator of leadership potential. Personality testing plays a much less significant role in law firm selection processes, which means there tends to be much greater variety in personality traits than cognitive ability. Identifying those lawyers with the personality traits that are markers of leadership potential, allows law firms to identify those individuals with the greatest potential to become successful partners, early in their career.

The High Potential Traits Indicator (HPTI)[7] developed in 2016 measures six personality traits that research has shown are foundational or growth dimensions of leadership potential.[8] It is important to note that the relationship between each of the six traits and leadership potential is curvilinear. This means there is an optimum range for each trait; having either too little or too much of a trait is likely to have a negative impact on leadership potential. The behaviors associated with each of the six traits are summarized in the box below.

Conscientiousness (foundational)
Highly conscientious people tend to make concrete plans, can motivate themselves to work and achieve goals. They are attentive to detail and ensure tasks are completed to a high standard, but there is a danger that over-conscientious individuals may undervalue more spontaneous insights and hunches, thus missing opportunities.

Individuals with lower conscientiousness are more casual about detail, deadlines and quality control. They may also have trouble setting individual and team goals. However, they are likely to be very adaptable, open to new insights, and tend not to get stressed or overworked.

Adjustment (foundational)
People with low adjustment scores tend to think more negative thoughts and become preoccupied with negative emotions. They are more likely to be self-conscious about their work, their actions, and how they behave around others. They can become preoccupied with the opinions of others and may spend excessive amounts of time worrying about what others would see as trivial issues.

High adjustment is often related to feeling positive about one's own work, performance and relationships. Those with higher adjustment can shrug off stresses and strains, and are more confident about their performance.

However, too much adjustment can also be a problem. It can make individuals seem cold, disengaged, and may make them more prone to hubris.

Curiosity (foundational)
Highly curious individuals tend to search for new information and alternative methods of getting work done but may undervalue existing work methods. Overly-curious individuals risk implementing change for change's sake, which can demotivate others and lead to perfectly good, established ways of doing things being abandoned unnecessarily. Less curious individuals value tried-and-tested approaches, can be suspicious of new information, and may dislike experimenting with new techniques. Individuals who are not open to new information may stick to old ways of working long after they've become problematic or inefficient.

Risk approach (growth dimension)
This indicates how someone deals with challenging, difficult or threatening situations. People with a high-risk approach consider a broad range of options, choose whichever they believe to be the best one and then act quickly. They are willing to confront challenges directly and immediately. Individuals with lower risk approach tend to avoid challenges or conflict until they have no other choice.

Ambiguity acceptance (growth dimension)
This describes peoples' reaction to complexity and contradictory information: situations where outcomes, decisions, argument and evidence are not immediately obvious or clear.

Individuals with high ambiguity acceptance enjoy such situations and will often thrive in organizations which have flexible policies, and which value individual decision-making and independence.

Individuals with low ambiguity acceptance prefer straightforward problems, situations and solutions. They may be better suited to organizations where clearly documented and rigid hierarchies, business processes and guidelines are the norm.

Competitiveness (growth dimension)
Individuals with higher competitiveness need to feel that their achievements are recognized and appreciated. Higher competitiveness can drive performance and a desire to self-improve. Competitiveness is positive when it is used to encourage group performance improvements, but not when individuals pursue selfish goals.

Individuals with lower competitiveness feel less need for control and are less focused on rewards or recognition. Where group efforts are key, individuals with low competitiveness may be better able to draw out the varying talents of others.

How do partners differ from other lawyers?

Research with over 100 UK-based, commercial lawyers (27 partners and 76 non-partners) using the HPTI showed that the personality traits of partners differ from non-partners in two statistically significant ways. On average, partners scored higher on measures of risk approach and ambiguity acceptance than non-partners. This suggests that partners are likely to be more comfortable than non-partners when dealing with complex problems and that they will approach challenging situations differently to other lawyers.

The size of these differences would be described as "medium" in statistical terms. This means if we were to pick a partner and non-partner at random, there is an almost two-thirds likelihood that the partner would score higher than the non-partner on each of these traits. We can therefore be confident that the observed differences are very unlikely to have arisen by chance and that they are non-trivial in nature.

The mean partner score for each of these traits was also closer to the optimal range of scores for a leader than the non-partner scores; this was especially true for partners holding senior management roles. These traits are, therefore, likely to prove useful markers of leadership potential early in a lawyer's career. The other four traits measured by the HPTI showed no statistical differences between the scores of partners and non-partners, suggesting that these are less likely to be useful markers of a lawyer's leadership potential.

There was evidence that partners with senior management roles also scored significantly higher than other lawyers on measures of *conscientiousness, curiosity and competitiveness.* However, the relatively small number of these partners in the overall sample means further research is recommended before firm conclusions can be drawn.

Implications for law firms and lawyers

Lawyer selection processes

It has been argued that an over-reliance on academic performance as a selection criterion restricts access to the legal profession and reduces diversity.[9] The lack of significant correlations between personality traits (such as those measured by the HPTI) and cognitive ability indicates that law firms are likely to benefit from including both in a model of potential. More specifically, when identifying individuals with leadership potential it would be useful to consider traits such as *risk approach* and *ambiguity acceptance*. Making these changes to both external selection processes and internal talent management has the potential to improve both firm performance and lawyer diversity.

Law firms must avoid defining potential in a way that is either overly restrictive or too broad. The former can cause talented lawyers to be overlooked, while the latter can lead to lawyers being promoted into unsuitable roles.

Lawyer development

Law firms must avoid defining potential in a way that is either overly restrictive or too broad. The former can cause talented lawyers to be overlooked, while the latter can lead to lawyers being promoted into unsuitable roles. A multi-faceted approach to talent management, with different categories of potential and related career paths, should help firms provide their lawyers with opportunities that will help them fully develop their potential. This will in turn mean lawyers experience increased career satisfaction, leading to improved retention. Adopting such an approach would represent a significant change in many firms. Clear communication of the revised categories of potential – how they were developed and the benefits that they offer to lawyers – must consequently be prioritized during implementation.

Personality testing would help law firms identify high-potential lawyers, making it easier to give these individuals the experience that will help them develop their leadership capacity. Risk approach and ambiguity acceptance are both growth dimensions of potential, which means individuals require guidance and opportunities in order to utilize these traits to their full potential. Finally, feedback from personality testing can be used to increase lawyer self-awareness. This can help lawyers better reflect on how they can best make use of their abilities (whatever they may be) and identify a career path that will maximize their chances of career success. Following such reflection, for some the goal will remain partnership, but for many it will not.

This article first appeared in the 2018 publication, *Legal Leadership: A Handbook for Future Success,* published by Globe Law and Business.

Edward Walker is an independent consultant who works with law firms and in-house legal teams as a coach, facilitator, and trainer. Prior to this he worked for over a decade in resourcing and talent management, during which time he managed trainee solicitor recruitment for a leading international law firm. Edward holds MScs in Psychology and Organizational Psychology and is currently undertaking doctoral research that focuses on the experiences of legal professionals who use artificial intelligence at work.

1 Empson, L. (2013). *Who's in charge? Exploring Leadership Dynamics in Professional Service Firms.* London, UK: Cass Business School.
2 Clance, P.R. and Imes, S.A. (1978). The Impostor Phenomenon in High Achieving Women: Dynamics and Therapeutic Intervention. *Psychotherapy Theory, Research and Practice*, 15(3).
3 Pendleton, D. and Furnham, A. (2012). *Leadership: All you need to know*. Basingstoke, UK: Palgrave McMillan.
4 Silzer, R. and Church, A. (2009). The pearls and perils of identifying potential. *Industrial and Organizational Psychology*, 2(4), 377-412.
5 Ree, M. and Earles, J. (1992). Intelligence is the best predictor of job performance. *Current directions in psychological science*, 1(3), 86-89.
6 Barrick, M., Mount, M. and Judge, T. (2001). Personality and performance at the beginning of the new millennium: What do we know and where do we go next? *International Journal of Selection and Assessment*, 9(1/2), 9-30.
7 Thomas International (2016). High Potential Trait Indicator *(HPTI)*, www.thomas.co/assessments/high-potential-trait-indicator-hpti-assessment
8 MacRae, I. and Furnham, A. (2016). *High Potential Traits Inventory: Leadership Capacity Report Testing Manual*. London, UK: High Potential Psychology Ltd.
9 Sullivan, R. (2010). *Barriers to the legal profession*. London, UK: Legal Services Board.

Culture, diversity, and ESG

Empathy – do lawyers need it?

Sophie Cameron

October is World Menopause Awareness month

Five years ago that might have been a surprising statement to read in a legal journal or to hear in a corporate environment, but lately the menopause has definitely been having a moment. In 2021, a well-received TV documentary fronted by UK TV presenter Davina McCall sought to challenge many preconceptions about the menopause, and was followed up by a coordinated campaign involving a number of prominent female public figures which ignited a public debate. Demand for hormone replacement therapy (HRT) medication has increased by 42% between 2021 and 2022 and a special taskforce was set up to coordinate supply chains modelling the approach taken with the Covid vaccine. Menopause specialists like Dr Louise Newson and Dr Jennifer Gunter have come to prominence by debunking myths on social media and providing support networks for menopausal women. A #MakeMenopauseMatter campaign is aiming for 150,000 signatures on a petition to parliament demanding mandatory menopause training for all GPs, and menopause policies in every workplace. In the United Kingdom there is now an All-Party Parliamentary Group and in 2021 a Private Member's Bill was introduced which seeks to abolish prescription charges for HRT.

As chair of Women@TR – the women's employee network at Thomson Reuters – in 2021 I worked with colleagues to organise two panel sessions to discuss the menopause and its impact on women in the workplace. Over 300 TR attendees globally attended to hear from two experts – one medical and one in women's wellbeing issues, and myself

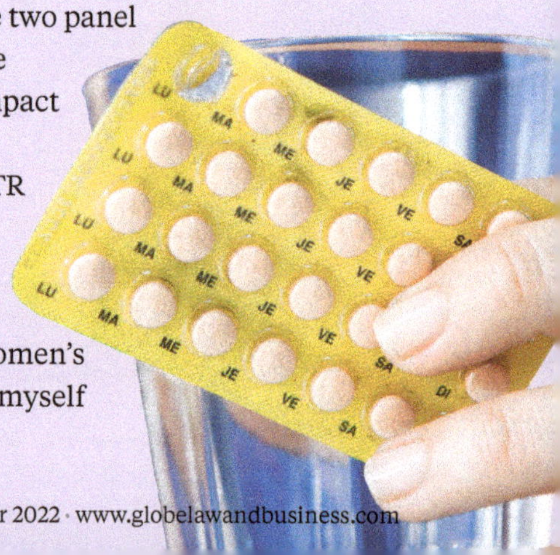

and several other employees shared our varied personal experience of perimenopause and menopause.

We received a record amount of positive feedback following these panel sessions and subsequently organised a series of small group coffee sessions on different aspects of the menopause and for different groups of employees and also produced a guidance toolkit to support employees and managers.

Two pieces of feedback in particular resonated with me:

So empowering to hear a group of women openly talk about how our bodies actually function and how that plays into the workplace. Thank you so much! [US participant]

I can't tell you how informative and healing the panel event was for me. It helped me rebuild my confidence and not look at my own experience in isolation. [European participant]

By making space for a conversation about menopause we had created the conditions for empathy. Empathy is the ability to emotionally understand what other people feel, to see things from their point of view, and to imagine yourself in their place. Creating empathy with your workforce is crucial in an age when authenticity and diversity of thought and experience is lauded and when employees and job seekers are placing an ever-higher premium on being able to bring one's whole self to the workplace. In global organisations, empathy can help build common ground between virtual teams based in different locations and reduce silos. Building empathy can also engender deeper connections with colleagues working from home in hybrid arrangements.

Arguably, the business case for diversity and inclusion (D&I) has now largely been proven – it is generally accepted that diversity of thought and views lead to better business outcomes and as such inclusion is of strategic value and importance to organisations. Law firms have D&I practitioners and policies in place. But what that means in practice for our workforces and for client services is still evolving. Too many people still view lack of inclusion and diversity, or exclusion, as requiring blatant and visible manifestation. If we think back to the summer of 2020 and the resurgence of the Black Lives Matter (BLM) movement following the murder of George Floyd in Minneapolis, there was a welcome focus on being 'anti racist', taking active steps to go beyond obvious examples of discrimination and to build self-awareness, to explore our bias and privilege and the experiences of those who have experienced discrimination and to guard against white fragility. In other words, to build empathy with others. Thomson Reuters is headquartered near Minneapolis so we felt the impact of the BLM movement particularly keenly and local staff have made a massive contribution to the rebuilding of the Minneapolis community both physically in terms of clearing up after the riots and by supporting local community organisations via volunteering and sponsorship. The TR Black Employee Network was also instrumental in introducing listening sessions for employees across the organisation.

Empathy is the ability to emotionally understand what other people feel, to see things from their point of view, and to imagine yourself in their place.

Understanding your workforce better and, crucially, acting on this understanding is likely to create a more inclusive and safer environment for them to be themselves and to thrive at work. But how do organisations identify the issues important to their employees and clients and how do they address them in tangible ways? There can be a lack of clarity about which issues should be addressed and in what order which can in itself create fear and discomfort and sometimes lead to paralysis.

Why does the menopause matter?

So why did we choose to focus on the menopause last year? There are about 13 million British women who are either peri- or postmenopausal right now, with about 4.5 million of those in the workplace. By 2024, the US Bureau of Labor Statistics estimates that there will be over 55.1 million women aged 55 and over in the US workforce – a far greater number than the 18.5 million women aged 16–24. Some three out of four women experience menopause-related symptoms with one in four experiencing serious symptoms. Menopausal women are the fastest growing section of the workforce and recent studies have shown that there is a spike in the number of women aged 45–55 leaving the workplace at a critical point in their careers due to the hidden symptoms of menopause such as reduced confidence and increased anxiety. So, crucially, if we want older women to stay in the workplace and if we want to maintain and increase female representation at a senior level, we need to find a way to talk about what women need from their employers during the perimenopause and menopause.

Building trust and a sense of belonging is a vitally important aspect of working with employee networks.

At the TR Thomson Reuters US menopause panel, 44% of those who responded to a poll question had experienced menopause symptoms that impacted them in the workplace. At both panels there was support for manager training, the development of a toolkit to help managers and employees and possibly a support network. It is important that allies are aware of the challenges menopause may bring for some women but the complexity and breadth of symptoms means that women have different experiences so it is important not to assume that female managers will automatically have all the answers either.

Some of these issues go to wider challenges with women's access to health services, and there are major intersections with other areas of inequality. Just as black women are three times more likely to die from a pregnancy-related cause than white women, women of colour may have additional challenges in terms of menopause symptoms and accessing healthcare and have higher instances of uterine fibroids and hysterectomies. Multiple factors contribute to these disparities, such as variation in quality of healthcare, other underlying health conditions, structural racism and implicit bias.

Empathy for lawyers?

As a senior director with Practical Law and chair of an employee network, I felt a very strong need to share my experiences of the perimenopause and to model an empathetic approach, especially to our majority female legal editorial staff. We were lucky to have several other senior leaders from the TR legal business who were also comfortable sharing their experiences. This was an exercise in bringing our whole selves to work and modelling vulnerability. For me, building trust and a sense of belonging is a vitally important aspect of working with employee networks. I had found working with other business resource groups a really rewarding experience and wanted to reach more people with this approach. We were really taken aback with the response the menopause panel sessions received. Hosting the sessions on Microsoft Teams meant we were able to include employees from many different regions and business units and provided an easy platform to share the recordings and follow-up actions.

We had positive feedback from the demographic already experiencing perimenopause or menopause (as quoted above) but also crucially from younger women who told us that they felt better educated and prepared for their future and supported by an employer who was prepared to host these discussions. It was agreed that knowledge is power – sharing information and experiences with colleagues helps empower us and demystifying and destigmatising this topic is vital in order to access the tools to deal with it.

We discussed dialogue with managers, the importance of maintaining and realising the benefits of a flexible work environment, being open with colleagues when necessary so women feel able to bring their whole self to work. Minor adjustments to a working environment can bring great benefits.

We did have a few – but not enough – male attendees. Hopefully, however, we started the discussion and opened the door to more male managers and allies actively educating themselves and being ready to have discussions about the needs of their female team members.

We did, however, receive some negative feedback from a senior leader from another jurisdiction. In her opinion, conversations about the menopause should be reserved for 'a woman and her physician' and were not for the workplace and we had overstepped the mark with the guidance we had produced. We had involved HR colleagues in our planning meetings as well as women's network colleagues from other jurisdictions and most of our positive feedback had in fact come from the same jurisdiction as this negative feedback. There was clearly a need for more open dialogue on the impact of menopause in the workplace in some jurisdictions but also that need meant that it should be handled more sensitively and we needed to get more buy-in from local leadership.

Therefore, actively developing empathic skills should assist organisations in building an inclusive and psychologically safe environment in which senior management understands their workforce needs. This is a great end goal in itself of course, but will this help lawyers in their client work?

Empathy towards clients

Increased legal risk and complexity in a global environment and rising competition for legal services means that law firms and legal services providers need to find ways of differentiating themselves. The lingering vivid examples of Covid and BLM together with renewed focus on the need for urgent climate action also demonstrate the need for and value of empathy in increasing the ability of business to respond to novel situations and known unknowns.

Most of us work in self-described 'client-obsessed', 'client-centric', or 'client-focused' environments. Being able to empathise with client experiences, anticipate risks and challenges and put forward solutions for their legal challenges has long been recognised as the secret sauce which marks out a sought after trusted adviser rather than simply a competent technical lawyer. Lawyers need to be able to put themselves in a client's shoes and consider broader business impacts and, increasingly, social issues. Planning the TR panels definitely increased my consciousness of menopause awareness-raising work going on across the legal profession and in-house legal teams.

Actively developing empathic skills should assist organisations in building an inclusive and psychologically safe environment in which senior management understands their workforce needs.

Further, lawyers take instructions from individual clients. These individuals may have grown up in different jurisdictions, have hidden disabilities, have caring responsibilities. We may leverage their love of rugby, tennis and theatre for client entertainment purposes and we should not shy away from seeking to understand their whole selves.

How to build empathy

Taking intentional steps to build empathy with colleagues and employees and also with clients will speed up progress towards a more inclusive workplace and also improve client focus and service delivery. Precise actions will vary from organisation to organisation but there are some key themes. In some organisations and regions, building empathy may require significant culture change or close examination of existing structures and practices which might not be comfortable for everyone. However, it is important that if progress is to be made there is an acceptance that existing practices may need to change and in that process mistakes may occur. The journey is important.

Seek feedback
Make it easy for feedback to be shared via a variety of channels and be prepared to either action the feedback or, if that isn't possible or appropriate, to share reasoning. One person's inclusive and safe environment may not be another's, especially where there are regional or other cultural differences in an organisation. As I shared above, feedback alerted us to this with the menopause panels. Be open about your organisation's journey and iterate it. Don't get too caught up in concerns about language – do your research and be mindful but you are likely to make some mistakes along the way so be ready to learn from them. We navigated the UK/US menopause language barrier – for some reason we refer to hot flushes in the United Kingdom and hot flashes in the United States!

Use surveys and listening exercises with clients at different touchpoints across the organisation and at different stages in the relationship. Don't wait for the end of a project to seek feedback. Lawyers need a deep understanding of client strategy and not just the work that is sent to them so encourage and facilitate curiosity.

Support and enable employee networks
I am a great believer in the power of employee networks to share experiences and build empathy and a sense of belonging. At Thomson Reuters there were some incredibly powerful sessions of our Black Employee Network in 2020. Enabling employees to self-organise means you will hear authentic voices from the bottom up. But put in place genuine feedback loops and make sure HR and senior management are accountable to them.

Leverage employee networks
Those employee networks can also support the organisation's activity and amplify messaging, and when they work together you will see change. I have seen this work well with vital campaigns around improving employee personal data records in order to measure D&I performance.

Model empathy and embed in the workplace
Everyone should be encouraged to adopt an empathic approach and to model empathy wherever possible, particularly leaders. Inviting people to speak in meetings or setting up one-to-ones is a great way to do this. Invite people to tell their stories, especially if they have different life experiences. Of course, it is essential that these are authentic approaches and you will need to create safe spaces for these discussions to take place. It can take time to create these conditions. Not everyone will be willing to share personal information and no-one should feel compelled to do so.

Tell stories
Storytelling is important as is modelling vulnerability. Sharing my personal experiences about the perimenopause was a very cathartic process for me. I was nervous and I was conscious of my privilege. I definitely felt that I was making myself vulnerable and I was relieved to hear (mostly!) positive feedback afterwards.

Put policies and benefits in place

After seeking feedback and listening to employees, do your research, benchmark against other organisations and walk the talk in terms of what benefits and entitlements you offer your employees.

Conclusion

Nearly all discussions about the power of technology and digitisation to transform legal services end with an acknowledgement that legal services are still a human business and lawyers still need to be good managers and inclusive practitioners and empathy is at the heart of this – start small by listening to those around you.

Sophie Cameron was until recently a senior editorial director and chair of the Women's Network at Thomson Reuters where she worked in a variety of editorial roles with Practical Law over the last 17 years. During that time she also served for eight years as a councillor at the London Borough of Hackney. She was formerly a practising lawyer at both Freshfields and Bates Wells.

Waste not, want not – recalibrating legal

Eimear McCann

How can the legal industry operate more sustainably? Eimear McCann explores how lawyers can work smart to eliminate waste.

How often do you think about global waste? Predictions are that by 2050 worldwide waste generation will increase by 70%, driven by socio-economic factors and behavioural shifts. Only 20% of this (3.4 billion metric tons by approximation) will be recycled: a genuinely shocking statistic. In a state of overwhelm, most of us will be blinded to the remaining 80%, simply because we struggle to contemplate something which feels much larger than our lived, human experience. Our inaction is not necessarily reflective of indifference, but rather a feeling of impotence in the face of the enormity of the collective task.

I remain in awe of the astrophysicist, tasked with presenting a visualisation of the universe, even though our universe was not built for human minds to comprehend (in fact, only 5% of the universe is normal, observable matter). Our inherent cognitive limitations are further compounded by culture, mindset and a conditioned way of thinking and assessing. Apparently, as humans, we have blind spots for a myriad of cosmic phenomena that simply run counter to our intuition and understanding; for example, we erroneously perceive patterns in the spacing of stars and of the planets in the solar system, seeing them as though arranged in a specific order. Apophenia or otherwise, our human perceptions often get in the way of seeing the truth.

Our legal universe is vast, and often indecipherable to those who do not inhabit it (trying to explain the dichotomous billable hour is often an exercise in self-ostracism). For many of us, law is all we have known, and it can be challenging to step outside of our cosmos and set aside flawed perceptions and patterns. Historically, law has been populated by lawyers and practitioners who have never resided in other worlds. Cross-pollinating was not a thing, and the law had its own unique orbit, which was simultaneously exclusive and inclusive, depending on the nature or duration of your residence.

Evolution is happening rapidly across all segments of the profession, and yet, as welcome as the transformation is, there is still so much waste on a global scale. Intangible and often impossible to measure, this waste – an elusive chameleon – is largely ignored.

The widespread adoption of technology within legal has inexorably diminished our reliance on paper, with a global push for greener ways of working. Working electronically has never been more seamless, or more desirable. Thanks to an escalation in the use of the cloud and a renewed focus on tech-enabled working on a business-wide level, paperless is becoming the norm. There is a sense that as we save on one resource, we overlook others.

Fundamentally, technology, for all its ubiquity, is only useful when it is properly implemented, understood, and, as obvious as it sounds, has full buy-in from the end users. Legal tech is still a relatively new market, and the waves of new products and functionality will continue to flow. Amidst talk of market saturation and record levels of investment, I can still picture stressed-out lawyers sitting at their desks, feeling entirely detached, not only from this exciting market, but from the new software that feels more like an imposition than a welcome addition.

The chasm between decision maker and end user has still not completely narrowed, and anecdotally many law firms find that uptake across the business can be low to moderate. Aside from the wasted cost of procurement, and the time lost on implementation and likely integration, there is a deeper sense of futility for all involved. Without internal marketing and buy-in, new platforms will experience a gradual atrophy of usage, which does little to displace some lingering reticence to engage new software in the first place. The land and expand strategy has a crucial role in many legal tech success stories, with a focus on internal champions and an empathetic style of engagement. It may sound basic, but a product is only useful if the story resonates with the user; otherwise, it's just another platform to contend with in an omnichannel overload.

Our adherence to Microsoft packages seems unwavering, and yet large chunks of the functionality of the Office 365 package are under-utilised. I'm not sure I've ever used Excel for much more than data capture and simple calculations. I suspect that most of us have access to platforms on desktops and laptops that we surface, but don't fully engage, and all the while new products with new integrations emerge; a steady flow of new ideas captured in software.

With this increasing digitisation, we face further challenges. The nature of a lawyer's autonomous inclinations is a standard part of the legal vernacular, but I wonder how far that desire for autonomy stretches? Our lives are busy, and our brains are busier. Thirty years ago, we tended to delegate; both personally and professionally. Armed with our multi-functional smartphone, we are very much in control. In fact, we can organise our entire lives from a device which could be said to be the digital encapsulation of autonomy. And yet, aside from the generic distractibility arguments, how much time do we waste as a consequence? With emails and instant messaging so accessible, do we send messages that are superfluous? Do we migrate away from complex work too often to check emails that simply don't need our attention?

Thirty years ago, we tended to delegate; both personally and professionally. Armed with our multi-functional smartphone, we are very much in control.

Unless, or until, we have a more cohesive way of working, I fear that we are fuelling the myth of multi-tasking, which not only increases the production of cortisol and adrenaline, but also leads to overstimulation and an inevitable scrambling of thought. Just when we think we are saving time and energy, we are wasting some of our most precious resources – our clarity of thought and judgement – indispensable in the mind of a lawyer.

Conversely, the same tech can be remarkably efficient at saving time, energy and cost in the overall automation of workflows. This is factually undisputed. Technology, coupled with legal design, is arguably even more effective, although the latter is still handled with caution by many, not yet persuaded of the potence of visuals and iconography in the serious business of law. Legal design, as a concept, is a novel one, and innovation will always leave the door ajar to some cynicism; however, I believe that these misconceptions around legal design will dissipate, leaving more room for human-centred design thinking and ideology.

Legal design, in my view, is primarily about accessibility, in whatever form that may take. I love words and language, but we waste a lot of them in legal drafting. Do we need to be so verbose? Do contracts need to run to hundreds of pages? Does the language itself need to be so incongruous with the real world that we inhabit? I wonder how alive we are to the disparities of tone and language, and whether we are wasting an opportunity for new and innovative ways of communicating.

Legal design, in my view, is primarily about accessibility, in whatever form that may take. I love words and language, but we waste a lot of them in legal drafting.

Running in tandem with legal design thinking is the push for standardisation. OneNDA (a crowd-sourced, open-source Non-Disclosure Agreement) is an excellent example of a desire to stop legal waste. Like most great ideas, it started with asking a simple question – what if there was a homogenous starting point, with the same template? Wouldn't that save enormous amounts of time, money and effort? It makes commercial sense. No one wants a protracted negotiation; everyone gets the deal done quicker and lawyers have more time to spend on complex work. Not all legal documents are capable of standardisation and there will always be a place for the detailed and the tailored, but we could simply look to save where we can by streamlining language and by simplifying categorisation.

To do so, we need to embrace collaborative ways of thinking and working. The amount of knowledge that is wasted and forever lost within the profession cannot be captured by metrics, but it must surely be expansive. Before transitioning over to the world of tech, I had never heard anyone allude to the 'bus factor' (which essentially refers to the number of people in your team/business who could put a project in trouble if they are hit by a bus). It sounds brutal but it's an important component in the mechanisms of a project or within a business, particularly smaller ones, where the bulk of the knowledge and the core skillset tends to fall on to one or two people.

Knowledge-sharing in legal is sporadic, although the necessary duality of awareness and desire is growing. Noslegal and Liquid Legal Institute are two disparate initiatives that are a call to action for lawyers globally to share knowledge, experience and awareness; while they have a very different manifesto, they both aim to bring cohesion and transparency to a world lacking both, with education firmly underpinning their work across the sector.

Much could be explored on the wasted opportunities to share knowledge within and beyond the confines of our legal cosmos. As a starting point, I wonder why paralegals, trainees and junior lawyers aren't encouraged to share ideas and observations to a much greater extent, joining law firms and businesses with fresh minds and an initial objectivity that will naturally diminish over time. A question of rhetoric, but one worth asking is why aren't lawyers more consultative in their external engagements? Wouldn't it say a lot more about the profession if there was less "it depends" and more of "let's work this through together"? Would this not encourage knowledge-sharing, within and beyond the profession?

And yet it all starts where it is most equivocal – law school – the springboard for everything else. With some wonderful, notable exceptions, legal training can be oxymoronic and outdated. Rather than experiential and experimental, it is mainly study-based and light years away from current practice. Such a waste of brilliant minds and extensive resources. Imagine if kinaesthetic learning dominated, with law students utilising the tech used in practice, from document automation through to visual workflow tools and data analytics. Imagine too that students were taught design thinking (by designers), business development skills, and actually spent time with clients, getting to understand their pain points and the importance of collaboration. The study of law is tough, but it could also be fun; more importantly, legal training could really move future lawyers from positions of heightened anxiety to a place of psychological safety. A new generation, armed with enough experience, confidence, and competence to feel at home in law – that would really be something.

Law and technology share a mutual criticism in that regard; both maligned for their absence of humanity. There are wasted opportunities in both. Professionalism has finally been granted its proper definition, shedding years of uptight stereotypes. The opportunity now is to really demonstrate that lawyers, intelligent and competent, are simply humans, who can not only empathise and think creatively, but who can also suffer burnout and exhaustion. External perceptions matter much less than the internal culture within legal. We have an opportunity to reframe and to give lawyers a chance to express themselves, to have permission to fail, to make mistakes and to be supported in the process. If there was ever a time to change, this is it – a time to recalibrate. With attrition rates at an all-time high, I can only think of the waste of training and talent, as more and more are choosing to leave the profession behind.

As to the tech, do we need to explore sensory experiences, particularly in the contentious sectors? Arguably, all virtual experiences are hybrid; we are physically present, even if our communication may be digital, and we need to have technology that reflects that. How can we ensure that our hybrid experiences retain humanity? Should hearings be more immersive, with an interdisciplinary focus, looking at the roles of neuroscience, art and music?

The amalgam of law and tech is a human one. We design the technology and yet the tech shapes how we behave and how we work. We decide where the tech slots into workflows and processes and, in theory, the tech ameliorates our experience. We therefore have a responsibility to design the tech to augment our humanity, otherwise we risk creating a deeper chasm between them and us.

With a richness of data, there are many possibilities to create stories that bind together the human and the tech. Data stored and organised is powerful, but the uses are infinite and still untapped. Once we start to analyse the data to identify trends and patterns, our relationship with tech is less fractious and more harmonious, with analytics empowering decision-making and strategy. Creativity and autonomy marry well at this intersection of legal tech.

Perhaps we are already on the path to a more ecological legal world. Thinking around office space and business travel has changed, tech has liberated us from long commutes and there is a growing sense of urgency in the need for deep cultural change within the profession.

Returning to my awe of the astrophysicist, rather than focusing on the vastness of our legal cosmos, and how insignificant a place we may hold, maybe it's time to flip the narrative and instead see the potential of the individual in exploring exciting new ways to eliminate waste and to recalibrate legal.

Eimear McCann is a former lawyer, and currently commercial director of TrialView, an AI litigation platform. She also lectures in legal tech and innovation at BPP University and is a member of the Law Society Technology & Law Committee.

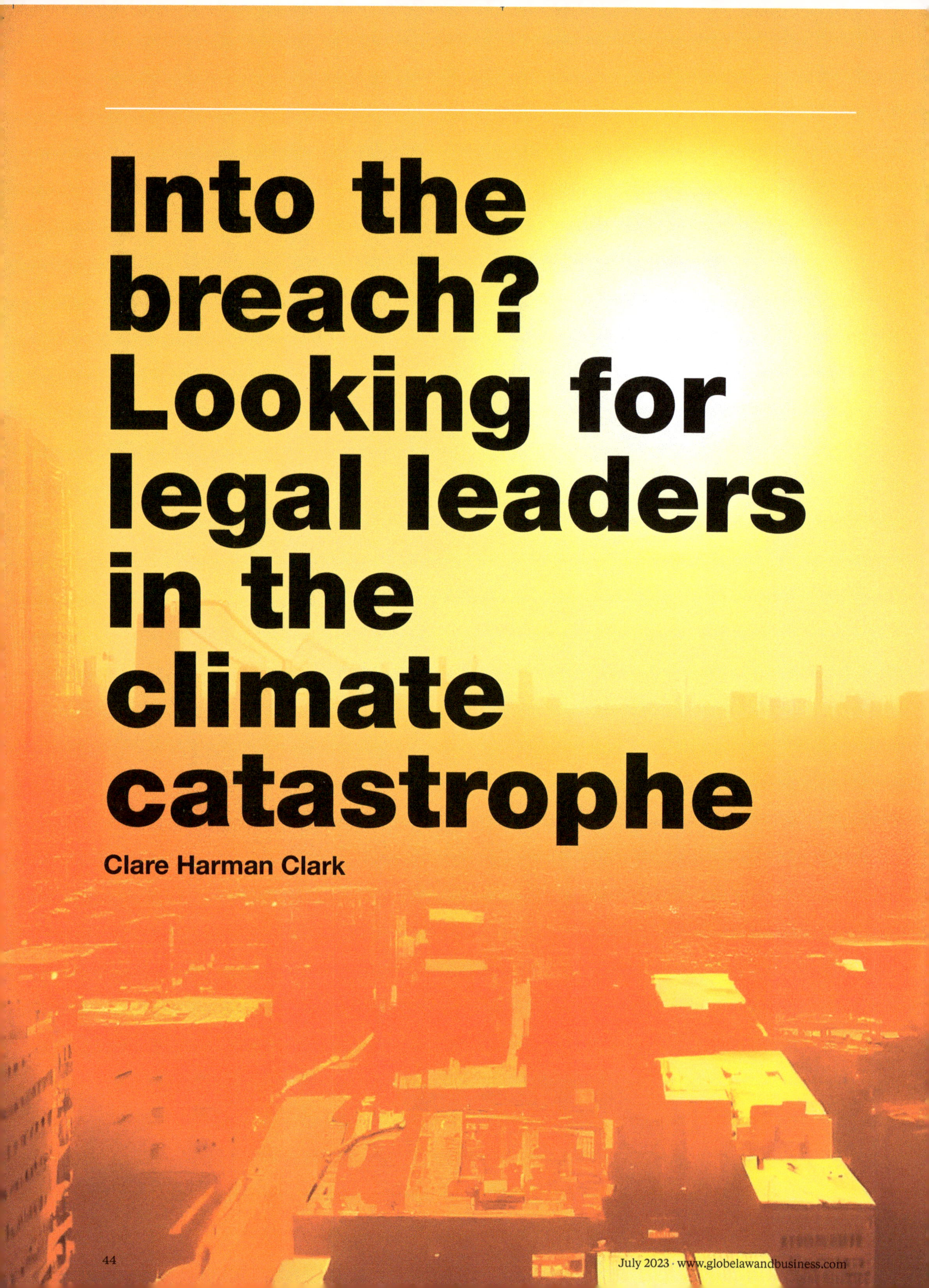

Into the breach? Looking for legal leaders in the climate catastrophe

Clare Harman Clark

It's time.

Climate change is making its impact felt across the globe. We're facing *another* summer of record extreme temperatures, more heat-related deaths, devastation from spreading wildfires, droughts, storms, and significant disruption. Closer to home, it *again* highlights the UK's critical climate vulnerability; the exposure of its cities, its infrastructure, its communities (human and animal), and its economy. And the risks are only getting worse.

Fifteen years ago, the UK was actually the first jurisdiction to put what are colloquially called net zero targets on a legislative footing, with the Climate Change Act 2008. The government was making all the right noises. In 2016, it ratified the Paris Agreement to the United Nations Framework Convention on Climate Change, publicly committing to a goal of holding the increase in global warming to "well below 2°C", and ideally a maximum of 1.5°C above pre-industrial levels.

Despite this promising start, however, there remains "very limited evidence" that the country has been equipped at the scale needed to face the climate risks. The independent Climate Change Committee (CCC), which was established under the 2008 Act, was recently damning in its biennial report of progress on climate change adaptation,[1] a key part of the looming decarbonization deadlines. CCC chair Lord Deben introduced the report clearly, saying "The UK has lost the clear global leadership it once held". He continued:

"The [Government's] current approach is not leading to delivery on the ground and significant policy gaps remain… Action cannot be delayed further."

Indeed, the CCC concludes that, without action, "our confidence in the UK reaching its targets has materially reduced".

Clearly, as every general knows, strategy without tactics will not win a war. And if there is no top-down tactical leadership, no road map for actual change, we must all look collectively to get our own houses in order.

All eyes on the lawyers?

To be fair, many industries have already made vanguard movements against this complex and intractable enemy. Many have articulated and demonstrated their own commitments to net zero in the absence of any actual government plans or regulations. And many think it's right that the legal profession now shows its own leadership, not only in the board room but also across the (albeit virtual) negotiation table.

We're facing *another* summer of record extreme temperatures, more heat-related deaths, devastation from spreading wildfires, droughts, storms, and significant disruption.

The Law Society has long agreed. Back in October 2021,[2] it made a Climate Change Resolution, promising to "develop plans and take rapid action, in a manner which is consistent with restricting global warming to 1.5°C, by adopting science-based targets". Among other things, it vowed to urge "solicitors, always in a way which is compatible with their professional duties and the administration of justice, to engage in climate conscious legal practice". This resolution was a clear signpost of things to come and on 19 April this year, it published detailed *Guidance on the Impact of Climate Change on Solicitors*,[3] with the clear message that, one way or another, the time has come for the legal industry to polish its armor and be prepared to place both our practices and our transactional advice in the context of climate change.

Battling in the boardroom

The first part of the note covers, arguably, the easy bit. As entities in their own right, law firms are already increasingly setting their own targets to reduce climate impact. It's no longer (just) about urging email recipients to think before printing; at the other end of the potential spectrum some firms

Our contracts are where the world is built, where obligations are set, relationships are forged, and our clients' impact and potential is writ large. Where our pens are potentially mighty swords.

have created far-reaching environmental, social, and governance (ESG) strategies detailing how they will do business. Some have been actively operating within a "Green Pledge" from Campaign for Greener Arbitrations,[4] while others have committed to implement sustainability-improving practices. Most recently in June this year, the first eight members, including Taylor Wessing LLP, have even signed up to the ambitious Legal Charter 1.5 initiative, which aims to galvanize the entire legal sector to drive transformative change.

Against this active backdrop, the Law Society guidance helps firms with the design and implementation of their own climate-conscious corporate strategy. These strategies will undoubtedly vary dramatically depending on the size and impact of the relevant firm, and the application of any mandatory (or voluntary) reporting obligations. Nonetheless, whatever your step on this journey, there is also much to learn in terms of understanding scientific *language* that can obfuscate this foe. The note discusses "science-based" targets, for example, the calculation of greenhouse gas (GHG) emissions, and explains simply how these arise (including the nature of "advised" or downstream emissions, which lawyers can effectively pick up as a result of their association with the matters and transaction it advises on). It also offers advice on greenwashing and, crucially, how to identify physical and transitional climate risks.

The Legal Charter 1.5[5]

The Charter consists of a set of common principles that signatories commit to support, to make the best contribution to reduce greenhouse gas emissions at the speed and scale necessary to restrict global temperature increases to no more than 1.5°C.

Participating firms will make a public commitment to eight core principles:

- *Principle 1: Leadership* – reducing their own law firm's emissions in line with science-based targets and influencing clients in this regard.
- *Principle 2: Advised emissions* – supporting the development of a methodology on advised emissions to deliver a 1.5°C transition.
- *Principle 3: Commitment to the "Global Goal"* – working to restrict global temperature increases to no more than 1.5°C whilst also supporting efforts to address and not exacerbate the related challenges of biodiversity loss and social injustice.
- *Principle 4: Reforms and public policy* – identifying and promoting constructive reforms and informing public policy.
- *Principle 5: Accountability and reporting* – all firms commit to reporting annually on their activities and progress across the principles and projects of the Charter. These reports are designed to offer examples of best practice and case studies as to how best to implement the Charter principles.
- *Principle 6: Education and upskilling* – of staff across the legal profession.
- *Principle 7: Focused pro bono* – to leverage firms' combined resources and influence.
- *Principle 8: Meaningful offsetting* – working as a collaborative group, both signatory firms and dialogue partners will explore how to develop a large-scale offsetting project that will help to leverage greater impact from the offset spend across the legal sector.

Out in the field

So far, so good, but arguably the big guns in the *Guidance on the Impact of Climate Change on Solicitors*, and the best potential for genuinely effective, bottom-up change, comes with an exploration of professional duties.

Every lawyer, advising on any type of law, is bound by professional duties and the note looks in detail at the way these are likely, ultimately, to stretch to accommodate a necessary analysis of those climate change risks. It looks in detail at the duties of care, to warn, to disclose, and to uphold service and competence levels, and the Law Society's conclusion that we will need to place every instruction or piece of advice within the context of climate change. Of course, all of this analysis is likely to be fact- and context-dependent (including in relation to the extent of client sophistication in this field), but it is also worth considering various SRA Principles – the fundamental tenets of ethical behavior for solicitors. The note particularly focuses on a need to apply professional judgment and take a balanced approach to meeting duties, whilst prioritizing conflicting principles that safeguard the wider public interest (such as rule of law) over individual clients.

We can expect more detailed guidance of how this might be done *in different practice areas* in due course, but, for the time being, the message is that our existing professional duties to clients have already started and will continue to flex to incorporate understanding and advising on climate legal risks.

Mightier than the sword?

Of course, the potential for change being driven by the legal profession is something groups such as The Chancery Lane Project (TCLP)[6] have argued compellingly for years. As TCLP rallied practitioners for ambitious, collaborative exercises in legal planning and drafting, it has been very clear – in the absence of top-down strictures, we must all change the world from the bottom up, one contract at a time. Our contracts are where the world is built, where obligations are set, relationships are forged, and our clients' impact and potential is writ large. Where our pens are potentially mighty swords.

Note: The Law Society launched a consultation on 19 September 2024 on its new climate risk and conveyancing practice note.

Clare Harman Clark is a senior counsel at Taylor Wessing. She has specialized in commercial property for nearly two decades, advising on complex and high value transactions. She chairs the property section at the Law Society, sits on the editorial board of the Landlord and Tenant Review, teaches the LPC at the University of Westminster, and writes extensively on legal developments. *A Practical Guide to Green Leases for Property Professionals* was published in November 2023.

1 www.theccc.org.uk/publication/progress-in-adapting-to-climate-change-2023-report-to-parliament/
2 www.lawsociety.org.uk/topics/climate-change/creating-a-climate-conscious-approach-to-legal-practice
3 www.lawsociety.org.uk/topics/climate-change/impact-of-climate-change-on-solicitors
4 www.greenerarbitrations.com/
5 https://legalcharter1point5.com/
6 https://chancerylaneproject.org/

Let's get physical!

Getting real about body inclusion

Bendita Cynthia Malakia and Morgan Reams

Would you ever tell someone that they might win over a diverse jury because they "look exotic"? Would it be acceptable for a colleague to ask another of South Asian descent, "Where are you really from"? Would it be ok if an LGBTQ+ attorney was passed over for a leadership role because it wasn't clear how the client would receive them?

In each of these instances, the answer is a resounding NO (maybe even with an expletive)! These examples reflect implicit biases that are often experienced based on gender, race/ethnicity, and LGBTQ+ identity. If we are not comfortable with these types of comments, then why do so many of these types of comments pass unnoticed or are even supported? Let's look at a few more examples:

"We need a lawyer that will be disciplined; at their weight, it's definitely not them."
"He is 6'2" so he just looks like he should lead."
"I hate to say this, but it's just improbable that we'll put someone that unattractive in front of a client."
"Their teeth will be too distracting for a jury."
"She's bald so she's either ill or a ballbuster – either way I don't want her."
"I don't know how they are going to get through an interview with their face like that."

These types of comments are examples of physicality bias.

Physicality bias is too often deemed acceptable and justified

While explicit and implicit biases implicating gender, race/ethnicity, and LGBTQ+ identity are widely recognized as unacceptable in the legal profession, physicality bias is an explicit bias that is often deemed justified. In fact, as one person who we surveyed noted, physicality bias "is so pervasive that I have a million stories, there is no purpose in recounting one. This is just what I live with."

The Implicit Association Test (IAT)[1] is designed to uncover individuals' subconscious associations between concepts and stereotypes. The tests have been taken millions of times by individuals around the globe on the basis of a variety of demographic identity and social concepts. In a 2014 IAT study,[2] Sean M. Phelan, PhD, MPH and colleagues revealed that weight bias tends to be more tolerated than biases related to race, gender, or sexual orientation.

Physicality bias is broader than just about weight, although weight plays an outsized role in the research and discussion. It is the implicit or explicit bias based on an individual's appearance outside of characteristics like gender, race/ethnicity and disability – although these identities certainly play a role and physicality bias impacts different people differently. Often, physicality bias is a specific category of appearance bias focused on physical attributes that are immutable or not "easily" changed.

Physicality bias is broader than just about weight, although weight plays an outsized role in the research and discussion.

Known by various names such as beauty bias, lookism, attractiveness or appearance discrimination, and pretty privilege, physicality bias impacts each of us in overt and subtle ways. For those with sight privilege, humans are predominantly reliant on visual cues, and our primitive brains instinctively form judgments based on traits that are identified as aligning to a better chance of corporeal and genetic survival. In addition to weight, physicality bias may arise with respect to body shape/proportionality, height, facial symmetry, teeth whiteness/alignment, or hair texture/absence of hair (e.g., baldness).

There are myriad stereotypes that align with physicality bias that may be readily identifiable. For instance:

- Fat (and note, we use "fat" here rather than "overweight" or "obese" as those are medical diagnoses, whereas "fat" is based on perception) employees may be unfairly perceived as lazy, unmotivated, undisciplined, and unprofessional.[3]

- Taller individuals are often regarded as more capable, dominant, and charismatic.[4]
- Individuals with symmetrical facial features are deemed more successful long-term.[5]
- Women with larger breasts are unfairly dismissed as unintelligent.[6]
- Individuals with naturally curly hair textures are scrutinized for appearing unkempt and unprofessional.[7]

These are just a few manifestations of how physicality bias permeates daily interactions.

While many perceive weight and body type to be within one's control, there is enough evidence that many other factors can impact one's weight and body type, including genetics, environmental factors, race, ethnicity, gender, etc.

Co-author Bendita Cynthia Malakia periodically hosts trainings on various subjects to boards, executive teams, individuals, and organizations on inclusive leadership and to support them in leveraging an equity and inclusivity perspective in their roles. For leaders to do this, it is imperative that individuals interested in increasing their inclusivity quotient focus on their capacity for empathy, humility, and vulnerability. One of the many ways this plays out is to ask participants to share a bias that they have with the group. Whether live or virtual, participants can share orally or via writing to be accessed by all (e.g., the chat function or post-its on a board). To lead by example, Bendita always shares her implicit biases first, as revealed to her by many years of taking the IAT and observing (and correcting) her own behaviors.

Unsurprisingly, this is a hard exercise. For lawyers or business professionals in legal organizations, individuals are prone to ask themselves: *Am I really acknowledging that I have biases? Am I really admitting to my biases to others, publicly? I can go along with this "unconscious bias" concept, but my culpability and liability increases markedly once I admit it.* It usually takes participants a bit of time to get their bearings, process all the emotions (typically fear, nervousness, anxiety, etc.) and then remember they pledged to occupy brave space and a growth mindset during the session. The vast majority of the time, participants do one of three things:

1. They are silent and non-responsive (~10%).
2. They are evasive, providing answers such as: *I am sure I have something, but I can't think of anything right now. They ARE supposed to be unconscious, right?* (~35%).
3. They will assert a physicality-based bias, usually weight-related, such as: *Well, I DO think that fat people lack control / are undisciplined / aren't organized / are lazy / are unmotivated / other stereotype about fat people* (~50%).

We all have implicit biases on traditional categories too, and I suspect more of us know what ours are than we admit. The idea that of all the biases, the one individuals feel most confident in pronouncing publicly is about the perceived moral failings of fat people. Identifying as a fat fluid individual, having occupied many weights along the spectrum from 163 lbs to nearly 400 lbs during her professional life, Bendita is both disheartened and intrigued by weight bias being the bias that individuals are most willing to openly express. In our view, this demonstrates a level of ignorance about weight and physicality more broadly that one might have seen levied against women and racialized individuals in a less enlightened era.
A focus on weight and body type in this instance is intentional – the other areas of physicality bias have less stigma because society doesn't tend to assign as much responsibility to an individual for their height, or their dental structure (though they may correctly or incorrectly assign a socioeconomic class), their facial features, or their perceived attractiveness. While many perceive weight and body type to be within one's control, there is enough evidence that many other factors can impact one's weight and

body type, including genetics, environmental factors, race, ethnicity, gender, etc. Deciding one is "at fault" for their condition is often enough for individuals to feel justified in their having a physicality bias. Whether a factor is at play that is perceived within one's control or not, perceptions on physicality impact one's progression and experience in the legal profession.

Physicality bias impacts inclusion and advancement

A directed focus on body inclusion in the context of the legal profession feels incongruent, not least because legal professionals tend to be highly educated and analytical and are valued for those attributes. A focus on appearance may feel shallow or overblown because it is often thought that it is intellectual heft that matters, not how attractive one is. One can imagine the overly tread phrases from the land of racial defense retorts: *I don't care about what someone looks like – they can be green, purple, blue, or whatever – I care about what they can do; I care about the merits*. That was not accurate then and it isn't accurate with respect to physicality. As a society, and as a profession, we care about appearance and our brain operates using schemas to align social ideas to physicality attributes.

We posit that the inequitable benefits and detriments that align with that caring results in those with atypical physicality experiencing inordinate barriers to access and progress within the legal profession. Physicality bias also has an impact on feelings of inclusion, belonging, and wellbeing, which impact retention and performance. When you are distracted by microaggressions or feelings of exclusion, it is a challenge to do your best on your substantive work and to connect with others. While the research on physicality bias in the legal profession is scant, the legal profession isn't immune to the explicit and implicit biases experienced on the basis of other demographic and social identities.

From multi-stage law school admissions processes to the complex dynamics of navigating a path to partnership, the overt and subtle sways of physical appearance mold opportunities, perceptions, and outcomes, perpetuating disparities and undercutting the bedrock tenets of meritocracy and the promise of diversity, equity, and inclusion (DE&I). Some examples and implications of physicality bias follow, primarily in the contexts of the law school experience, recruitment, access to opportunities and interactions, intersectionality, the legal landscape and proxy protection, and compensation.

When you are distracted by microaggressions or feelings of exclusion, it is a challenge to do your best on your substantive work and to connect with others.

The law school experience

Recruitment practices, coupled with the biases of educational administrators, have a compounding effect. Research by David L. Wiley in 1995[8] unveiled this reality, exposing how educational administrators often favor physically attractive students over similarly qualified but physically unattractive ones. Consequently, retention rates plummet, and class participation wanes as individuals shrink from drawing attention to themselves. The negative self-concept that results stifles future advancement as negative perceptions of immutable attributes persist throughout individuals' professional careers.

Recruitment

Sharon Grant and Toby Mizzi note[9] that individuals that are obese are judged as less attractive and less hirable; that overweight people are 35% more likely to experience bias in higher profile jobs; and that overweight women are more likely to experience bias than overweight men. Additionally, in "Weight Bias in the Workplace" in 2013, Grant & Mizzi report that obese applicants received 20% fewer interview

Individuals with normalized physicality and ideas of professionalism often enjoy advantages, ranging from heightened perception of promotability to easier networking access.

calls than average weight applicants, suggesting that it isn't necessarily capability that gets the interview.

Opportunities and interactions

Mentoring, training, leadership opportunities, and an overarching sense of belonging are also impacted by physicality bias. Individuals with normalized physicality and ideas of professionalism often enjoy advantages, ranging from heightened perception of promotability to easier networking access. A survey by Matt Gonzalez in 2023[10] revealed that half of managers expressed a preference for interacting with employees who are not overweight. Additionally, legal headhunter Tariq Sheikh observed in 2023[11] that attractive individuals are commonly perceived as more trustworthy, confident, and likable – qualities highly valued in the legal profession and, one can imagine, among colleagues and clients alike. While physical attributes ought not be leveraged as proxies to determine access to opportunities and success, in the absence of other guidance and monitoring, societal norms perpetuate physicality biases leading to disparate outcomes for those with normalized and atypical physicality.

Intersectionality

Identity is multi-layered. While we have attempted to fictitiously separate traditional demographic identities like gender, race/ethnicity, and LGBTQ+ identity from the physicality conversation, as one might expect, there are interlinkages. Some people have more license to be tall (e.g., white men) than others (e.g., Asian women). Socioeconomic class or social mobility are often inferred by the straightness and whiteness of one's teeth. Villainization of hair texture has received considerable treatment as being indelibly linked to various race/ethnicity and gender permutations. Adding an additional marginalized identity like a physicality bias for an individual that already navigates life with other marginalized identities can often only complicate their experience in a way that is synergistic and not merely additive, causing them to experience profound exclusion and additional barriers to access opportunities. Affinity bias (or being unconsciously inclined to offer more benefits and assign fewer penalties to those like them) is real, and overcoming obvious dissimilarities to find more substantive, but perhaps hidden, commonalities may be a bridge too far. By acknowledging the intersectionality of weight bias, we can work towards creating workplaces that embrace diversity in all its forms and foster a culture of belonging for everyone. As one might imagine, the impacts ripple beyond individuals and significantly impact organizational culture and practices. An intersectionality analysis highlights that when appearance is perceived to align with competency, DE&I efforts may suffer.

The legal landscape and proxy protection

From a US perspective, there are not many jurisdictions that offer specific legal protections for those based on their physicality. In other words, in most jurisdictions it is lawful to deny individuals opportunities based on perceived attractiveness, weight, height, body type, facial asymmetry, or other physicality attributes. Jurisdictions that have anti-discrimination laws on the basis of height and weight in one or all of employment, housing, and places of public accommodation such as airlines, hotels, and restaurants, include the cities of Binghamton, NY, Madison, WI, New York, San Francisco, Santa Cruz, CA, Urbana, IL, Washington, D.C., and the state of Michigan. Other states, including Massachusetts, New Jersey, New York, and Vermont have pending legislation on the basis of height and weight discrimination. Some believe that disability laws protect individuals from physicality bias, but there is only partial protection available for those who fit under the Americans with Disabilities Act framework in the US, such that atypical physicality impacts what is deemed to be a major life function. We are not aware of other disability legal frameworks, but are hopeful that other jurisdictions offer additional protection and support to those with atypical physicality.

The CROWN Act[12] has received more traction. CROWN, or Creating a Respectful Open World for Natural Hair, prevents legal discrimination on the basis of an individual wearing their natural hair and styles that are central to specific racial/ethnic groups. Having been passed in 24 US states and 40 additional localities, the CROWN Act may be evidence that proxy protection works or that there was some mileage from the impact of the murder of George Floyd.

Given inconsistent and often nonexistent legal protection on physicality, intersectionality offers the hope of proxy protection, which is defined here as leveraging legal protections for overlapping or aligned identities such as membership of a legally protected class, like gender, race/ethnicity, or LGBTQ+ identity. An illustrative example lies in the historical discriminatory practices surrounding entrance and promotional exams within certain police departments. Prior to the 1970s, prospective male candidates were required to meet a height requirement of at least five feet and nine inches to be eligible for recruitment. This criterion posed a significant obstacle for individuals of Mexican descent, whose average height tended to be lower compared to other nationalities. Addressing this issue, the Latino Justice Puerto Rican Legal Defense and Education Fund, a prominent Latine legal advocacy group based in New York, undertook a decade-long legal battle aimed at increasing access to law enforcement agencies. According to Suzanne Gamboa in 2020,[13] such barriers were successfully removed through litigation against the New York Police Department. This exemplifies a noteworthy instance where race-based protections offered an avenue to combat physicality bias in a way that would support a broader population, also serving as an excellent reminder that equitable practices for one group tend to have a broader positive impact.

Compensation

Such findings echo M. Dittman's 2004 research,[14] revealing that, on average, individuals towering at six feet tall earn nearly $166,000 more over their careers than their counterparts that are five feet five inches tall. These statistics underscore society's inclination to put a monetary value on those extra inches, assigning a success value with increased height, irrespective of similar educational and professional backgrounds.

From a US perspective, there are not many jurisdictions that offer specific legal protections for those based on their physicality.

Earnings are also impacted by weight. In 2021, Nico Pronk reported[15] that obese women earn as much as 12% less and are more likely to be in low paying jobs than thinner women. Additionally, Pronk found that men impacted by obesity are underrepresented in managerial and professional positions and are paid less than men not affected by obesity.

This quick trip through various employee lifecycle stages and the scant legal protection currently offered demonstrates that there is much to do to protect the experience and opportunity of those with atypical physicality.

What can we do?

It is our hope that you are convinced that people should not get paid less because they are short, nor should they have fewer opportunities because others perceive them to be unattractive. With so many factors at play and the broad acceptability of physicality bias, one might wonder what can and should be done. Below are some institutional and individual opportunities that we recommend embracing if one wants to expand their inclusivity capacity to include physicality, whether through their organizational operations, as a leader or manager, or as an individual who wants to be a more supportive colleague.

Pay attention to legal requirements. Is important for both institutional and individual protection to be aware of the jurisdictions that have legal protections for appearance discrimination.

Institutional opportunities

- *Take allegations seriously.* As organizations ought to do with individuals from any marginalized background, believe the stories of individuals with atypical physicality when they share them with you. They may experience shame and may anticipate ridicule, which can be (re)traumatizing. It is important that organizations do not minimize their experience and take allegations of physicality bias or differential treatment seriously. Allegations of appearance discrimination and physicality bias deserve investigation and further inquiry.
- *Pay attention to legal requirements.* It is important for both institutional and individual protection to be aware of the jurisdictions that have legal protections for appearance discrimination. Incorporate awareness of the requirements into any standard employment/HR training that you perform related to discrimination and harassment.
- *Create a zero-tolerance policy on weight discrimination.* Make it known within your organization that discrimination on the basis of weight, as the most pervasive physicality bias, is not permitted and ensure that such policy or any attendant guidelines are part of your standard employment/HR training.
- *Apply dress codes fairly.* Ensure the equitable coverage and enforcement of dress codes, making sure that individuals of different weights, heights, and body types meet the same expectations for professionalism. Notwithstanding the foregoing, it also remains important to be supportive of personal decency in the fair application of dress codes.
- *Educate your people about physicality bias.* In the same way that there are trainings and additional education about other demographic identities that experience bias, make sure your colleagues understand the legal and cultural understandings of physicality bias and how to identify it, prevent it, and remedy it.
- *Understand the intersectional and pretextual impact.* Even if a jurisdiction doesn't offer legal protection against appearance discrimination and physicality bias, understand that the organization may still be at risk of liability owing to proxy protection given some physicality characteristics aligned with protected classes. Understanding how atypical physicality intersects with traditional demographic diversities can make for a more robust DE&I offering and ensure that members of protected classes aren't experiencing disproportionately negative outcomes through pretextual actions.
- *Expand your understanding of what constitutes diversity, equity, and inclusion.* Introduce physicality bias as a component of your DE&I strategy, especially from an inclusion and belonging perspective.
- *Make resources easily accessible.* Create a one-pager of any physicality-supportive resources, from benefits to alternative adjustments to wellbeing supports.
- *Beef up your benefits.* Make GLP-1s (e.g., semaglutides like Ozempic, Mounjaro, and Wegovy) a part of your health benefits and eliminate discriminatory policies such as Body Mass Index requirements around insurance requirements.
- *Establish systems to evaluate external opportunities.* Whether it is thinking about

who gets featured on the website, is interviewed, or is established as a liaison to clients, the community or other external stakeholders, ensure that skills and capabilities drive appointments and designations rather than appearance.

- *Consider the photos you use.* Eliminate or significantly reduce the practice of photographers editing school or office portraits to fit a firm standard (e.g., reducing gaps in teeth, adjusting hair volume, providing facial symmetry, or reducing ear size), which often makes assumptions about normalized physicality. At the very least, ask the individual before editing and give them an option.
- *Consider seating, access and activities.* Pay attention to seating, especially static chairs attached to desks or permanent seating fixtures, to ensure a variety of body sizes and heights can learn and work comfortably. Think about where events are hosted. Is that rooftop accessible via elevator or only a staircase? Think about whether there are meaningful opportunities at that amusement park gathering for all members of your organization to enjoy themselves. Scrap those weight loss competitions and reframe initiatives to support health-based practices.
- *Consider seating, access and activities.* Think twice about gifts and swag that are size-based, whether clothes or accessories. It may be beneficial to avoid clothing entirely or, alternatively, ensure that there are a large variety of sizes and lengths available.

Individual opportunities

- *Interrupt inappropriate comments.* When you witness any physicality-based microaggressions, or other biased or unacceptable comments, interrupt the individuals in the moment or privately, as appropriate. Allowing inappropriate comments on someone's body to remain uninterrupted is an implicit validation of the sentiment behind the comments and can make the subject of the comments feel even more excluded. Going further, it is suggested that it is never appropriate to comment on other people's bodies, unless you want to inform them about a circumstance that could potentially be embarrassing for them, such as an unzipped zipper or lipstick on one's teeth.
- *Quit the jokes.* The adage *"There is truth in jest"* feels instructive here. For those who have experienced physicality bias, body-related jokes are extremely harmful and often lead to those individuals feeling less included. Physicality-based jokes don't have a place in the workplace.

Avoid comments about the amount or types of food that others are eating, whether it is intended as a compliment or criticism.

- *Avoid certain food commentary.* Avoid comments about the amount or types of food that others are eating, whether it is intended as a compliment or criticism. Praising a fat person for eating healthily may be just as offensive as a weight-based slight, and may be received as a microaggression. Unless serving as a requested nutrition accountability partner or providing a requested opinion, there is little to gain from an individual feeling as if their consumption is being monitored.
- *Keep learning.* Include ongoing learning about physicality bias in your continuing education, especially areas where physicality is normalized or there is less familiarity. Incorporate and share any learnings with others.
- *Avoid making decisions based on physicality.* Notice when internal assessments or conclusions are drawn based on appearance

in everyday life. Be aware of any observed defaults and ensure that decisions made are not based on those biases.

- *Use the terms "skinny" and "fat".* This may be controversial because "fat" can be a loaded term and some could receive it negatively based on their own histories. Here we follow the trends of body positivists and physicality progressives that suggest that using the terms "skinny" and "fat" are more appropriate than terms like "underweight", "overweight", and "obese." The latter terms are considered to be medical diagnoses that those who are not medical professionals are not qualified to determine. "Skinny" and "fat" are perceptions, whether self- or other-imposed, and best encapsulate the positive, neutral, and negative connotations that most are trying to communicate when using those terms.

The way forward

Like other areas of discrimination and bias, physicality bias – or lookism, pretty privilege, beauty bias, appearance discrimination – has a significant impact on the ability of individuals with atypical physicality to enter, experience belonging, and advance in the legal profession. Unlike other areas of discrimination and bias, physicality bias tends to be justified by those that hold it, as if having atypical physicality is a moral or competency failing. Continuing to self-educate and encouraging organizational education about physicality bias is an initial action that should be taken to combat this explicit and implicit bias. Whether it is ensuring that organizations take allegations of physicality bias seriously or interrupting body-based jokes, making progress on the institutional and individual actions that can make body inclusion real should be a priority in the DE&I landscape.

Bendita Cynthia Malakia (she/her) is a Black bisexual fat-fluid woman who aims to ensure that individuals that are underrepresented, underserved, and underestimated can thrive in the workplace. She is the director of diversity and engagement at O'Melveny & Myers, is president of the National LGBTQ+ Bar, and coaches and advises boards and executive teams on increasing their diversity, equity, and inclusivity capacities. Previously, she was a finance lawyer at an AmLaw 100 firm, at Goldman Sachs, and International Finance Corporation. She matriculated at Barnard College and Harvard Law School. A catalyst and connector, Bendita is down for the folx.

Morgan Reams (she/her) is an accomplished professional within the social sector, demonstrating a profound dedication to advancing racial justice, economic equity, and inclusive democracy. In her role as co-founder of BlackWomen&, she not only amplifies Black women's voices but also drives strategic growth, cultivates partnerships, and advocates for diversity, equity, and inclusion. With extensive experience garnered at Title Nine and the William and Flora Hewlett Foundation, Morgan possesses a comprehensive skill set in program development, grant administration, and organizational effectiveness, with a notable emphasis on empowering marginalized communities and catalyzing systemic change. Recognized as a collaborative leader, Morgan remains steadfast in her commitment to fostering positive change and advancing social justice initiatives.

1 https://implicit.harvard.edu/implicit/
2 IAT, Implicit and Explicit Weight Bias in a National Sample of 4,732 Medical Students: The Medical Student CHANGES Study, www.ncbi.nlm.nih.gov/pmc/articles/PMC3968216/
3 Ibid.
4 Melvyn R.W. Hamstra, "'Big' Men: Male leaders' height positively relates to followers' perception of charisma", 2014, *Personality and Individual Differences*, Elsevier, Volume 56, pp190-192, www.sciencedirect.com/science/article/abs/pii/S0191886913012178
5 Elizabeth B. Cooper, 2019, "The Appearance of Professionalism", Fordham University, https://ir.lawnet.fordham.edu/cgi/viewcontent.cgi?article=1995&context=faculty_scholarship
6 Michael Conklin, "Unlocking Beauty from Within Title VII: Arguing for An Expansive Interpretation of Title VII to Protect Against Attractiveness Discrimination", *American University Journal of Gender, Social Policy & the Law*, 2023, volume 31, issue 1, https://digitalcommons.wcl.american.edu/cgi/viewcontent.cgi?article=1854&context=jgspl

7 Rangita De Silva De Alwis, "Addressing Allyship in a Time of a 'Thousand Papercuts'", 2021, Penn Carey Law, https://scholarship.law.upenn.edu/cgi/viewcontent.cgi?article=3801&context=faculty_scholarship
8 David L. Wiley, "Beauty and the Beast: Physical Appearance Discrimination in American Criminal Trials Comment", *St Mary's Law Journal*, vol 27, no.1, 1995, https://commons.stmarytx.edu/cgi/viewcontent.cgi?article=2164&context=thestmaryslawjournal
9 Sharon Grant, Toby Mizzi, "Body Weight Bias in Hiring Decisions: Identifying Explanatory Mechanisms", 2014, *Social Behavior and Personality An International Journa*l, 42(3) www.researchgate.net/publication/262882830_Body_Weight_Bias_in_Hiring_Decisions_Identifying_Explanatory_Mechanisms
10 Matt Gonzales, "Laws, Policies Can Counter Weight Discrimination at Work", 9 May 2023, www.shrm.org/topics-tools/news/inclusion-equity-diversity/laws-policies-can-counter-weight-discrimination-work
11 Tariq Sheikh, "The Unspoken Bias: How Attractiveness Influences Hiring Decisions in Law Firms", 23 No 2023, www.linkedin.com/pulse/unspoken-bias-how-attractiveness-influences-hiring-decisions-sheikh-cfcff/
12 www.thecrownact.com/
13 Latino officers are helping diversify police. Can they help reform the ranks? www.nbcnews.com/news/latino/latino-officers-are-helping-diversify-police-can-they-help-reform-n1230351
14 M. Dittman, "Standing tall pays off, study finds", *Journal of Applied Psychology*, July/August 2004, Vol 35, No. 7, American Psychological Association, www.apa.org/monitor/julaug04/standing
15 Nico Pronk, Ph.D., M.A., FACSM, FAWHP, "Weight Bias and Discrimination in the Workplace: Addressing a Diversity and Inclusion Issue", Health and Fitness Journal, https://journals.lww.com/acsm-healthfitness/fulltext/2021/05000/weight_bias_and_discrimination_in_the_workplace_.15.aspx

Talent

Smart collaboration: increasing the odds of productive lateral hiring

Heidi K. Gardner

Introduction

One of the biggest challenges in today's law firms is recruiting laterals into the firm and then finding ways to integrate them, retain them and help make them sustainably productive. Many of today's law firm leaders agree that the war for talent is at least as brutal as the battle for clients. Yet, once hired, firms mismanage and ultimately undervalue their newly acquired partners because they do not have an actionable, data-driven strategy to help them flourish. In this article, I draw on years of empirical and qualitative research to show how cross-practice, smart collaboration is one of the essential elements for increasing the odds that a lateral hire will be successful and productive in their new firm.

How exactly does smart collaboration help? Smart collaboration helps firms to better utilise and maximise their greatest asset which is the collective expertise of their lawyers. Smart collaboration is a means to an end, rather than an end in itself – a team of talented problem-solvers with specialised legal expertise integrating their collective knowledge to tackle and solve their clients' thorniest problems. To be clear, smart collaboration is not delegation, sequential teamwork, cross-selling, or the mere assembly of experts. While it may not involve direct, face-to-face work, smart collaboration does require repeated interactions that, over time, allow the creative recombination of different people's information, perspectives and expertise.

For new lateral hires, a firm's collaborative prowess determines how easily they will be integrated and how quickly – and whether – they will thrive. Collaboration helps bring lateral hires up to speed with the firm's practices, allows them to get to know their colleagues (and vice versa) and, most important, builds trust between lateral hires, their peers and new clients. The trick, of course, is making sure that your firm is set up to foster this kind of lateral-incumbent collaboration. Supported by my extensive empirical research at Harvard University, this article will outline how firms can foster collaboration between newly hired and existing partners by using specific systems in the pre-hire, recruiting and onboarding phases. Doing so will increase their chances of making lateral hiring more successful.

Speed is key

We can now demonstrate empirically that smart collaboration is essential to ensuring that lateral hires can become successful and productive, post-move. For more than a decade I have been studying issues related to leadership, teamwork and talent development in professional service firms. During my time on the faculty at Harvard Business School and now at Harvard Law School I have amassed a database comprising millions of data records across multiple law firms, including a decade's worth of their time-sheet, personnel and financial records. Statistical analyses reveal patterns in the data that can be difficult for the human mind to detect. Together with my research team, we marry these quantitative findings with insights from hundreds of in-depth interviews with lawyers and other professionals, law firm leaders and clients as well as thousands of research surveys.

Our analyses show that collaboration has to happen quickly – if laterally hired partners are to be successful at their new firm, they must be sufficiently integrated with incumbent partners and clients within the first 18 months, if not sooner. Specifically, two things both need to happen in that short time – laterals need to have had the opportunity to work on at least a couple of the firm's incumbent clients (on pitches, if not actual projects), and they need a couple of long-term partners to help on the client work they generate (either clients they have imported or new clients). If either is missing, new hires are at a higher risk of leaving; if neither happens, they are very likely to leave the firm by their

Figure 1: Collaboration and lateral hires

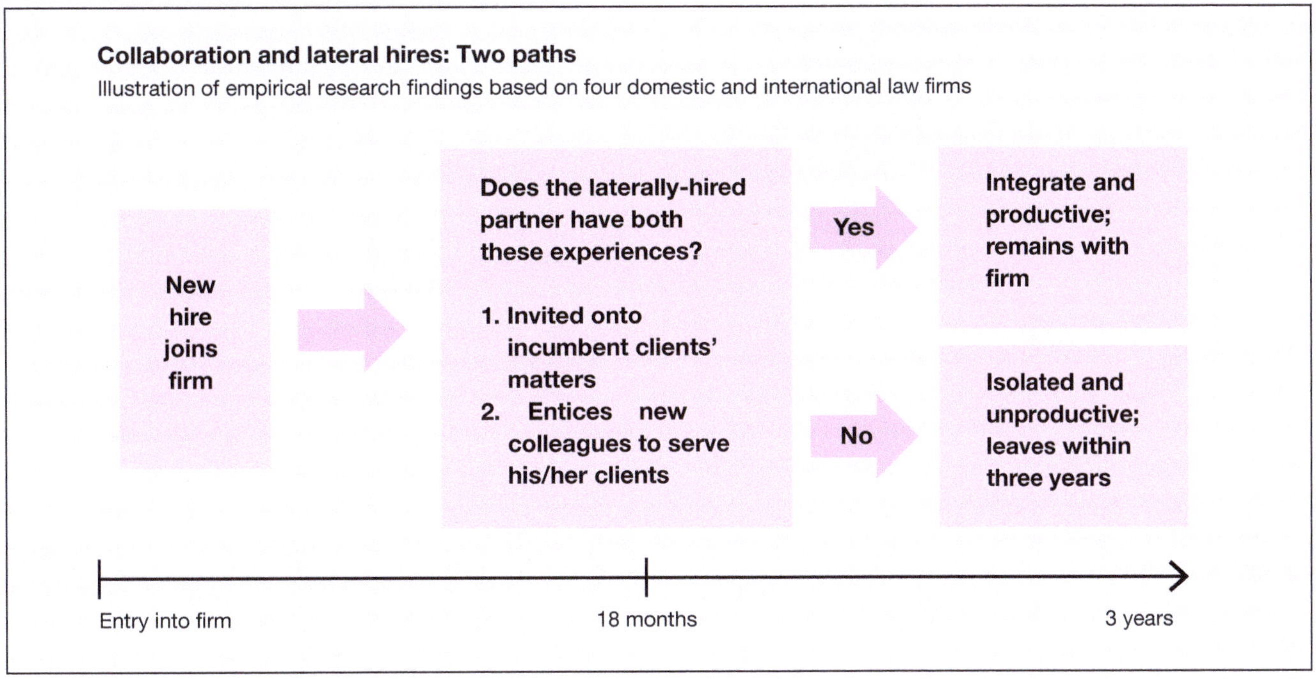

three-year anniversary, as illustrated in figure 1.

Our analyses are what researchers call a 'conservative test' because only statistically significant findings from across multiple firms are reported. Partners in two firms outside my dataset – one law firm and one accounting firm – explained that analyses of their own firms' data revealed that the critical window for achieving collaboration is as short as six months after a laterally hired partner joins their firm! Clearly, firms need a well-constructed plan, flawless execution and clear accountability processes if they expect to help laterals achieve two-way collaboration quickly and efficiently.

Market distortions and client demands

Client demand for solutions that are both deep and broad-based leads to some predictable distortions in the labour market, as multiple firms try to build up whichever practice group is most in demand at the moment. An excellent example is cyber security. Across most economic sectors, clients are deeply troubled by having their data and systems compromised. Experts who can credibly advise on these risks open the doors to client c-suites and boardrooms. The predictable result is that every law firm playing in this particular game wants to have the best cyber security experts in their stable, rather than someone else's. And the rise of various advisory firms – ranging from the Big Four accounting firms to specialist boutiques – creates even more demand for the experts.

Today's law firms are increasingly engaged in a war for talent – a war that is being fought on a number of fronts. In many places, increased partner mobility has fostered the emergence of a free-agent mentality. Encouraged by growing legions of headhunters, experienced legal talents today have a keen sense of their value in the marketplace, and face far fewer cultural taboos about jumping ship for a more lucrative offer. In some of the hottest areas, it is not unusual for professionals with an in-demand specialty to receive multiple calls every week from recruiters or competitors.

Layered on top of this is the breakdown of the former gentlemen's agreements that divided up the legal landscape into what might be called 'spheres of influence'. In the legal field – as well as in many other professional fields, including accounting, engineering and consulting – the entrance of international firms into previously domestic markets has fuelled competition for top-end partners. As many readers will recall, when US firms began their push into London, many City lawyers massively spiked their income by joining the first wave of partners to sign up with those newcomer firms.

This trend is also visible in formerly stable localised markets like Bogota, Munich, Phoenix and scores of other cities around the world. For example, when firms such as DLA Piper or CMS expand their Latin American presence, their arrival causes a significant uptick in labour market competition – not only for partners, but also for associates. Tales abound of lawyers doubling their salaries overnight, and then subsequently negotiating for additional perks like preferred parking, flex time and increased holidays. In many jurisdictions, a 'new normal' has descended concerning salaries and poaching. Many Chilean law firms have reportedly skipped over their direct competitors by recruiting lawyers from in-house positions into a range of practice areas. Full-scale lift-outs of firms' entire practice groups are likely to become the next phase for recruiting in these hot legal markets. Yet, the odds of success for all these lateral hiring efforts is worse than a coin toss, and the highest attrition is seen at the leading edge of a firm's geographic expansion – the Middle East, Latin America and Moscow.

Beyond expense – the risks of poor lateral hiring

While firms fiercely aim to recruit and hire the industry's best and brightest, the strategy of accumulating stars without a strategic plan and simply hoping for the best does not work very well. In fact, after spending vast sums to build and buy stables of thoroughbreds and extend their geographic reach and practice breadth, today's premiere law firms have reached a sobering conclusion – all that talent cannot be harnessed for competitive advantage or profit enhancement *unless they find a way to get partners to collaborate*. To maximise the worth of those expensive individuals, firms must integrate their partners' diverse and distributed knowledge in a way that clients value.

Most firms recognise – and research confirms – that it takes three to five years for a lateral hire just to reach the level of performance they displayed in their old firm, let alone to become even more productive. In reality, though, most laterally hired lawyers who are struggling to become productive in their new firm simply do not stick it for more than a few years at best.

Lateral hiring can also cause internal strife about the compensation system among long-term employees because firms generally need to pay much more for individuals brought in from outside in order to compensate them for the risk of changing firms. In US law firms, for example, the pressures associated with lateral hiring can lead to enormous disparities in compensation between partners within the same firm. Although the median spread between the highest and lowest-paid partners inside a US firm is 10 to one (already quite a gap), that ratio swelled as high as a staggering 23 to one in one firm where lateral hiring was rampant.

Finally, the biggest risk might be the dilution – or worse – of a firm's culture. Sometimes the addition of employees with different perspectives can be hugely beneficial for firms by opening up new ways of thinking, which can breed positive change. But unless you are deliberately seeking and hiring candidates with a specific, diverse set of characteristics, you are leaving the evolution of your culture to chance by hiring people who come from firms with cultures radically different from your own.

Figure 2: Critical actions steps for integrating lateral hires

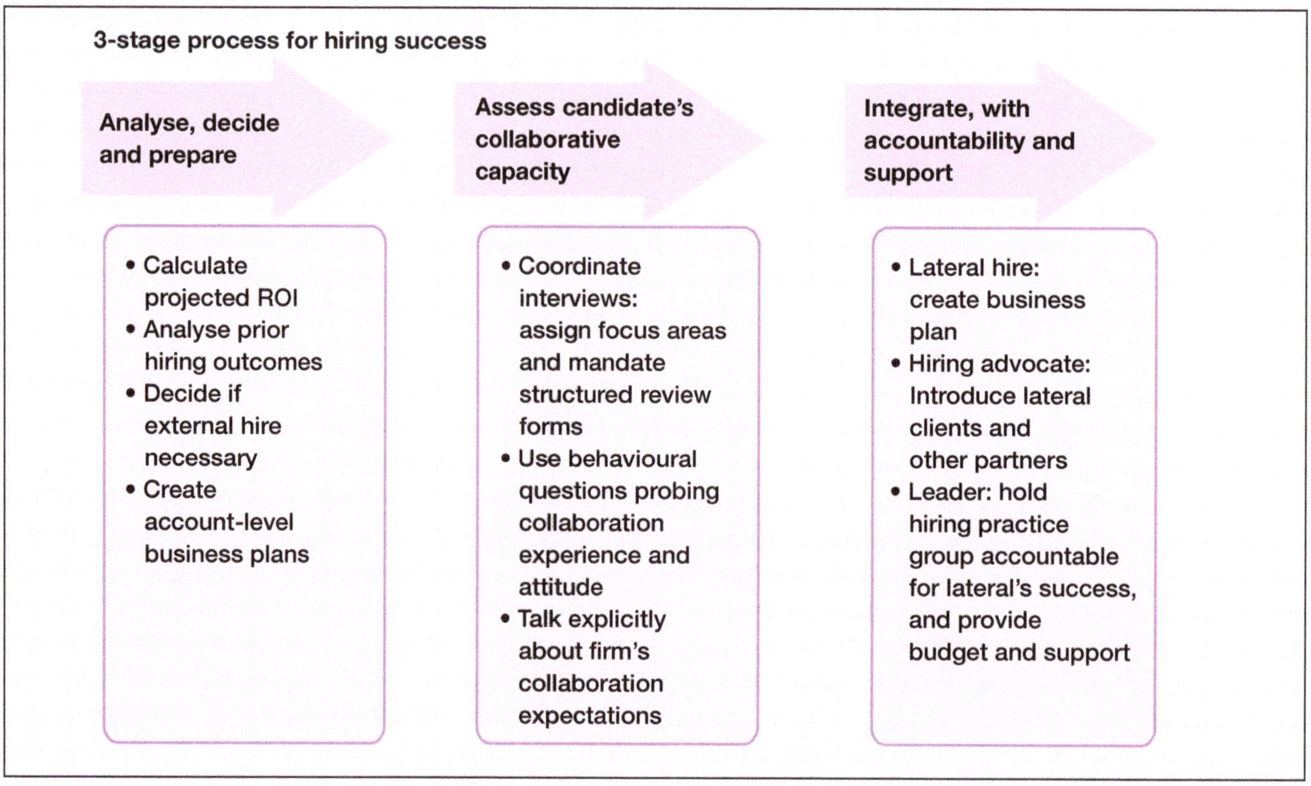

Most firms recognise – and research confirms – that it takes three to five years for a lateral hire just to reach the level of performance they displayed in their old firm, let alone to become even more productive.

Critical action steps to improve lateral hiring

Assuming that your firm concludes that the potential upsides to hiring laterals outweigh the downsides, you can better your odds with laterals by following these critical action steps. They fall into three phases that correspond to the pre-hire, recruiting and onboarding stages: an analytics-driven business plan, a structured assessment of a candidate's collaborative capabilities, and post-hire mentoring and accountability processes, as illustrated in figure 2. Let us consider each in turn.

Analytics-driven business plan

First, you need a robust, data-based analysis that forms the business case for each lateral hire. Many firms believe that they have already got such a system in place, but most of the plans I have reviewed are more about arguments than analyses – which is not surprising given that they were written by lawyers who had neither been supplied with data nor trained to perform quantitative analyses. Instead, engage your financial and business development experts to collect and dissect both internal and market data to calculate anticipated returns on investment (ROI) for each proposed candidate. Even more specifically, analysts should work with partners in both the proposing practice group and adjacent ones to understand a range of realistic scenarios, and then calculate how sensitive the initial, projected ROI is to these differing assumptions.

Whether to hire and how many to hire should be based not only on these financial models, but also on strategic factors, such as expanding business opportunities, new offices in specific geographic markets, partner turnover, and newly developed (or growing) practice or sector-focused groups. Each of these factors analyse current capacity and utilisation to reveal whether the emerging market needs can be covered by an internal, existing resource. Set the bar high to convince yourself that a lateral is the only option.

Objectively gauge your organisation's readiness to absorb a new partner. Is the practice group appropriately leveraged? If you hire a lateral partner, will she have adequate associate support for her business? Has that office or practice just hired a cohort of other laterals that are consuming all the onboarding attention and energy? Your ability to answer these questions ties directly to your ability to help a newly hired partner succeed.

Aside from financial considerations, firms should dig deeper to uncover which practices have a track record for successful lateral hire integration. Gather and review your lateral hiring data from the last five years or so, with a specific focus on who pushed for or sponsored the request, and how well each of those laterals fared, once hired. You may discover a strong correlation between certain partners' or practices' attempts and success rates or pockets of 'churn and burn'. Do not be discouraged by an historically high churn rate. Instead, view it as a growth opportunity. Generally, offending groups fail to strategically consider their hiring requests, use the wrong hiring criteria, or lack the proper means to integrate laterals once they arrive. Gaining a full understanding of exactly what is broken helps a firm pinpoint a sustainable, practical and long-term fix.

If your firm decides that a lateral hire is the best option based on convincing evidence and a sound strategic plan, then you should produce a business plan towards that end. The plan should include specific client objectives with a named individual responsible to see it through to completion. Accountability is critical.

Structured assessment of a candidate's collaborative capabilities

Some law firms already have well-established processes for assessing a candidate's merits – especially their technical, legal capabilities and often their reputation with clients. If those processes are actually getting the results you want, then use them. Additionally, consider augmenting them with additional techniques that can help you collect evidence about a candidate's suitability to become the kind of partner who can truly leverage your firm's full set of expertise in order to solve clients' most complex, high-value problems. In other words, figure out a candidate's collaborative capacity.

One important, yet basic technique is to use multiple interviews in order to mitigate the risk of bias from a single opinion. Some firms put interviewees through dozens of interviews with staff members and partners, in multiple geographies and offices. But merely setting up multiple, unstructured interviews is basically a waste of time, however, because partners outside the candidate's area of expertise will only walk away with vague impressions of the cultural 'fit'.

To ensure that multiple interviews are productive requires significant coordination within the firm, both before interviews and afterwards, in order to uncover gaps, probe possible weaknesses and provide feedback for the next interviewer. For example, in one consulting firm that I have worked with, as interviewers meet with a particular candidate, they provide feedback and make suggestions about issues that can be probed in subsequent interviews. Eventually these interview notes should be mined to reveal competency gaps where the successful candidate needs to improve, setting the stage for an integration and training plan for the prospective employee.

In interviews, the current best practice is to use behavioural questions, rather than hypothetical ones. Ask candidates to describe particular situations they have faced, how they handled them, their personal emotional response, and what they learned from the experience. For example: "Can you provide me with an example of when you made a bad decision?" The objective is to break the candidate out of predictable and standard responses, thereby enabling the interviewer to gain more insight into the candidate's problem-solving approaches and emotional intelligence.

Clearly, this kind of interviewing is new to most lawyers. It requires training and practice, which many partners will resist. But consider this – partners who become excellent spotters of collaborative candidates are the ones who are better equipped to discover client opportunities in the candidates' collaborative tendencies and emotional intelligence.

How can you directly assess a candidate's actual collaborative capabilities? My advice is to get the issue on the table well in advance of the interview. If you are using a search firm, make sure it is extremely well briefed on your demands for collaboration, and is prepared to pre-screen candidates for this quality. Candidates turned off by this will rule themselves out.

Once the candidate is in the chair, first use the kinds of behavioural questions described above to explore their past experiences with collaboration. Table 1 lists additional key competencies associated with strong collaborators, with sample prompts that the interviewer can use to probe. Next, tackle collaboration head-on with the candidate.

Clearly explain the firm's expectations for collaboration, articulating as many specific examples as possible. Describe how collaboration will be measured and rewarded, how much the firm cares about origination versus execution, and how those activities are tracked. Explain the extent to which the firm values and rewards non-billable activities. Clarity helps to weed out non-collaborative candidates through self-selection, which is a very efficient way to weed.

Post-hire mentoring and accountability

Most firms already have a nominal 'buddy system' for incoming hires, but far too few of those programmes actually work. To create the highest chances of a lateral hire being successfully integrated, you need to take some specific steps to ensure that mentoring happens (in multiple directions, as discussed below), and that all parties are held accountable for delivering post-hire collaboration within the first 12 months:

- Work with laterals as soon as they join to develop

Table 1 – Key collaborative competencies to test with candidates

Key collaborative competencies	Sample interview prompts to elicit response
• Adaptability • Conflict management • Initiative and follow-through • Integrity • Learning motivation/curiosity • Listening and probing • Networking • Perseverance • Persuasiveness (leading without authority)	• Tell me about a situation when you teamed up with colleagues to solve a really tough client problem. • Follow on: How did you find the right expert? How did you know they were capable? How did you convince them to join the effort? What role did you play after the team was formed? Describe a time when you needed a colleague's input on client work, but that person did not respond to requests. What did you do? Give me an example of a time when you uncovered an opportunity to serve a client with a multi-practice team. What ultimately happened?

a strategic client service plan, which identifies specific opportunities for them to involve incumbent partners. Leaders should facilitate those introductions, and make it clear to incumbents that they are expected to participate.

- Assign a peer mentor for new hires to help them learn the firm's culture–insider knowledge, such as people who serve as 'honest brokers' in the firm to help connect partners with client or other work. Ideally, this mentor will be someone whom the new hire met and connected with during the recruiting process so that they have already established a level of interpersonal trust.
- Gain commitment from a few specific people in the hiring group (practice, office, or ideally, both) who are responsible for introducing the newcomer to several pre-determined accounts or other kinds of strategic contacts, as outlined in the pre-hire business plan. And require them to report on progress – to you, or at least their practice leader (whose feet you then hold to the fire), not to a functionary in HR. Again, the key here is *specificity* and *accountability*.
- Use competency grids to assess the collaborative and mentoring abilities of both the newly hired partner and those in the surrounding practice. (If you do not have these tools, your professional development staff needs to source or create them.)
- Provide a budget for laterals to visit colleagues, even for exploratory conversations, and set the expectation that they will use the full budget (appropriately) within the first six to eight months. Expect laterals to report back to you with opportunities they have uncovered, and when, how, and with whom they are taking action.
- Hold formal internal roadshows for laterals to present their client work to offices, practice groups and sectors. Make sure the local leader has spoken with the lateral ahead of time to suggest specific people or account opportunities that the lateral can reference during their presentation, and to ensure that the highest-potential collaborators attend the roadshow.
- Make it clear to hiring groups that their ability to hire future laterals will depend on how successfully they integrate each newcomer. You might not be able to measure immediate financial results, but you can track activity – how many partners have used the newcomer's expertise to develop joint pitches or to create new IP such as white papers? When partners do create these opportunities, celebrate them across the firm. Recognition for good behaviour not only encourages more partners to engage in it, but also helps spread the newcomer's reputation as a collaborative, value-adding asset within the firm.

At the end of this rather long list, it is probably worth putting in a plug for good citizenship within your firm. Good citizens in the senior ranks of your firm typically are willing to contribute – their time, contacts and knowledge – generously, without calculating direct returns. They act with faith that building up their colleagues' capabilities is the right thing to do and trust that they may ultimately benefit from this in an indirect way. They do not keep score or mentally track reciprocity. Leaders need to recognise these citizens for the tremendous value they bring.

Central to all the techniques cited above for setting the stage for post-hire collaboration is culture. Our research shows that culture – more than processes – enables, encourages or inhibits collaboration; processes merely reflect culture – whether it is flourishing or stunted. As you venture into this new, complicated and rewarding realm, watch for signs of cultural chafing, and attend to what needs to be fixed.

Within the larger strategy

While the collaboration as a remedy for bolstering the success of lateral hires has been the focus of this article, it is worth noting that collaboration is critical to the success of your firm more broadly. Collaboration between partners in law firms is essential for developing and maintaining a competitive advantage. As clients' problems become increasingly complex, firms must respond by pulling their experts out of narrowly defined practice areas and encouraging them to collaborate – for the sake of the firm, its clients and individual lawyers.

The financial and talent-related benefits for firms that foster multi-practice collaboration are impressive – the more practices that serve a client, the more revenue the client generates for the firm each year. As the following graph shows, moving from one to two

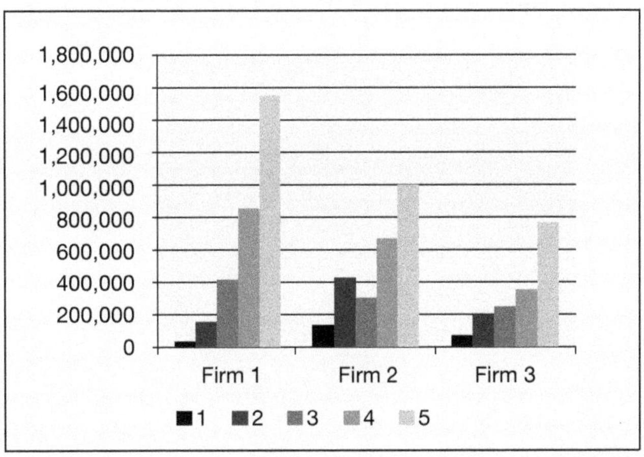

practices serving a client triples that client's revenues, and the addition of each subsequent practice continues to grow fees. Clearly, if 1 + 1 = 3, then the lawyers who are involved in cross-practice service are doing more than just referring their colleagues to provide their own siloed work.

Further, cross-practice collaboration allows lawyers to gain access to senior executives who have broader responsibilities, larger budgets and more sophisticated needs. This complex work commands higher margins, revenues and hourly rates, as one partner said: "The clients are much more generous on fees because if it's so big, the deal's got to get done, and they cannot waste time negotiating or nit-picking." While single-specialty is often viewed as a commodity awarded to the lowest bidder, cross-practice work is less subject to price-based competition.

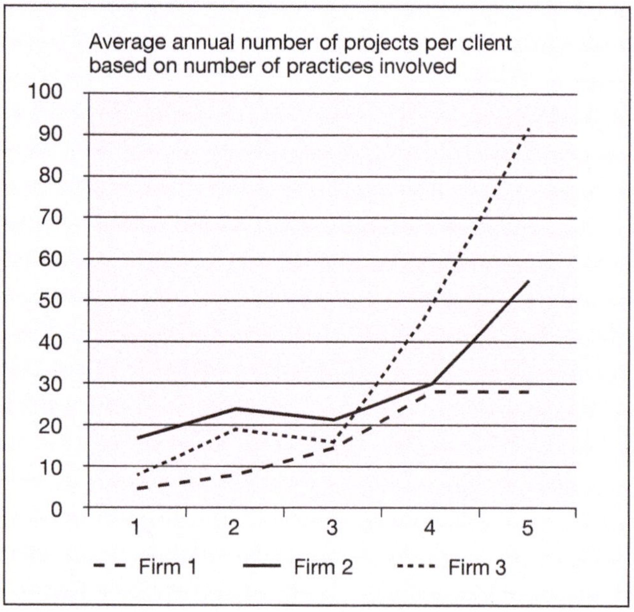

Superior solutions pay off. When it is done right, cross-practice collaboration makes clients stickier in the long run by creating switching barriers. As the general counsel of a Fortune 100 company explained, "Despite what they think, most individual lawyers are actually quite replaceable. I mean, I could find a decent tax lawyer in most firms. But when that lawyer teamed up with colleagues from IP, regulatory, and ultimately litigation, I couldn't find a whole-team substitute in another firm." And its collaboration, by and large, that enables you to embrace and overcome complexity, on behalf of your client.

Most importantly, a commitment to collaboration is a commitment to a collaborative culture. Firms that actively foster and celebrate collaboration are better able to retain, motivate and inspire their employees to perform at their best – a benefit with powerful financial implications. Collaboration does not just make people *feel* as if they are in the right place. In fact, it is a self-fulfilling prophecy – collaboration among long-term partners and newcomers makes the 'fit' better, makes the hard work more efficient and effective, and thereby makes the firm more successful. If firms neglect to purposefully integrate newcomers into their overall collaboration strategy, they risk leaving heaps of untapped talent and revenues on the table.

Conclusion

In today's competitive marketplace, your firm's ability to attract, integrate and ultimately retain lateral hires is critical. Smart collaboration is not optional – it is a business imperative for the strategic growth, profitability and sustainability of a firm. Collaboration done 'right' requires strong leadership, sustained efforts and deep commitment from your partners at all levels to collaborate with the newcomers. The money and energy your firm puts into fostering smart collaboration – including the recruitment and retention of key laterals – will pay you back many times over.

Heidi K Gardner is a Distinguished Fellow at Harvard Law School's Center on the Legal Profession, a Harvard Lecturer on Law, and Faculty Chair in the school's executive education courses. Previously she was a professor at Harvard Business School, a consultant with McKinsey & Company, and a Fulbright Fellow. Dr Gardner's best-selling book Smart Collaboration: How Professionals and Their Firms Succeed by Breaking Down Silos *was published by Harvard Business Press in 2017.*

Are non-execs the key to future success of law firms?

Claire-Elaine Arthurs

Helen Foord

While other professional service industries have embraced the opportunities for change presented by more corporate business structures, the legal sector continues to lag behind. Solicitor and Non-Exec Director, Claire-Elaine Arthurs, and Marketing & BD specialist, Helen Hammond, discuss the opportunities presented by Non-Exec Directors with skills and experience that extend beyond finance to include strategic planning and marketing.

One only needs to glance at the press to see that the legal services market is experiencing unprecedented change. Disruptive business models are emerging to challenge the more traditional law firms, driven by technology and an increasingly flexible approach to the provision of legal services. Against this backdrop, and with client expectation and competition increasing, traditional firms are racing to keep up, merging to survive or going out of business altogether.

At the beginning of 2019 the Solicitors Regulation Authority recorded 10,383 law firms in England and Wales. Of those 4,812 (46%) are limited companies and 1,542 (15%) are limited liability partnerships. The majority of larger firms have chosen to embrace a more corporate structure to enable them to adopt better financial structures and to limit the personal exposure of the equitable owners of the business. Yet, the reality is that beyond this little has really changed. The same 'equity partners' make up most boards and the structure, agenda and content of board meetings is frustratingly familiar, month on month, quarter on quarter and year on year. While other professional service industries have embraced the opportunities for change presented by these corporate structures, the legal industry seems to be lagging behind.

It must be acknowledged that solicitors are great at working 'in' their businesses. Inevitably, partners are intelligent and commercial business people, capable of digesting complex data and providing innovative advice and support. They understand the regulatory and financial aspects of their business in detail and are able to drive their teams to meet their monthly, quarterly and annual billing targets.

However, when it comes to working 'on' the business, we start to see cracks in the system. Most have had no formal business management training, which is why board meetings tend to focus only on recent or immediate financial performance and short-term business development goals.

This approach may have helped many firms survive the financial crisis, but it no longer works in the current climate and certainly does not lend itself to supporting the longevity of the firm. If a business is to survive, then it must thrive, grow and evolve to meet the market's needs. Where focus remains firmly *in* the business, no one is working *on* the business.

The executive team's focus should be on the day-to-day management, whereas the board purpose should be oversight and longer-term strategy. Where the board is made up only of internal managers, there can be a strong tendency to focus on the day-to-day running of a firm. It then becomes increasingly difficult to step back, critically evaluate performance and focus on future vision, which is what the business needs to do in order to move beyond its current position.

The other issue that restricts the ability of firms to adapt to and embrace change is a lack of diversity on their boards. Having a diverse range of perspectives and skill sets at the table will inevitably lead to a more rounded view, a more flexible approach and an increased problem-solving capability. There is no question that steps are being taken to encourage more solicitors, who happen to be female or from ethnic minorities, into more senior positions in the industry. This is something that needs to continue but is unlikely to be enough on its own.

Even on the most 'diverse' boards, there may still be a significant skills deficit if each member has a similar 'legal' skill set and the same view of the market. It has been possible to register alternative business structures (ABSs), which may have a non-solicitor in the position of director, since 2012 but only a small proportion of

All directors should be capable of stepping back and seeing the firm and business from a broad perspective, though this certainly comes more easily from the NED perspective as they are not restricted by playing an internal management role.

active legal service providers, approximately 10% in 2018, have taken advantage of this. The SRA has taken steps to streamline the process of conversion and stands ready to support any firms wishing to make the change, but many still appear reluctant to take up the offer.

Of the firms which have sought to diversify their board, this has often been limited to adding on the head of finance. Very few have moved beyond that to include other disciplines, and fewer still have opted to invite someone with an outside perspective to join their board.

In other professional service industries, the need for an external perspective, diversity of background and opinion has been long-established. In firms in comparable industries it is common to appoint non-executive directors (NEDs) to assist firms in obtaining and maintaining market advantage. NED appointments have traditionally been the domain of retiring executives – used as a means of keeping their hand in, sharing their experience and earning a little additional income. However, these days, a NED is as likely to be a marketing expert in their 30s as an ex-CEO in his 60s, as focus is more on skills-based boards that include a range of experience and expertise.

NEDs perform a crucial role in many companies. The Cadbury Report in 1992 identified that NEDs "should bring an independent judgement to bear on issues of strategy, performance and resources including key appointments and standards of conduct". To be effective they should be independent of management and free from business or other relationships that might interfere with their judgement. They operate from a position outside of the business, giving them a unique perspective and the ability to provide insight and act as a critical friend. They are often active in the wider market and able to draw on that experience, offering a fresh perspective and alternative skill set. Professionals with extensive knowledge of the legal market will be more attractive candidates as they not only lend outside perspective and accountability but have the ability to understand the market and the unique challenges faced by a law firm.

While any NED brought into an ABS law firm would need to meet the suitability test (and understand the necessary compliance and conduct requirements, being of 'good report' and willing and able to comply with the principles set out in the SRA Handbook) these are no more onerous than those in other industries. Common sense would suggest that any NED a law firm would seek to appoint would meet these criteria in any case. Where an ABS is not attractive, it is possible to find a wide range of solicitors who have left the profession, requalified and now bring with them not only an intimate knowledge of the legal practice but also a breadth of additional insight.

NEDs are usually chosen because they have a breadth of experience, are of an appropriate calibre and have particular personal qualities that will complement those already present on the board. In addition, they may have some specialist knowledge in areas such as business development, marketing, PR or IT, which is not already available within the business. They may also bring with them key contacts in related industries, which may mean they can assist firms in communicating with a wider network.

Some firms draw on consultants to offer an outside perspective on a particular issue, with an intense period of involvement. Many NEDs are also consultants but the skills being deployed, and the contribution made in the two roles, are very different. Where traditional consultants trouble shoot or project manage, the commitment and continuity of the involvement of a NED offers the opportunity for greater strategic input. The UK Corporate Governance codes states: "Non-executive directors should have sufficient time to meet their board responsibilities. They should provide constructive challenge, strategic guidance, offer specialist advice and hold management to account". NEDs are concerned with the wider view and helping to drive the long-term strategic success of the business and have a unique ability to act as a critical friend, to bring fresh ideas and contacts to the table.

All directors should be capable of stepping back and seeing the firm and business from a broad perspective, though this certainly comes more easily from the NED perspective as they are not restricted by playing an internal management role. This means they can bring a degree of objectivity to the board's deliberations and play a valuable role in monitoring executive management. Their external role as a critical observer makes them well suited to assisting with the risk, audit and compliance functions of the board. They also provide accountability for implementation of strategy and the monitoring of performance.

Managing partners and heads of department can also find it difficult to express their doubts, frustrations and concerns to those they lead or work with on a daily basis, sometimes feeling that they need to appear positive and decisive at all times. The appointment of a NED allows for a confidential sounding board at a senior level. They are also well placed to assist in the effective resolution of work place disagreements or grievances at a senior, yet independent level. This often helps to facilitate the smooth running of the business.

The knowledge and resource of a NED is available to the business in a cost-effective manner. This calibre of individuals can be very expensive if they are to be engaged as employees or contractors. Further, a NED has a more vested interest in the success of the business, as they share the same responsibilities and liabilities as any other member of the board. Unlike consultants, they can also be called upon more strategically for their input over a period of time. Having said that, most NEDs are also only appointed for a year or so, with the option to renew. If their input remains useful, they can be retained. However, if the business has moved on and now requires another skill set or input from a different external perspective, then that can be easily replaced to meet the business need. Something that is much harder to do with an employee.

Comparing practice in the legal industry with that of other professional service industries, it is clear that legal firms are lagging behind in their ability to adapt and drive change. One catalyst that could efficiently make a significant impact would be the introduction of more NEDs to boards, particularly where those appointments are coupled with specialist skills or particular industry knowledge not readily available within the firm itself.

A practical example: appointing a NED for growth

Big Building Law Limited was formed in 2009, when a group of 10 property lawyers left Magic Circle Law LLP. Despite tough times in the UK property and construction sector, Big Building Law has grown steadily, taking on new fee-earners and staff as needed. They now have 12 partners, 15 solicitors, three paralegals and an administrative team of 25 (including PAs, finance, a marketing executive and an office manager). Their HR and IT requirements are met by outsourced providers.

In 2014 Big Building Law decided to adopt the ABS to allow their head of finance to take on a director role and join the board. The other partners felt this would make board meetings more productive and ensure that decisions were being made in a more responsible way. The hope was that this would lead to greater growth and a stronger focus on strategy, rather than tactical matters.

With the advent of Brexit and other changes in the UK property market in 2018, the board became increasingly aware that the organic growth, enjoyed in the firm's first 10 years, was slowing down. The partners were busy managing their own caseloads and had little time to dedicate to growth plans, or their delivery. Furthermore, the current marketing executive, although hard-working and capable at a tactical level, did not have the knowledge required to help them identify opportunities and set out a strategy for achieving them. Importantly, the outsourced IT and HR support, being one step removed from the business, made it difficult for the board to understand any requirements the firm might have for personnel or technology developments, to support any growth strategy. Finally, members of the board were doing an increasing amount of international construction work, as well as mediation/arbitration, and were keen to explore international growth, as well as possible mergers.

The board recognised that guidance was needed. Looking back at their time in Magic Circle Law they recognised that the marketing and business development director provided high-level strategic guidance from a position of being 'within' the organisation, understanding the people and culture. However, they felt that the salary requirements of recruiting this expertise were beyond the firm at that point. Members of the board spoke to a number of consultants and felt they would benefit from the objectivity they would bring, but would miss out on the sense of their being 'part of the team' and invested in

Comparing practice in the legal industry with that of other professional service industries, it is clear that legal firms are lagging behind in their ability to adapt and drive change.

collective success. As a result the decision was taken to recruit a NED with experience in marketing and business development, as well as, ideally, the property and professional services sectors.

Sarah spent 20 years working in-house in law firms, within the marketing and business development teams. Her last role was as head of marketing and business at another Magic Circle firm. She left this role, after five years, in 2015 to work as a consultant and NED, when her family relocated out of London. Since then she has held NED roles at a number of accountancy and property firms, as well as supporting other law firms through consultancy roles. In one particular firm she was responsible for managing the marketing and communications elements of an international merger.

Sarah joined Big Building Law in January 2018 as a NED. She is a full member of the board, attending monthly meetings as well as having a further two days a month to prepare for the meeting, read board papers and sit on any relevant sub-committees.

When Sarah joined the board, as their first external member, they decided to hold an away-day, designed to help them all get to know one another, as well as to give management a chance to step back and consider the firm's longer-term strategic vision. Sarah used this opportunity to ask challenging questions – perhaps not previously considered – and was able to draw on her experience of what had worked well in other professional service organisations, as well as the lessons learned through those experiences.

Following the away-day Sarah was able to assist the board in making decisions that made a clearer distinction between their strategic oversight and the executive team's tactical delivery. This allowed for some positive long-term changes to be made in the business.

Sarah shared some examples of other firms that she had worked with and how they had tackled reporting on marketing and business development at board level. She helped the board to understand how their current financial reporting when reviewed in isolation gave little understanding of how or why figures were going up or down.

The board decided to task the executive team with developing recommendations for a clear reporting system, using the firm's practice management and CRM software. What came back to the next board meeting for approval included not only this but a simple template report on marketing activity and enquiries, expenditure and return on investment, as well as lapsed clients and lost jobs (enquiries that did not convert to instruction). This recommendation from the executive team did not simply share facts and figures, it explained them within the context of past performance and future objectives and helped the board to make informed strategic decisions about where to direct effort and resources, to really get results.

By adding this analysis and 'blue sky thinking' section to the board meetings the board found itself moving, naturally, to a way of working focused far more on directing strategy than on micromanaging the day-to-day. This impacted on the other areas of the agenda. With this in place the productivity of board meetings changed dramatically. Over several meetings the board was able to agree on the type of client they wanted to attract and retain, as well as developing a clearer idea of the areas of focus they would have over the coming months and years. Focusing resources more effectively in these areas.

Having seen the potential impact of giving more focus to this area of the business, the board resolved to set up a business development sub-committee, which Sarah was invited to chair. The group would meet monthly, before the main board meeting, to drill down into more of the marketing and business development data, before making recommendations to take back to the board. This allowed for increased scrutiny, without making full board meetings unwieldy.

Sarah continues to sit on the board as a NED. She is now acting as a critical friend to assist the board in constructively interrogating the reporting coming before them to assess impact and opportunities for future development. The board is now having a much more informed discussion about the various supplier and technology changes required to better support development of the firm, as well as considering the business case for the launch of the firm's first office in the Middle East. If that project goes ahead then the board are considering another NED appointment of someone with specific knowledge of that market.

Claire-Elaine Arthurs enjoys a portfolio career. As well as providing non-executive support to flourishing businesses, she is also a solicitor, judge, and mediator, making her uniquely positioned to offer support and insight within the legal industry. Under the banner of Orthelian, she also facilitates training, coaching support, and immersive development experiences for senior leaders.

Helen Foord is CEO of legal sector marketing agency ELE. Having held a number of senior internal marketing and business development roles, Helen formed ELE and now works with both US and UK law firms and chambers on strategic and tactical marketing development. Helen is often called upon to advise boards on strategic planning, related governance, and communications matters.

Want to attract the best and brightest? Embrace social and technological change

Janet Taylor-Hall

How *not* to become a casualty of legal's ongoing war for talent.

In the past, successful legal careers followed a predictable pattern. Law firms would survey the latest graduate cohort, select the top candidates to become trainees, then set them on the path to eventually become a partner.

It operated like a sales funnel – fill it with prospects at the top so that a determined and lucky few can battle through to the end. But despite enduring the same long hours, stress and exhaustion, most found themselves struggling to reach a goal that was never really attainable.

To avoid reaching mid-career and looking back with regret, today's best and brightest arrive in the legal profession with different ideas about what constitutes success. They have a modern view of achievement and actively seek work environments geared towards solving problems, gaining new experiences and respecting social values.

They want to use the latest tools and technology. They don't want yesterday's paper- and office-based grind or a daily competition to see whose jacket is still on the chair at midnight.

The question is, how many law firms and in-house legal teams have absorbed just how much has changed?

To a large extent, our profession stands aloof from the talent marketplace, operating by rules from a bygone age and expecting new joiners to follow traditional career journeys that aren't relevant for the majority.

One example is a business culture still dominated by the perceived hierarchy between lawyers and other skilled professionals working within the legal profession, while lack of respect for competencies like data analytics and design thinking is another.

Those are precisely the kinds of skills today's newly-qualified want to use on the job. They're also increasingly the kinds of abilities clients want to buy. The fact that they haven't been fully embraced by the profession points to pervasive, old-school thinking, which is increasingly unpopular with candidates and clients.

When you're trying to attract the best and brightest, that's a problem.

A 2020 study by the World Economic Forum (WEF)[1] analysed the skills required to succeed in the digital age. The study found that bread-and-butter legal aptitudes like problem-solving and critical thinking are still vital to success.

But so are skills like emotional intelligence, collaboration and creativity. They're now seen as equally essential for the legal positions being filled today as well as the new roles still being created.

Collaboration is key to building better delivery ecosystems for talent to thrive, in that it ultimately provides clients with solutions that are focused on solving their problems. If we are going to succeed at being more sustainable and solving the world's most pressing issues such as the climate crisis, then we will need to be less competitive and openly work together. Whilst this is a big mindset shift for a sector that currently has no short-term economic incentive to change, the potential gains are significant.

If we are going to succeed at being more sustainable and solving the world's most pressing issues such as the climate crisis, then we will need to be less competitive and openly work together.

A chasm between expectations and delivery

After two decades working in, and for, top law firms and corporate legal teams, it's clear to me that a gap has opened up between client expectations and the profession's capacity to satisfy them. It's happening because legal leaders are failing to grasp the technological and societal changes that are driving digital transformation.

Legal professionals at every stage of their career have more choices available to them in terms of roles, workstyles, lifestyles and geographic options than ever before. Meanwhile, corporate clients are increasingly demanding a more responsive, flexible and impactful kind of legal service. Clients still want their legal providers to protect the business, but they're also asking for more support in identifying risks and uncovering commercial value.

Since law schools are still adapting their curricula to address these changes, most lawyers already working in traditional settings won't have acquired the necessary skills.

New joiners want what clients want

Clients increasingly want to buy the same capabilities that trainees hope to gain on the job, mixing legal expertise with data science and other aspects of the modern economy.

Clients want lawyers to be data-driven, agile, proactive, sustainable and collaborative. Young lawyers want to support clients with solutions to business challenges.

That approach requires a comfort level with all things digital that only those who have grown up amid digital transformation can fully grasp. A report from Gartner, a technology research and consulting company, suggests that less than one-quarter of legal teams understand the issues around digital transformation well enough to provide effective legal insight and support.[2]

Clients want lawyers to be data-driven, agile, proactive, sustainable and collaborative. Young lawyers want to support clients with solutions to business challenges.

The lack of understanding is evident in the pervasive idea that only lawyers can deliver legal services. In other sectors, rapid uptake of digitally-driven modes of service delivery is accepted as proof that transformation is well underway.

In legal, the view is more ambiguous.

The wide adoption of legal operations, for example, might be accepted, but its practitioners don't enjoy the same status as those in legal SME roles. And that won't change until legal culture recognises the importance of business agility, collaboration, sustainability, gender pay equity, diversity and lifestyle choice in today's legal workplace.

To deliver services in the digital age, legal leaders have to build operations staffed by people prepared to work at the intersection of law, business and technology. Labels like 'full-time' or 'project-based' matter less and less.

The sheer challenge of cultural change is explored in a powerful piece written by Isabel Parker, "Rethinking law firm culture and purpose",[3] where she closes with a challenge to law firms:

> *It's time to think more expansively. Law firms should follow the example of the New York Fed. As purpose becomes an ever more pressing imperative, they should seize the opportunity to shrug off the wig and gown of lawyer exceptionalism and learn from others.*

Your colleague is a computer

Technology isn't just altering skill sets and workstyles; it's arguably making working in the legal profession more rewarding. Automating manual tasks related to things like simple contracts and discovery frees people to focus on high-value activities that directly support clients' strategic objectives.

In practical terms, it means new joiners expect legal to be like other professional services – hybrid environments where people work alongside machines. Some responsibilities are carried out by humans, while more transactional tasks are handled by intelligent automation or by other specialists engaged virtually on the platform.

It's work as a space rather than a place, where everyone is part of an ecosystem of capabilities, and it opens up a host of different career trajectories. Be part of a core team, or be an independent specialist engaged on a project basis. Today both options can be the basis for a credible, long-term career strategy.

Either way, the skill sets we recruit for need to evolve. Working as part of an extended team might mean daily interaction between people who've never met in person. Managing relationships effectively using digital communications alone involves best practices that are still being developed.

And then there's the impact of legal analytics to consider. Data-centric legal teams are another defining feature of a hybrid legal workplace. The ability to mine contracts for insights that can inform a client's corporate strategy is already rising in importance.

Education, qualifications and experience will still be in demand, but so too will soft skills like creative thinking and emotional intelligence. This suggests the need to do more to draw from a wider pool of new or recent graduates and look beyond Oxbridge and the Ivy League.

Embracing flexibility and impermanence

If tomorrow's trainees are looking for a different kind of career and workplace, that opens up opportunities for legal leaders. Instead of staffing a legal firm or function with full-time permanent employees at a physical location, it can now be a blend of on-site, remote and virtual resources.

The blended operational models taking shape now resemble what's happening in other parts of professional services, where a 'hub' team of legal generalists is augmented by 'spokes' consisting of specialist resources.

It's a model that complements traditional legal roles with a more diverse range of skill sets in areas like data science, technology and operations that can be activated when they are really needed – or switched off when they aren't.

For GCs, it means flexibility to move up the strategic curve, using outside resources to release core teams from day-to-day tasks and focus on strategic responsibilities.

For fledgling lawyers, these changes open the door to new opportunities for shaping their careers. If a training contract isn't immediately available, gaining experience first with an alternative legal service provider (ALSP) offers the on-the-job experience necessary to increase an individual's prospects of securing training contract opportunities.

In our experience, lawyers and other professionals at ALSPs report feeling fully embedded with clients and often find their work is even more aligned with their client's business objectives than it might be if they were part of a traditional law firm's account team.

Others find that life as a hired gun suits them better. Lawyers who choose to work flexibly are drawn to ALSPs because their operating models cater to individual circumstances. Where temping was once seen as a stopgap between permanent roles, flexible working is now a lifestyle choice which has opened the door to a portfolio career. Then there is the added appeal of opportunities to work on interesting projects and use new technology. It goes well beyond notions of the gig economy.

Where temping was once seen as a stopgap between permanent roles, flexible working is now a lifestyle choice which has opened the door to a portfolio career.

The sector is also mature enough to see its own boomerang trend emerge. It's common now to see people starting their careers at an ALSP, moving on to a law firm or corporate team for a few years, then bouncing back to the ALSP to take advantage of better opportunities to work in their area of specialism, or simply to experience a wider array of clients, legal challenges and modern purpose-driven cultures.

Recruiting from the past

Legal professionals understand precedent, and we're trained to look at what's happened before to understand what's to come. But that approach won't deliver results where attracting talent is concerned.

In *The Second Machine Age*, futurist Erik Brynjolfsson points out that we're living through an age where "what's happened before isn't a reliable guide to what could happen next".

Up to now, legal hasn't embraced digital transformation or the changes it's bringing. You can see it in the profession's net promoter score,[4] which lags behind other sectors. If law firms and in-house legal teams want to attract the best people, acknowledging what's attractive to this generation in terms of career progression is critical.

In a recent LinkedIn poll, I asked my contacts what they thought talent would be looking for in 2022. More than 58% chose blended home and office working while 18% prioritised working for a company with a clear purpose that is lived. The opportunity to use the latest technology and build broader skill sets was voted third and fourth (with 13% and 12% respectively). Another senior legal leader commented that legal talent value defined career paths with responsibility.

What does this tell us? With salaries for newly-qualified solicitors in the UK heading skyward for some time (which then feeds into larger pay cheques for experienced hires),[5] experienced legal talent are in a strong position to look beyond material rewards for more holistic, long-term benefits.

You can see it in the dwindling interest amongst millennials in 'making partner'. A recent survey by Bloomberg Law[6] found that 59% of associates did not aspire to become partners at their current firms. The figure is borne out by another study[7] that found just 40% of millennial lawyers view partnership as their long-term career goal. Both analyses are US-focused, but they point to a direction of travel.

To be a talent magnet, legal teams need to become more sustainable, equitable, flexible, digital and diverse. The alternative is to start losing out to providers who already are.

Janet Taylor-Hall, Chief Executive Officer, Cognia Law. Janet founded Cognia to integrate how legal services are provided by bringing creativity, trust and sustainable outcomes. She is passionate about building efficient working models that enable legal professionals to realise their full potential to better serve their clients, stakeholders and communities in which they operate. Janet leads the organisation in listening to clients, adapting models to meet their needs and collaborating with partners to provide high-quality solutions to banks, global corporations and law firms. Building on her varied, international experience developed at EY, Clifford Chance and Integreon, Janet is a hands-on operator who brings her informed business acumen to work with clients in designing solutions to their challenges. This is made possible by Janet's commitment since Cognia's launch to building diverse teams that thrive and give clients access to the best talent.

1 www.weforum.org/agenda/2020/10/top-10-work-skills-of-tomorrow-how-long-it-takes-to-learn-them/.
2 www.gartner.com/en/newsroom/press-releases/2018-12-12-gartner-says-81-percent-of-legal-departments-are-un prepared-for-digitalization.
3 www.artificiallawyer.com/2021/12/10/rethinking-law-firm-culture-and-purpose/.
4 www.attorneyatwork.com/clio-legal-trends-report-in-context/.
5 www.thelawyer.com/trainee-newly-qualified-salaries-uk-law-firms/.
6 news.bloomberglaw.com/banking-law/survey-says-law-firms-need-not-fret-about-the-millennials.
7 www.mlaglobal.com/en-gb/insights/research/2019-millennial-attorney-survey-new-expectations-evolving-beliefs-and-shifting-career-goals.

For the people: can apprenticeships pave the way for a more diverse legal profession?

Lucie Allen and Jonathan Bourne

With the Learning and Work Institute[1] reporting that the skills shortage will cost the UK economy £120 billion by 2030, the legal sector is not alone in its struggle to recruit and retain talent. The Institute's analysis predicts a shortfall of 2.5 million of the type of "highly skilled" workers that law firms desire.

One school of thought gathering momentum across sectors and from senior industry leaders is to re-examine training and development opportunities for young people to address this skills gap. This could also contribute significantly to social mobility by widening opportunities into the professions to a much broader candidate pool. A recent report[2] by PwC UK and the Times Education Commission echoed this sentiment, suggesting that "with 85% of UK businesses experiencing or anticipating skills shortages, equipping young people for future jobs is vital to building a resilient and more inclusive economy".

When it comes to the practical solutions that can help to drive this forward, apprenticeships are growing in popularity, offering numerous benefits to both individuals and employers. This includes affordability, hands-on experience, and the ability to shape individuals based on the needs of the business. Nearly 750,000 apprentices participated in England in the 2021/2022 academic year, according to official figures.[3] Currently, there are 1,300 solicitor apprentices in England, according to the Government's Institute for Apprenticeships statistics.[4]

The tide is turning, with the legal sector waking up to the opportunities provided by the apprenticeship route as well as the need to provide alternative qualification methods to meet the evolving needs of the modern lawyer, driven partly by the integration into the solicitor apprenticeship of the new Solicitors Qualifying Exam (SQE). After all, among the reasons for the move away from the old Legal Practice Course (LPC) was a desire to broaden access to the profession and attract a wider pool of talent. This is already being embraced by firms, and the benefits of a stronger and more diverse pipeline are starting to become a reality. It's undeniable that the opportunities presented by apprenticeships in conjunction with this are significant and, for the first time, aspiring legal professionals no longer require a law degree – or need to complete a Graduate Diploma in Law (GDL) – to pursue a career as a solicitor. Indeed, the solicitor apprenticeship has created opportunities for non-graduates from a wide range of backgrounds to train to become solicitors – a clear benefit for those who cannot afford rising university fees or those who have previously been unable to fully pursue their career aspirations due to personal or financial restraints.

Traditionally, mid-sized firms have led the way in embracing apprenticeships, but the wider industry is now shaping new opportunities for this emerging pool of talent. For example, in June 2023 (on Social Mobility Day), over 50 City law firms joined forces with the City of London Law Society to launch 'City Century'.[5] This is a long-term program designed to "identify, attract, recruit, educate, qualify and develop" solicitor apprentices from a diverse talent pool. Led by Linklaters, alongside five flagship firms – Allen & Overy, Eversheds Sutherland, Hogan Lovells, Norton Rose Fulbright, and Osborne Clarke – City Century hopes to create 100 new partners by 2040 through the scheme.

Shadow Attorney General, Emily Thornberry, has lent her support to the initiative, saying:

> *"Apprenticeships are key to opening up access to careers for those who may otherwise be held back by financial barriers. Initiatives like these should be commonplace in all professions, but it's great to see many of the major City law firms finding new ways to support talented and aspiring young lawyers."*

So how do both firms and candidates benefit from the new solicitor apprenticeship route?

Seizing the opportunity

Understandably, often the first thing firms – and candidates – want to know when considering any type of training opportunity is the cost. However, with the apprenticeship option, financial barriers have been reduced. For larger law firms, the cost of training and the apprentices' two-part SQE fees are fully funded by the Government via the Apprenticeship Levy. For smaller employers who don't pay this Levy, the costs are still 95% funded by the Government and there is no employer's NI for most apprentices aged 25 and under.

In addition to this, the savings associated with using the combined apprenticeship SQE route to retain and train existing staff is also a compelling factor for many firms.

For example, retaining a good paralegal for the long-term whilst firms are competing fiercely for talent might seem challenging. However, if the potential and ambition are there, upskilling existing employees to become solicitors helps keep talent in the business by satisfying career aspirations as well as providing a consistent salary, while helping to create a strong future pipeline from within. The door to progression is well and truly open, and this can be particularly beneficial for smaller firms and in-house legal departments, where competing on salary with larger firms isn't feasible.

Traditionally, mid-sized firms have led the way in embracing apprenticeships, but the wider industry is now shaping new opportunities for this emerging pool of talent.

The other advantage of this route is that with the SRA's Qualifying Work Experience (QWE) requirement replacing the former training contract "seats", firms can take on both apprentices and standalone SQE students. The greater the breadth of experience that apprentices and SQE students can gain the better, and many employers will still "rotate" apprentices where possible. The experience gained counts towards the two-year QWE requirement, meaning candidates can earn while they learn (the SRA outlines[6] an 80/20 split between work (80%) and training/studying (20%)), firms don't miss out on the resource needed, and, importantly, apprentices get to apply the knowledge and skills that they learn in the workplace as part of their apprenticeship – all with reduced financial pressures.

As it supports workforce planning in a way that suits each employer's unique needs as well as the individual, this hybrid approach doesn't exclude candidates following a more traditional university pathway. It simply opens up a far larger talent pool, which includes a much broader range of people from different backgrounds and life stages – creating a richer, more diverse, workforce.

Yet it's undeniable that non-law graduates and those for whom the university route may have been prohibitive are those who are likely to feel the most immediate benefit. Therefore, as well as improving access to the profession, working alongside people who have different life experiences and viewpoints is hugely beneficial to enriching the existing workforce's diversity of thought. This can help to create more effective teams, identify blind spots, increase profitability and shape new, innovative ideas – amongst other things. Not to mention accommodating the vast spectrum of clients that firms represent and serve, helping to create a profession that better reflects today's society.

Enabling multiple routes to qualify as a solicitor can help firms create a diverse and inclusive workforce, supporting legal professionals from A Level through to graduate level and tailoring support as required.

Diversity in practice – Damar Training

Sharing common ground with the new SQE route to qualification, legal apprenticeship routes have been designed to be as flexible and inclusive as possible. They are available to any law firm, in-house legal team or legal service provider and employers will typically work with a training provider to offer the academic study required. While the exact offer will vary depending on the apprenticeship provider, Damar, for example, offers three routes to qualification as a solicitor for legal apprentices. Designed to be inclusive, the pathways are:

- *Shorter (18-month):* solicitor apprenticeship for those already working in legal jobs and who are law graduates, holders of a graduate diploma in law (GDL), or full-/part-qualified CILEX L6, licensed conveyancers or similar.
- *Longer (36-month):* solicitor apprenticeship for non-law graduates, successful paralegal apprentices, CILEX L3, conveyancing technicians, licensed paralegals and similar.
- *Five-year pathway:* for A-level leavers and non-graduate legal administrators. Two-year paralegal apprenticeship with Damar followed by a 36-month solicitor apprenticeship.

Enabling multiple routes to qualify as a solicitor can help firms create a diverse and inclusive workforce, supporting legal professionals from A Level through to graduate level and tailoring support as required. This takes careful planning, however. The CIPD's 2022 Inclusion at Work report[7] found that 47% of leaders don't have a formal equality, diversity, and inclusion strategy or action plan in place. So for firms truly committed to creating a diverse workforce (not to mention a strong pipeline of future talent), including apprenticeships as part of long-term workforce, design strategies should be a key consideration.

The commercial benefits of having a diverse and inclusive workforce are also widely recognized. The Solicitors Regulation Authority (SRA)[8] has quoted the Employers Network for Equality on Inclusion (ENEI) on the matter as part of its Benefits of Diversity in the Profession monitoring:

"The 'business case' debate is now well rehearsed and it is generally accepted through the business world that diversity is a strategic enabler, ensuring competitive advantage and positioning organizations as employers of choice."

Apprentices leading the way

Perhaps somewhat unfairly, the question is often asked if the new apprenticeship routes – which include non-law graduates and non-graduates – deliver as high-quality candidates as the traditional law degree route. This thinking has the potential to slow the speed of the industry's embrace of apprenticeships. However, we must not underestimate the SQE or disregard the reason behind its introduction – to put all candidates on a level playing field and to invite more diverse voices to have a seat at the table. Plus, it is challenging and arguably more demanding than the LPC, not least because it is designed to assess competence at the point of qualification rather than two years earlier (as with the LPC).

Yet, as the next cohort of SQE candidates prepare to sit their assessment (July 2023), the outlook for apprentices looks promising. Data from the SRA shows that more than 100 apprentices took the SQE between September 2021 and August 2022, with marks that were 8% higher, on average, than non-apprentices. This is arguably going some way to support changing perceptions around apprenticeships across the industry.

Although it's early days, the regulator has suggested that the mix of practical and formal learning that apprentices undertake on their journey to qualification is a possible reason for this SQE success. SRA chief executive, Paul Philip, says:

> *"Apprenticeships are a great way to encourage more talented people from all backgrounds to become solicitors. They are an attractive option for those who want a more affordable way into the profession and want to gain early legal practice experience. It can also be a good option for employers looking to recruit and shape new talent."*

A case in point

As long-term advocates of opening up the legal profession to a greater diversity of candidates, BARBRI and Damar Training partnered earlier in 2023 to broaden access to the apprenticeship route and support the needs of the industry. Working with a wide range of law firms and in-house teams, Damar embeds BARBRI's SQE learning technology into its apprenticeship programs, offering solicitor apprenticeship opportunities to a broad range of candidates across different ages, backgrounds, and socio-economic statuses, from school leavers to existing paralegals and law graduates.

Through flexibility around access points to training and technology, which enables personalized and tailored study to take place, the scheme has already created a diverse range of opportunities for employers and candidates.

The commercial benefits of having a diverse and inclusive workforce are also widely recognized.

Non-law-graduate Lewis Drew, a paralegal with Pennon Group, will be undertaking the three-year apprenticeship. He says of his decision:

> *"The new solicitor apprenticeship route to qualification is a perfect fit for me. Training as a solicitor has been my goal since school – I was inspired by a scheme I took part in run by the Social Mobility Business Partnership. Having later graduated with a degree in English Literature from the University of Bristol, continuing my studies via a graduate diploma in law was the only way forward for me – until the pandemic hit. Adapting to learning remotely came as a huge challenge and one that pushed me into the world of work as opposed to remaining in education. The ability to qualify over three years whilst gaining experience through my role as a paralegal is incredible, allowing me to build upon valuable foundations only possible through the new apprenticeship route – an opportunity I didn't think I would secure as a non-law graduate."*

From an employer's perspective, the benefits are also tangible. Cambridge University Press & Assessment is one such employer that recognizes this. Fiona Kelly, assistant general counsel for Cambridge University Press & Assessment said:

> *"We support alternative routes into the legal profession because they benefit both the individuals themselves and bring a valuable and different perspective to our team. The benefits go further than just having an extra pair of hands. We're getting new insights into our work from having*

colleagues who haven't done the standard university law school training contract route, both in terms of their approach to work and the new viewpoints they offer and in terms of the positive effect on other members of the team."

This positive experience is shared by Cambridge University Press & Assessment apprentice Branwen Cleaver, who says:

"The apprenticeship route is unique in that it enables me to combine my legal learning and practice within a supportive framework. My skills are developed in line with the SRA solicitor competencies, and I am entrusted with exciting, interesting projects. I'm thankful to work for an employer that is leading the way within the legal sector."

The future is bright

While initial progress has been made to embrace and shape apprenticeship opportunities, they arguably haven't yet been fully embraced across the industry for firms and in-house teams of all sizes. From our experience, we believe that the benefits are largely underestimated, especially for non-law graduates who may have felt excluded from opportunities in the sector under the previous qualification route. Plus, many are not fully aware that it's a possibility or to what extent it can reduce financial burdens for both the individual and the employer, so there is further work to be done to educate in this area.

However, as the SQE replaces the LPC and the transition period comes to an end in 2032, we'll likely see more apprenticeship opportunities emerging across the industry over the next few years thanks to the unique opportunity this presents. If we continue to see apprentices perform better than other candidates in SQE assessments – thereby seeing practical experience elevate academic understanding – the benefit of these schemes will become undeniable and unavoidable for both employers and individuals. It does have the potential to change the way the industry thinks about qualification, and we look forward to seeing how this progresses.

Lucie Allen is managing director for BARBRI. An established and energetic leader with over 20 years' commercial experience working across a variety of industries and verticals, Lucie spent seven years at Thomson Reuters prior to joining BARBRI in a global role as vice president in the legal segment where she works closely with global law firm leaders. Lucie has created organizational structures, built teams, defined propositions, and developed successful customer account programs throughout her career to deliver top line growth. She is recognized for her collaborative approach, influence, and ability to execute on her strategic vision.

After spending the early part of his career as a solicitor specializing in corporate law, Jonathan Bourne has been managing director of Damar Training since 2007, overseeing Damar's growth to becoming a national provider of apprenticeships in business and professional services. Jonathan brought together the consortium that created the first legal apprenticeship in 2013 and has been closely involved in the development and delivery of other legal sector apprenticeships. He is also a director of the Greater Manchester Learning Provider Network, a not-for-profit supporting skills provision in Greater Manchester.

1 https://learningandwork.org.uk/resources/research-and-reports/local-skills-deficits-and-spare-capacity/
2 www.pwc.co.uk/who-we-are/annual-report/stories/2022/supporting-the-times-education-commission.html
3 https://commonslibrary.parliament.uk/research-briefings/sn06113/
4 www.instituteforapprenticeships.org/about/newshub/news-events/solicitor-apprentices-outperforming-academic-counterparts-in-exams/
5 https://city-century.co.uk
6 www.sra.org.uk/become-solicitor/sqe/solicitor-apprenticeships/
7 www.cipd.org/uk/knowledge/reports/inclusion-work/
8 www.sra.org.uk/sra/equality-diversity/diversity-profession/

Business development

The perils and pitfalls of business development

Andrea Kennedy

Introduction

About 15 years ago I was asked to advise a law firm about business development. As part of the consulting agreement the firm wanted me to sign a restrictive covenant preventing me from sharing with their competitors, for at least six months, any magic, innovative or unique idea arising from my time there. I told them that I was flattered if they thought that I could offer them anything new in relation to business development. But in fact it was almost certain that I would not come up with anything that they couldn't find out for themselves by reading most books on business development and marketing for professional services firms. However, they would not get a competitive edge by reading all those books, or hiring consultants like me – that's easy. What would give them the edge was actually being willing to accept and apply what they read or were advised – that's hard.

And that remains the case today. There is nothing new about the basics of business development. What is new and different is the way in which communication, advertising and promotion is conducted via social media and the Internet. But that's about it. I think lawyers know in their gut what they need to do to develop their business, but sometimes it just seems too difficult.

This article will concentrate less on the 'how-to' of business development and more on the strategic challenges it presents. I will look at where it can go wrong in the planning and implementation, common mistakes that are made, and what makes business development effective. I will do this by taking the reader through a typical business plan and its various parts, offering practical tips along the way.

I won't use incomprehensible graphs, confusing jargon or management speak. Such things, I believe, put people off because it makes business development, which is primarily common sense, sound threatening and difficult. I will draw on my experience of over 25 years as a lawyer, a consultant and a client. I hope it will serve as an easy guide to an area that has been ignored, feared, loathed, misunderstood and, occasionally, embraced by lawyers worldwide.

The business plan

Any good business development programme starts with a business plan. In this article, I will talk about the business plan for a law firm, but the steps taken to formulate a firm-wide business plan or strategy can be applied equally to formulating plans for practice areas and individuals.

A business plan is crucial for any organisation to move forward in a coordinated and focused way. It should address three main questions, namely:

- Where are we now?
- Where do we want to be in x years' time?
- How do we get there?

Statement of business objective

A statement of the firm's business development objectives gives everyone a common focus and goals to bear in mind when carrying out any business development activities. It should be specific enough so as to be measurable and clear, but general enough to allow for flexibility and changes. Such a statement might read something like:

Our objectives over the next three to five years are to be the number one firm in the area of X and Y, to increase our income by X% by increasing both our client base and the value and volume of work, to gain five new clients in each of our specialist practice areas (eg, litigation, corporate, intellectual property, employment), to actively promote our practice areas and practitioners, to increase contact between ourselves and our clients and to encourage cross-departmental business development initiatives. In order to service our expanding practice we aim to increase our legal personnel by X% over the next five years through both lateral recruitment and internal, organic growth.

The agreed statement of objectives can serve as a backdrop of principles and goals against which the business plan is formulated.

Where it can go wrong: Treating the statement of business objectives as the business plan itself. The statement of business objectives addresses the 'what', but not the 'how' and the 'who'. Consequently, it makes business development and marketing impossible because everyone in the firm is left to figure out for themselves how they should go about it, making the process ad hoc, inefficient and expensive. I once worked for a firm as a marketing consultant and in order to know how to design an effective marketing plan I needed to see their business plan. When I asked them for it they presented me with something written on two sides of one piece of paper. It was effectively an extended mission statement, filled with platitudes and aspirations that were so broad as to be useless. As a result, trying to get people in that firm to engage with business development was impossible because no one knew what they were meant to be working towards. People became concerned about the firm's position in the market, and their own security in the firm, because it appeared that management hadn't thought about these things. Morale dropped through the floor and many people left.

A decent business plan should, at the very least:

- analyse the firm's position in the market by examining its strengths, weaknesses, opportunities and threats (a SWOT analysis);
- identify key clients;
- assess established clients' satisfaction;
- identify specific business development initiatives;
- consider growth via mergers and lateral recruitment;
- target specific new work/clients;
- identify sources of referral work;
- address the issue of following up initiatives and keeping in contact with clients/prospects;
- address who is responsible for managing and implementing the business development effort.

I will look at each of these elements in turn.

Analyse the firm's position in the market

The SWOT analysis

One of the most effective ways of looking objectively at a law firm's business is to perform the SWOT analysis (ie, look at its Strengths, Weaknesses, Opportunities and Threats). The SWOT analysis has been around for decades, but it does not mean it is an outdated method. It is still a fantastic way to start providing focus to an area that can be overwhelming. The following is an example of a fictional boutique English law firm's SWOT analysis:

Strengths

- Skilled lawyers
- Strength in breadth and depth of experience and expertise
- High profile/highly regarded individuals
- Energetic, eclectic team of individuals – can fit the best adviser to any particular client
- Team structure – provides cover and continuity for client
- Collegiate atmosphere
- High degree of client satisfaction – high standards
- Highly skilled lawyers
- Heavy presence in leading professional organisations
- Firm is No 1 in legal directories in some of its specialist fields and has been for a number of years running

Weaknesses

- Team structure may be too rigid
- Teams too self-contained – risk that knowledge is not shared
- Reputation of firm heavily reliant on the reputation of a few star individuals
- No formal know-how system in place
- No formal client contact database in place
- Some junior partners and assistants do not know how to market themselves
- Support staff to lawyer ratio very high, therefore harder to produce profit
- No individuals in 2nd tier of directory tables.
- Other specialist fields not represented in the directories

The SWOT analysis has been around for decades, but it does not mean it is an outdated method.

Once you have analysed your current client base and identified your key clients you may want to rush into a business development campaign.

Opportunities

- Arrival of high-profile practitioner and his team specialising in a new, but complementary, practice
- Growth of International work
- New legislation that will produce more advisory work
- New big name from rival firm recently recruited
- Potentially huge market in investment banks, American law firms and other firms which do not have similar practice. Potential referral work?

Threats

- Chief rival firm – more aggressive marketers and they market themselves as a global firm
- Our size – as we grow bigger it may be harder to maintain standards. Risk of fragmentation and loss of collegiate atmosphere
- The retirement/winding down of two top senior lawyers. No obvious successors
- Competitors will use retirement of senior people to their advantage and to brief against the firm

The idea is to try to maximise strengths and opportunities, and address and eliminate your weaknesses and threats. Only after these have been explored can the firm plan a realistic business development and marketing strategy.

Where it can go wrong: Not doing a SWOT analysis at all, and not concentrating enough on weaknesses and threats. Remember that new opportunities often present themselves out of perceived threats, so it is important to be as clear and honest as possible about weaknesses and vulnerabilities. There is an old saying, "A problem well stated presents its own solution." Pretending problems don't exist, or down-playing weaknesses, is counter-productive as they are rarely resolved on their own and can often become worse if not addressed.

Analyse your current client base

Having conducted the SWOT analysis it is now important to identify and analyse your current client base. Draw up a list of those clients who you consider to be your most significant clients, based on value or volume of work, or whatever other criteria you use. This is an important exercise because often your impression of how much work you get from a particular client (by value or volume) may be very different from what your records show. Working out how much work you get from your clients across the firm, within practice areas and in relation to individual lawyers, will help you to determine where to focus your business development efforts. For example, one client may give you a lot of employment work, but no M&A work. If you do both, you need to find out why they don't use you for both. Or you may find that your revenue from one business sector is lower than you thought. If this is a sector that you want to retain and develop, you need to find out what is happening. Alternatively, this data may alert you to the possibility that work in this area is declining in the market generally. Is it therefore worth pursuing and developing? How do you go about getting this valuable information?

Where it can go wrong: Relying on impressions rather than data. Doing this can result in developing a plan that does not accurately reflect the business reality.

Assess current client satisfaction

Once you have analysed your current client base and identified your key clients you may want to rush into a business development campaign. Before you do, you need to engage with them to determine how satisfied they are with you and your services, and to try to seek answers to the sorts of questions posed above. The best, and easiest, way to do this is simply by talking to them. Indeed, such conversations should take place regularly throughout the client relationship, not just when they are engaged with you on an active matter. This is sometimes easier said than done. The other way of assessing your clients' satisfaction is by conducting a client survey. A formal client survey can often elicit far more useful information than anticipated. Client surveys are a great way to gain intelligence about any number of things, such as the market's perception of you, how well you service your clients, what the competition is doing, and just generally to find out what really matters, as opposed to what you think matters, to your clients.

Where it can go wrong: Not seeking feedback from your clients at all, or only concentrating on those clients who you know are satisfied with you and your services. Some lawyers are nervous about seeking formal feedback from clients. They don't want to know if their clients are unhappy, and they don't want to bother them with a survey. But in my experience clients are flattered that they have been asked for their views, that you are taking the time to seek their views, and that you care about them. And if a survey elicits criticism in any way, it acts as an early warning system to give you the chance to address any issues before they escalate into anything more serious and irreversible.

Who do you ask and how?

This is entirely up to you depending on your, and your clients', culture and the relationship you have with your clients. You want to aim for a representative cross-section. I would divide the client base into those who instruct you regularly, those who instruct you less frequently or only in certain practice areas, and those who used to instruct you but no longer do so.

Even those clients who you think are 100% satisfied with your firm and your service will often have something constructive and useful to say. In addition, do not be afraid to approach clients who have stopped using you. There may be a perfectly good reason for this which has nothing to do with you or your firm. They may well have received poor advice or service from you, but there could be another, more benign, reason, such as a key client may have moved jobs, or the client may no longer do the sort of work that you do. One way or another it is useful to have this information so that you know how to address it.

The survey can be conducted in person, by telephone, by written questionnaire, online, or any combination of these methods.

What to ask?

That depends on what you want to find out. The most obvious thing is whether you are providing a good service and if your lawyers are performing well. But you may want to find out about what methods of marketing your clients find most effective, or why they no longer instruct your firm or certain lawyers. It is worth asking them about their own practice area with a view to identifying trends or trouble spots in the market. In a face-to-face interview the client will often set the agenda and be much more candid about talking about that which most concerns him or her, which can be extremely useful.

Who should conduct the survey?

You can either choose someone within your firm to conduct the survey or employ an independent third party.

Where it can go wrong: Employing an outsider who does not fully understand your business. An independent third party must have knowledge of the market, your business and culture and understand the relationship between you and your clients so as to be a credible representative for your firm and obtain the most valuable feedback. On the other hand, using someone from inside the firm could be awkward and may discourage your clients from being fully frank.

What do you do with the information from the survey?

Whatever you do with the information, you must realise that your clients' expectations will be raised simply because the survey was conducted. So you need to do something. However you choose to canvass your clients' views, remember that the purpose of the exercise is to meet their needs, not yours.

Where it can go wrong: Not taking on board your clients' comments and responding appropriately and positively.

Not sharing the findings with everyone in the firm – you must ensure that the results of any client survey are shared with your firm, at least by way of an executive summary of the findings, so as to encourage others to become engaged with, and feel part of, the process (see section below on who should do business development).

So far, so good. What next?

By now you have decided that you want to grow your business, increase your client base, your revenue and your profits. You have done your SWOT analysis,

Whatever you do with the information, you must realise that your clients' expectations will be raised simply because the survey was conducted.

Whatever initiatives you decide on, remember it will require some investment in time, manpower and money. You want to try to maximise your return on this investment.

identified your key clients, and have a good indication about how satisfied they are with your services. You have a good basis for a business and marketing plan. Now what?

Identify business development and marketing initiatives

Now you can start working out how to get to where you want to go. The homework you have done so far will give you a clear indication of how to move forward. You may decide, for example, to use one or more of the following:

- Embark on an advertising campaign to raise your profile in the market
  Remember that advertising in and of itself is unlikely to bring in work, but it is a quick way to raise your profile. However, it is expensive and has to be carefully placed to reach the optimum audience.
- Put on a series of seminars in your specialist practice areas
  Putting on seminars and taking part in conferences are good ways to raise your profile, get you in front of current and potential clients, and showcase your expertise but, as with so many other marketing activities, if you do not follow them up on a regular basis you might as well not do them. More on following up below.
- Use social media
  Like it or not, social media is here to stay. Depending on the culture in which you are operating, make sure that your lawyers are on LinkedIn or similar sites, consider blogging and using Twitter. Generation Y and the Millennials are current and future clients and operate in this space. Law firms and lawyers have to occupy a place in it. And if, as was suggested in a recent study, humans now have a shorter attention span than goldfish, blogs and tweets may be read more than long articles!
- Client entertainment
  Small-scale events like dinners and lunches, even breakfasts, allow relationships to develop and grow. As building and maintaining your client base is about establishing trust, this sort of face-to-face contact works very well. And you can all share a common, bonding experience: a nice meal! You can also entertain on a grander scale but it will almost certainly be expensive so you need to be discerning as to what events you do, how often, and for which clients.
- Write articles
  Despite our diminishing attention span, there is still a place for articles. The great thing about them is that they can be used in so many ways by so many different people. They can be re-printed and put in beauty parade packs, or distributed at seminars or workshops. They can be kept in electronic form and emailed to prospective clients when an enquiry is made. They can be put in a file and displayed in the reception area. And they can be reproduced on your website. But they take a long time to write and, depending on the topic, can quickly become out of date. That is why many prefer quicker and more immediate vehicles like blogs and tweets.
- We live in a world where communication is increasingly visual. A number of people respond more to videos than to reading something. Bear this in mind when you think of how best to reach clients or prospects in certain practice areas.
- Produce podcasts that can be accessed and downloaded by clients and listened to at their leisure.

Whatever initiatives you decide on, remember it will require some investment in time, manpower and money. You want to try to maximise your return on this investment.

Where these initiatives can go wrong

Rushing into any initiatives that are not supported by the analyses done and data presented. Marketing is expensive, and you want to get the best return on your investment. When met with a request to spend money on an initiative, a business plan will enable management to make sensible decisions based on the agreed strategy. Without an agreed plan, events will be ad hoc and inefficient, driven sometimes by departments or individuals who bill the most or shout the loudest.

Consider mergers and lateral recruitment

The legal press is full of stories about firms considering, or actually taking part in, mergers with other firms. It would appear to be a quick and easy way to fill gaps identified in practice areas, geographic reach or depth and breadth of staff.

Where it can go wrong: Not understanding the underlying cultural issues. Merging two firms is not just about merging practice areas, it is about merging cultures. Unless a lot of attention and work is put into the complex issues relating to cultural and organisational change and development, you are setting the scene for unhappiness and insecurity among your lawyers and staff. Clear communication is crucial.

Another way in which mergers can go wrong is when the sum of the two firms merged is less than the whole of the newly merged firm. Due diligence must be rigorous and comprehensive. Unless the merger creates a new entity whose sum of the two parts is greater than the whole it is probably a bad idea.

Finally, you must have a managing partner whose only responsibility is to oversee the merger and manage the new firm, free from fee-earning responsibilities.

The same issues relating to the clash of cultures when law firms merge apply to lateral recruitment. Some firms think that recruiting a lot of people laterally can fill gaps, and generate revenue, quickly. The rapid expansion of 'bums on seats', sometimes in direct opposition to your business plan, can dilute your quality and brand if they do not measure up to your professional standards, and may result in you carrying 'dead wood'.

Targeting new clients versus reinforcing relationship with current clients

A common mistake that many lawyers make is to spend too much time chasing new business and new clients at the expense of their current client base. It takes a long time to establish a trusting relationship with your clients, but once that trust is established, it is easier to sell further services to your clients, to persuade them to instruct you in different practice areas and to get referral work from them. All the ground work involved in building a trusting relationship, and the investment that represents in time, money and man hours, has been done. Take advantage of that. Build on those relationships. What other work do they do that you don't get? Can you get the same sort of work from them but of higher value? Are they referring you to others?

The process of going after new work is expensive. Selling to established clients is cheaper for the reasons mentioned earlier. If you are going to target new clients, or target new practice areas, you must conduct some sort of analysis, like a SWOT analysis, to ensure that it makes good business sense.

When you are pursuing new clients, get to know as much as you can about their business. This is particularly crucial when you pitching to new clients. One of the biggest complaints clients make about lawyers is that lawyers can't be bothered to put themselves in the client's shoes and get to know their business. I once sought feedback from a client to find out why a firm I was working for did not win a pitch. The client said that the whole pitch was about the firm and how wonderful it was. It was clear that they had not bothered to do their homework and find out as much as possible about the client. As the client said, "It was all about them and not enough about us and our needs."

Attracting new business through referrals

For the most part, clients choose legal advisers either because there is some previous connection to the lawyer or firm, or because they have received a personal recommendation from another trusted professional (eg, an accountant or lawyer) who has used the firm or has heard good things about the firm or a particular individual. Because a lot of new business for any law firm will come from existing clients and contacts, it is important to engage in activities that increase and reinforce your contact with not just existing clients but also with other professionals from whom you are likely to get work. The more widely known and trusted you are, the more the potential for referrals.

When you are pursuing new clients, get to know as much as you can about their business. This is particularly crucial when you pitching to new clients.

Keeping in touch with clients and following up contacts

Getting work is as much about timing and luck as it is about carefully planned business development and marketing, or even being a good lawyer. Let me give you the following example: In London it is common for small businesses to put their business cards or other advertising material through letterboxes. For years one particularly active sector was the replacement window business. Month after month I would get cards from various firms asking me if I needed any windows replaced. I ignored them all until one of my windows broke. The next company advertising window replacements that put a card through my letterbox got a phone call from me. I met them, liked them and they got my business. They got it because, apart from being good (that had to be a given), they had been in the right place at the right time.

What this story illustrates is that you have to stay in the client's mind so that whenever the time comes when they are in need of your services, be it in a month, a year or more, they will think of you. Remember, you are not the only one wooing them. If you think they are worth pursuing, others will think so too. We all like to think that people are thinking about us. Clients are no different. They like to feel cared about and valued. We lawyers tell them that their business is important to us, but how do we really show it? Ignoring them, or assuming that they are happy and therefore not in need of any extra attention, is dangerous. Look at your list of key clients and ask yourself:

- When was the last time that I had any contact with those clients? If it was more than three months ago it is probably time to get in touch again.
- What was the nature of the contact? If it was a mailshot of your firm's newsletter, it may be appropriate now to make a more personal connection, by way of a telephone call, a personal email, or organise some sort of face-to-face meeting.

Only you will be able to judge what sort of contact is appropriate for the particular client.

Following up on business development and marketing initiatives

This is the one area that is probably the most important part of business development and marketing, and it is the one area that is most ignored. Most marketing initiatives are likely to come to nothing if they are not followed up. The exchange of business cards is the beginning of the connection, not the engagement itself! Clients have short memories, and as much as they may be at the top of your contact list, chances are you will not be at the top of theirs. You have to gain their trust, which takes time, and give them a reason to remember you.

So, you have attended a networking event, either as a host or guest, met someone socially or made a business connection with them in some other way. What do you do now? Find a way to make contact with them again. The following are suggestions, although all will depend on the culture and context in which you are operating.

Send a brief email shortly after your meeting (within a day or two) referring back to something you might have said or shared. If appropriate, you can then suggest meeting again over a coffee or whatever. Make it simple and easy for them to accept. Offer to meet them at or near their offices and make it clear that you will not take up much of their time.

If they don't accept immediately, don't worry. Keep in contact at regular intervals and put reminders in your diary. You will be the judge of what regular means, but generally it's best not to leave it longer than three months. Other suggestions include:

- sending an article you read about their practice area or business sector;
- sending a copy of your firm's newsletter or blog and inviting them to join your mailing list;
- inviting them to a talk or seminar;
- offering to introduce them to someone who may be useful to their business;
- inviting them to connect on LinkedIn;
- if you talked about more personal interests, sending them something related to that (eg, notice of an art exhibition, a film review, a link to an interesting TED talk, something about their favourite sports team, designer or business guru).

Where this can go wrong

A big mistake many people – not just lawyers – make is trying to sell themselves at a networking event rather than connecting with people who may have a genuine need of their services at some point in the future. Going in too early with 'the sell' puts people off and can be counter-productive. It's better to walk away with one business card from someone with whom you have made a genuine connection that you can develop, than to collect a pile of business cards from people who are unlikely to give you any work, or who you won't realistically follow up anyway.

Think of how you follow up contacts in a personal context. If you were trying to develop a social connection in your private life you probably could think of all sorts of strategies and excuses to make contact. Use that same initiative and imagination to make and develop business relationships by following

The exchange of business cards is the beginning of the connection, not the engagement itself! Clients have short memories, and as much as they may be at the top of your contact list, chances are you will not be at the top of theirs.

up. Make some sort of connection with them on a regular basis, without being a nuisance, so that they will remember you. They cannot consider you for work if you are not on their mind. And never forget the role that luck and timing play in getting work.

Provide good service

Many lawyers find it difficult to put themselves in their client's shoes. But in order to win the client's trust and retain more client business, it is imperative to do this and to think, 'What would I want or expect from my legal adviser?', or 'How would I like to be treated if I were the client?' If you have conducted a client survey you will probably have a good idea about this. And if you have asked your clients want they need or want, you need to be prepared to deliver it!

Clients want and deserve good service from their lawyers. This may include big things like providing favourable rates for the work done, to *small* things like serving decent biscuits or refreshing their tea or coffee more than once during a long meeting. I put *small* in italics because they may seem small to you, but it is quite different for the client. It is very easy for small service failings to build up before you are even aware of them – the first you may know is after the client has decided to take their business elsewhere. Missed deadlines, surprise bills and delays in responding to their queries can all add up to make clients seriously question whether they are as important to you as you claim they are.

Small touches can make a huge difference. I once worked for a partner of a large firm who acted for two different candy manufacturers. When the one client came into the office for a meeting, all the candy bowls were filled with their products. When the other came in (never on the same day!) the bowls were emptied and filled with their candies. You may think this is taking things a bit far, but imagine how you would feel if you were one of those clients. You would feel flattered and valued and appreciate that your lawyers made that special effort. The partner in question, by the way, had the most profitable practice and loyal client following of anyone in the firm.

The great thing is that it doesn't cost much to deliver good service. What it requires is the will to do it. It requires a firm to operate with a sense of collegial spirit, with common goals and shared values. It requires strong leadership to ensure that everyone understands the importance of delivering good service. It requires listening to your clients. It may require that you provide training for your lawyers to understand the importance of good service, which does cost money, but it is money not just well spent, but well *invested*. Good service can give you the competitive edge. Bad service will lose you clients.

Who is responsible for the business development effort?

Finally, every person in the firm should be encouraged to take part in business development, and every person should think of themselves as an ambassador of the firm. People should feel proud of the firm and rewarded or recognised positively for the effort made.

Unfortunately, business development is often considered to be 'someone else's responsibility'. It is delegated to people or departments who themselves are not made to feel valued. There is an increasing trend in England for law firms to move their business development function abroad or to a city in the United Kingdom far removed from their home office. What message does this send to the lawyers, leaving aside the business development staff, about how these firms see the importance of business development?

It doesn't help that business development and marketing databases are rarely designed to be easy enough for lawyers to use themselves. Consequently, the lawyers often think such systems are a waste of time and money and are more than happy to let someone else maintain them. They fall into disuse, the data becomes useless because no one contributes to it, and they fail.

Lawyers are responsible for making and developing the connections that lead to successful and trusting business relationships. But they are under such pressure to record billable hours that they rarely have time to do anything else. If they are not given credit for business development, as a recognised part of their career development, then why should they bother?

Four years ago, at the IBA in Dubai, I attended a session called "Rethinking the law firm: can traditional leadership meet today's challenges – or tomorrow's?" The panel consisted of distinguished senior and managing partners from leading international law firms. Their message was that traditional leadership was not going to cut it in the changing legal landscape. Just doing what your predecessors did is not enough if you are going to grow your business and survive in an increasingly difficult and challenging market. Tomorrow's leader, they asserted, needs to be a maverick, think outside the box, attend an Executive MBA (or similar) course at a leading business school, be a brilliant manager of people, and be prepared to be 'disruptive'. And they were right.

But as I listened to them it occurred to me that it was going to be difficult to find anyone like that in a traditional law firm, at the time that you need them, to meet those criteria. I have worked in law firms, I teach leadership skills in leading business schools in the United Kingdom and Europe, I train and coach lawyers to help them develop their careers, and I consult on business development. One thing that I have noticed is that those very skills that are needed for tomorrow's (and today's) leaders are more often than not screened out at entrance interviews, or knocked out of lawyers within the first few years of training or qualifying. Trainee and young lawyers are not encouraged to be innovative, creative or to engage in business development. They learn early on that the way to survive and progress is through conforming and complying and working all hours of the day. Getting to the top of the greasy pole is not about looking backwards or sideways to see if someone is doing it differently. It's about looking in front to see how those who made it to the top did it before you. And you follow their lead, culturally and behaviourally. That being the case, where will those different leaders of the future come from when you need them, and how will things ever change?

Finally, business development is about people

Business development, and the business of law, is about people. It is also about:

- listening to your clients, learning and caring about their business and delivering good service;
- understanding the market in which you are operating;
- designing and implementing a business plan that you stick to, and communicate to your lawyers and staff, so that everyone in the firm understands his or her role and has a stake in the success of the business;
- developing, engaging and valuing your lawyers and supporting their business development efforts;
- making a good impression – everyone in your firm is an ambassador for, and reflection of, your firm;
- engaging in effective networking to establish strong relationships – it's not about the hard sell;
- staying in regular contact with your clients and prospects so as to be considered when they need your services. It is a lot about timing and luck.

Follow these simple rules because they work. Believe in them, invest the time and effort, and watch your business grow.

Andrea Kennedy works with leading law firms and barristers' chambers, delivering leadership skills training, coaching, and business development consulting. A California lawyer and former commercial litigator, she also delivers training and coaching to top business schools and other professional services firms worldwide.

Three power tips for growing a huge book of business

David H. Freeman

It can feel like there are a million ways to market legal services. But like anything else, when you dive deep and look at the core elements underpinning great truths, there are usually only a handful of key principles that provide the foundation for success. In this article, I'm going to boil down lawyer business development to three major factors that, if well executed, can make a significant difference in your career.

Get a 'watcher'

There's a reason why athletes have coaches, teams have managers, musicians and actors have agents, and kids have tutors.

They all have someone watching over them. Watching out for them. Making sure they stay on track, consistently doing what it takes to get the most out of their talent. There is a plan, and the watchers watch to make sure they're hitting that plan; building on their strengths and suggesting changes where needed.

Don't lawyers also deserve to get the most from their careers? Lawyers spend so much time working on their craft, but relatively little time on maximising the economic return that can come from delivering that craft. Like anything else, if you're going to do it, why not do it as well as possible?

In your role as a lawyer, who is *your* watcher? Who is your handler, your personal accountability partner who helps you develop a great plan and keeps you accountable to relentlessly execute it? Take a moment, close your eyes and imagine the kind of practice you could have if you were fully engaged. It can be pretty intoxicating. But you need a team, and one of the most important players on that team is your watcher.

One lawyer I'm coaching set up several watchers. She has her assistant watch over her list of important contacts, making sure she stays in touch frequently enough to stay top-of-mind. She has another watcher, a partner who she meets with monthly to brainstorm marketing ideas and they hold each other accountable for completing their commitments. She also has a standing monthly meeting with a member of the firm's business development team to tap into their wisdom, and the firm's resources, to find new opportunities to get out in front of targeted potential clients. Engaging your watcher(s) can set you up to achieve a whole new level of success.

Lawyers spend so much time working on their craft, but relatively little time on maximising the economic return that can come from delivering that craft.

Don't let them forget you

As a species, we often take some of our best relationships for granted. We don't shower them with enough love and attention to make sure they don't leave. Marriages end, friendships sour, clients move on, prospects choose other lawyers, and referrals give work to someone else.

All too often, we hear potential clients or referral sources say some variation of 'I'll keep you in mind', but we know that's not always the case. In fact, in your own mind the game here is to flip that statement – instead of hearing 'I'll keep you in mind', you must translate that into 'I invite you to stay in my mind'. It's not their responsibility to remember you, it's your responsibility to be remembered. The goal is to find elegant, valued and welcomed ways to do just that.

For example, some lawyers have Google Alerts set on their top targets, and when something worthwhile shows up in the news about that contact, they reach out. Other lawyers use techniques like offering on-site presentations, conducting office hours, making valuable introductions, joining clients when they're conducting their own internal strategic planning sessions, and setting up social events.

There is a statistic I've seen which says that about two-thirds of the leads which professional service providers collect in their career are not followed up. One great way to prevent this from happening is to make a list of your important contacts, note the last time you contacted them, and revisit that list often to make sure no-one goes stale. If time has passed, come up with a good reason to reach out, and make that contact. Many lawyers I've coached have told me that after reaching out to someone they hadn't spoken to in a while, they received a piece of work shortly thereafter. Again, it's not their job to remember you, it's your job to be remembered.

You must rise above the noise of others to stand out and stand for something they need.

Become famous

You may be a tree. A big, beautiful, talented and highly experienced tree. But if you fall deep in the forest and no one who wants to buy lumber hears it, it doesn't really matter how great you are.

Which means you must make a noise. Good noise, welcomed noise, noise you want potential clients to hear. You must rise above the noise of others to stand out and stand for something they need. Your future clients are out there, looking for you – but it's your job to be found.

For our purposes, famous doesn't mean worldwide Elvis, Beyonce or Warhol-like fame. It is about being known within your specific circle of high-value people – those who have the power to hire you or refer the kind of work you want to attract.

Let's say you're an employment lawyer and you're looking to get work from mid to large companies in London. Are you known by those decision-makers? Do you have personal relationships with a good number of them? Do you go to the events they attend, write for the publications they read, or conduct presentations when they gather in meetings? Do you join and take leadership positions in their groups? Do you send out press releases relating to your successes? Are you visible on social media and are you interviewed by the traditional media?

One lawyer I recently coached was a skilled presenter and our strategy was to get him in front of as many high-value rooms as possible. He wrote articles and submitted them to organisations to demonstrate his expertise. After receiving a few invitations, he was so well received that others reached out to ask him to speak at their organisations. This exposure, this 'fame' attracted many new clients.

The fact is, people want to work with those who look successful, and by utilising the exposure afforded by fame-making institutions they can amplify you and make you a 'famous' authority on subjects that attract your targeted clients. Use this psychology to your advantage.

So there you have it. Be watched. Don't let the people you've already met forget you. Get famous so you can attract new clients. Three keys that can open some very lucrative doors to the kind of practice others can only dream about.

David H Freeman, JD is a member of the National Law Journal Hall of Fame for being voted the top law firm business development coach and consultant in the United States for several consecutive years. He is a two-time best-selling author who has written and co-authored 15 books on law firm leadership and business development, he has trained and coached over 10,000 lawyers and leaders in hundreds of firms worldwide and he is the creator of Lawyer BookBuilder®, an online, self-study programme that shows lawyers how to transform themselves into major rainmakers. David can be reached at david@lawyerbookbuilder.com or 310-773-7691.

How to future-proof your career

Joanna Gaudoin

What does your career plan look like? Do you even have a career plan? The legal profession is seen as a solid, reliable career choice, where progression is well structured and easy to manage. But of course, it's competitive and often highly reliant on the relationships you have as well as your technical capability.

In this brave new world, where ways of work are changing and technology such as AI is seen as threatening by some and transformative by others, it can be tricky to predict where your career might go from here – or even what a legal career might look like in five years' time. So now is the time to think about investing in the skills you need to stay a step ahead.

Put bluntly, most people's legal qualifications are comparable. You're expected to have a baseline of expertise and experience in order to progress. If you're in a room with 20 people who all have the same technical ability as you, how are you going to stand out from the crowd? What will your future employers be looking for, and how can you make sure you can deliver what they need?

Law isn't just competitive for those working within it; it's competitive when it comes to finding and retaining clients. As your career progresses, you will become part of a team that has to attract clients to your firm. Someone who will understand the power of reputation building. Someone who can be a driver – and a role model – for success.

The need for law firms to have so-called "soft" skills alongside technical excellence is borne out in research carried out by the Law Firm Marketing Club.[1] Interviewing people from across the UK, the research showed that clients want to feel that their law firm is approachable, that they will contact them ahead of key dates, that they will be proactive in raising potential issues, and want to be supported throughout their case.

The better your firm can do these things, the more likely you are to win repeat and referral business – no matter what area of practice you are in. Clients are human, after all.

Five key skills for career progression

Of course, lawyers are human too. You probably think you already have pretty good people skills. And perhaps you do – but are you making the most of those skills and using them in a way that will future-proof your career?

In this article I highlight the top five skill areas that I know will help, based on my individual and group work with lawyers and other professionals who have discovered that understanding the power of these skills and putting the work in to improve them where needed produces great results.

Skill 1 – Engage with clients meaningfully

Often, law firms can get into the habit of dehumanizing clients. They become names on a page, accounts to be invoiced. Whatever area you specialise in, from family law to corporate law, you are dealing with people – who are often experiencing difficulties, whether personal or commercial. Those people want to feel that you are genuinely interested in them and their matter, and that they have a relationship with you – a relationship that means they can trust you.

Of course, your technical skills are important, so that you can achieve the best outcome for your client – no matter whether you are dealing with commercial cases or private individuals. But you must also show empathy and take the time to listen properly. This helps you to build trust with your client and that in turn leads to higher levels of credibility – for you and for your firm.

Part of better engagement is about good communication. This is not only about the quality of language in your client letters. It's about setting out exactly how and when you're going to communicate with your client and then keeping those promises. It's about being proactive in your communications so that clients feel that their matter is important to you and your firm. Establishing this at the outset and delivering on your promises will build a strong relationship with your client.

What does this mean for you and your firm? It means a greater likelihood of repeat business. It means warm referrals that can turn into new business, and, crucially for your firm, it means that clients are more likely to accept fee increases. Clients will also ask for you by name, boosting your personal brand within your firm.

Skill 2 – Consider your personal brand and profile

Following neatly on, your personal brand is important to future-proofing your career. This is more than being "known". You want to have a reputation for the right reasons. How can you be positively memorable? It's important, especially if you work in a large law firm, or in an internal legal department of a large organization.

What is your personal brand? I often explain this in terms of PIE, a concept explored by Harvey J Coleman, author of Empowering Yourself, The Organizational Game Revealed in the 1990s. His breakdown of what influenced promotion may be surprising:

- 10% – your performance.
- 30% – your image.
- 60% – your exposure.

How do these break down in terms of looking at your career?

- Performance – how good you are at your job and how good the results are of what you do.
- Image – you and how you are perceived. In the 1990s, the term "personal brand" was used even more widely than it is today.
- Exposure – this is all about how well people know about what you do; not just your immediate boss or supervisor but the level(s) above them, as well as the leaders and partners in other departments.

You can't help but have an impact on others. From the way you answer your phone to the way you walk into a room, people will start to form an opinion about you.

For this tip, I'm concentrating on the "Image" part of the PIE. To begin with, think about these three things:

- Appearance.
- Body language.
- Voice.

These are all important to create a positive personal impact. Professional services firms have always required a certain standard of appearance, and although some of the more traditional rules have been relaxed – particularly as a result of the pandemic – lawyers are expected to give a professional impression. This applies both to your contact with clients and to your internal relationships. Make sure your dress and attitude are appropriate to the sector you work in – media lawyers may look and behave differently to corporate banking lawyers, for example. Appearances – and first impressions – do count.

As much as 70% of your communication in an in-person meeting is through body language. It's part of the impact you have on people, and so it makes sense to be aware of the body language you are using. This includes eye contact, posture and gestures – but it's a much wider field than that, and something that's worth further investigation.

We know that communication is a critical soft skill. This is about what you say and how you say it. Tone is very important here, as is pace. If you speak too quickly, it can be hard for clients or colleagues to follow you. This can lead to confusion and a lack of clarity, as people might feel too intimidated to ask you to repeat yourself or slow down your delivery – particularly if they are junior to you. Similarly, if you speak too quietly or without conviction, people may make assumptions about you. Whilst these may be completely wrong, it is still unhelpful for people to perceive you that way.

Skill 3 – Bring your personal brand to life

You can't help but have an impact on others. From the way you answer your phone to the way you walk into a room, people will start to form an opinion about you. As we know from our own experience of forming opinions about others, it can be really hard to reverse a negative opinion, even if it is unwarranted.

It's important to do as much as you can, not just to understand how your personal brand can influence others, but also to consider how you can make it work in practice. Don't forget that confidence is catching. If you feel confident about yourself, you project confidence onto others. I once heard about a high-profile lawyer who wore specific underwear on days when he had a big case. Of course, nobody else could see them, but they made him feel good!

As with everything in this article – and everything to do with planning your career – you need to adopt a strategic approach to bringing your personal brand to life. Think about things like:

- Where does your personal brand matter? With clients, with your team, with your line manager and senior partner, with your professional network, with any committees or professional bodies you belong to? You need to be consistent in your approach across all these situations, but with a flexibility that allows you to react to circumstance.
- Where else does your brand exist? Consider your LinkedIn profile, your firm's website, any biographies you have for articles you've written or papers you've contributed to. All of these areas support your overall personal brand, and you should make sure that they reflect your approach.
- How can you extend your reach? Visibility is one of the best ways to improve your personal brand and to ensure that people think of you when they are looking for someone with your

skills and abilities. You can easily use your LinkedIn profile to showcase your expertise and build your credibility, whilst demonstrating that you are approachable and personable. Why not contribute an article to a suitable journal, or look for opportunities to be a guest on a podcast, or a panel member on a webinar?

Skill 4 – Build positive internal relationships

This advice is about how you can develop the skills you need to progress your career. It's important to consider the relationships you build with the people in your current firm. Building better relationships isn't about clawing your way to the top – it's about being in an environment where you can do your best work, help others to do their best work, and contribute to your firm's reputation for excellent advice and customer service.

There needs to be a strategy for building your internal relationships:

- Your immediate team. The better the relationships in your team, the better work will be delivered. This results in happy clients, repeat business, and referrals. It can be easy to get bogged down by competitive relationships within your department, but by taking a positive approach and working on those relationships, you can build a great personal reputation and increase productivity.
- The person you report to. This is a critical relationship. This person holds the key to much of your career progression. They can recommend you for promotion, they can approve additional training, they can put you onto certain matters or clients. A positive working relationship here can bring considerable dividends for your career – as well as making your day-to-day working life much more pleasant.
- Other senior people. Your immediate senior associate, department head, or partner shouldn't be the only most senior person you build a relationship with. Particularly in large firms or organizations, it's easy for you to be one of many people at your level. Look for ways to make a difference and get to know senior people who are more distanced from your daily work. Offer to give a presentation on something that showcases your skills or special interests. Write something for the internal website or newsletter. Taking part in social or charity events can also raise your profile with those at the top. This is the "Exposure" part of the PIE model mentioned earlier.

Don't forget that, even internally, people will only refer their valuable clients to you if they know about you, understand your skills, and trust you to handle things well.

Don't forget that, even internally, people will only refer their valuable clients to you if they know about you, understand your skills, and trust you to handle things well. Building these relationships helps them to understand how you can help their clients – and vice versa –which, will generate cross-selling opportunities. You might be surprised by how many lawyers and firms don't focus on this – which means clients are going elsewhere for advice and expertise that you have in your own firm.

Skill 5 – Nurture external relationships

What are the things that make you valuable to your firm? Your technical skills, of course, and your ability to conduct and close matters successfully. But firms also value your ability to bring new business to the firm, increase business with existing clients, and look for opportunities to grow the firm's range of services.

To do this, you need to be able to build trusted external relationships, with both potential clients and potential referrers.

This applies whether you are hoping to move to a more senior position in your current firm, or move to a role in a new organization. Your case history and successes are likely to be one of the deciding factors in the selection process, and firms will also consider your ability and potential to contribute to the firm's commercial success. If you do not have a good, nurtured external network at this point, it may count against you.

When I speak to lawyers about networking, there's always a bit of anxiety about attending gatherings with other lawyers, but I'd advise you to actively go to events where you know other lawyers will be attending.

For this reason, the sooner you can start developing your networking skills and building a valuable network, the better. Even if you are in a junior position, there are plenty of opportunities available. Networks take time to develop – you can't start six weeks before a job interview and hope to have a suitable network in place.

Like all the skills in this article, adopt a strategic approach. Look for suitable networking events where the people you want to meet are likely to be. This might include the sector you specialise in, local and regional professional networks, places where you can acquire new skills, or groups with similar commercial interests.

Once you have defined the groups that are most suitable, take a deep breath and sign up! Many people find networking tricky when they get started, and fall into the trap of trying to sell their services. In fact, conversations are more natural and more revealing when you express a genuine interest in the people you're speaking to, and explain the impact your work has, rather than just stating "I'm a lawyer". The more you do it, the more natural those conversations will become. Never open with the question "What do you do?". There are so many more interesting questions to ask – about the venue, the weekend's sport, their last holiday... these questions open up a much better conversation and so build a much better relationship.

When I speak to lawyers about networking, there's always a bit of anxiety about attending gatherings with other lawyers, but I'd advise you to actively go to events where you know other lawyers will be attending. These are people who may need your skills and be able to refer clients to you. They are people who may have interesting things to say that spark your interest and drive you to make changes in your own practice. And of course, they may be in a position to offer you a job in the future.

Going to a networking event is just the beginning. Like all relationships, you need to build them up over time. Connect with people you've met on LinkedIn and engage with them there. Arrange to meet people for a one-to-one coffee or lunch to find out more about them. Invite them to events your firm is holding. Attend your chosen networking events regularly and offer to give a talk or presentation to your group to give them more detail about you and your work. These are all ways to build your network, both of clients and potential referrers – something that will be important to future-proofing your career.

What next?

You may feel you have some of these skills already – a great network, for example, or a confident internal brand. This is an opportunity to take an audit across these skills and others, to see where there might be gaps and what you need to focus on. My advice to professional clients usually follows these steps:

- Identify the areas you need to work on, and prioritise them as high, medium, or low importance.
- Define the specific actions you need to work on, and commit to how and when you will do this.
- Review your progress quarterly to maintain motivation and accountability – and also to change focus if that feels necessary.
- Put regular "career time" in your diary to work on your career skills – you might not be

able to devote time to this every week, but if it's in the diary, you're more likely to get on with it.

- Outline the support you need to reach your goals. This might include support from your colleagues and managers, outside help from a third party, relevant career books and guides.

Why this is important for you

If you want to progress your career, you need a plan. That plan must be a "whole picture" – an understanding that it's often not the people with the best technical skills who rise up the career ladder, but those with a range of people, communication, and networking skills too.

Knowing that, it makes sense to take an objective look at where you already have skills you can build on, and the areas you need to work on. The sooner you can do this, the better it will be for your career. Review everything from your LinkedIn profile to your internal personal brand and make a plan that has objectives and outcomes attached.

If necessary, find someone to hold you to account. If you ask the right person inside your firm, you've already made a start on enhancing your personal brand. Equally, you might want an external party to give you that support, so that you have an objective third party to challenge your plan and applaud your progress.

Alongside your skills strategy, you should also build a job strategy. What do you really want out of your next role, and what are the "nice-to-haves"? This might be practical considerations like working hours and environments, or it might be access to training and development. This will help you to focus on applying for the right roles, either internally or externally, making the most of your time and allowing you to focus your CV and applications on the roles you really want.

Don't forget that these skills are important for your current role too. By improving your working relationships both internally and externally, building your network, and paying attention to your personal brand, you will find you're able to be more productive and satisfied in your current role – and maybe thoughts of moving jobs at all are premature! It's certainly true that these skills are skills for a lifetime career, and not just something you do to get on the next step of the ladder. Build them genuinely and put them into practice authentically and career opportunities will naturally follow.

Joanna Gaudoin, managing director of Inside Out Image, specializes in helping lawyers excel at relationships in different professional situations, helping them improve performance and achieve their goals. She offers tailored training programs for law firms and works one-on-one with lawyers. She is the author of *Getting On: Making work work* and a co-author of the second edition of Globe Law and Business's book on Business Development for Women Lawyers. Discover more about Joanna's Business Development Accelerator, designed specifically for mid-size law firms at https://insideoutimage.co.uk/services/business-development-for-law-firms. This program equips your firm with the essential foundations and tools to build on your marketing efforts, win more business from existing clients, increase referrals, and attract new clients. To receive Joanna's eBooklet, 'Nine Skills needed for Career Success', go to: https://insideoutimage.co.uk/articles/career-success-booklet

1 "What do law firm clients really want, need and expect?" Law Firm Marketing Club. *www.lawyer-monthly.com/2022/01/what-your-clients-want-research-from-law-firm-marketing-club/*

The art of conversation

Michelle Elstein

For over 20 years, I have observed hundreds of people work their way up the partner promotion process in law firms and have found that the majority carry insecurities related to their ability to hold an effective business development conversation with clients and potential clients. In this article, I explore why partners find this challenging, what you can actually learn from rainmakers, the breadth of conversations that you need to have today, and how you can take steps to be a great business developer. There is so much untapped partner potential and I know that, with a little bit of courage and some practical insights, we can unlock it.

Starting with empathy

I should start by saying that I have huge empathy for partners in law firms. It's a tough environment in which to willingly go out of your comfort zone. Twenty years on, I find I am still encouraging partners to be braver in their business development (BD) focused conversations.

I equally have empathy for GCs. We coach and consult with many GCs, legal operations directors and their teams, and discuss very openly the challenges they deal with. Never have their roles been more interesting and varied. The advent of AI will change the provision of legal services irreversibly and so their roles will become increasingly expansive. The need to be capable of holding an insightful, constructive, and valuable conversation has never been more critical for partners to secure robust, sustainable, and trusted client relationships. At the root of these conversations are empathetic and creative mindsets. This isn't always on the job application for the partner role but now is the time for the industry to go broader and bolder in their art of conversation.

Why business development conversations feel hard

Let's define what an effective business development conversation might include:

- *Very clear purpose and expectations.* I still hear partners tell me that they only start to think about the meeting in the cab on the way over. Would you get in your car if you didn't know where you were going? A meeting needs a direction of travel and everyone needs to know where they're heading.
- *A breadth in scope of the conversation.* There is no need for a hard sell and you shouldn't feel it necessary to have all the right answers or all the right people in the room to have a broad or deep exploratory conversation.
- *Attentive listening.* This means picking up on signals, cues, reading the room, and an ability to reflect back what you're hearing to confirm what the real problem is, why, and how the client feels about it. You can also use it to test ideas out.
- *Careful and confident facilitation.* A conversation has to be guided to a set of outcomes, even if that outcome is not the one you expected to achieve. Going back to the car analogy, someone has to be the driver in order to determine whether you stay on the road or make a diversion. Without strong facilitation, you can easily waste time.

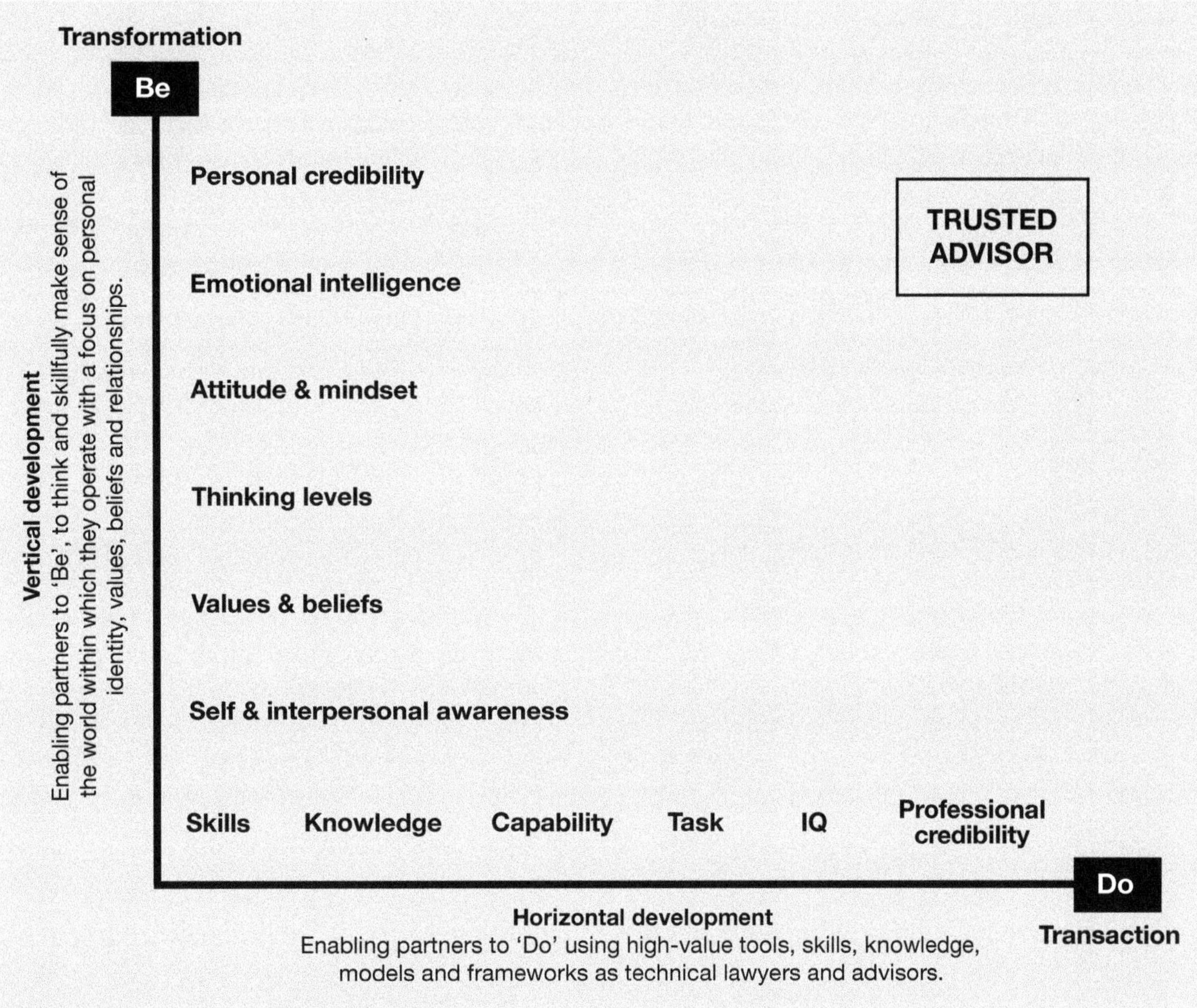

Figure 1: Vertical vs horizontal development. Adapted from N. Petrie (2014).

It all sounds very sensible, so why is it so hard? To shed some light on this, we need to consider the difference between being in "lawyer mode" and "BD mode". You are one person, but you need two modes of being. When in "lawyer mode", you draw on and provide technical expertise. The emphasis in "BD mode" is on building relationships and uncovering needs.

To help explain the difference, I shared the diagram shown in Figure 1 with a cohort of junior partners in a US firm to see where they felt they might have strengths and where they might need to do some development work.

During the lively discussion that followed, the partners concluded that they have essentially been wired since law school to focus on the horizontal axis. They felt that they don't develop along the vertical axis until much later, and in some cases, too late. The industry reinforces this with awards and rankings, acknowledging a professional and transactional track record. It's at the cost and to the detriment of learning along the vertical axis early on, which is critical to achieving trusted advisor status. I use the word "wired" because neuroscience tells us that we can wire and rewire our brains. If we're naturally inclined or conditioned to a certain way of operating, e.g. driven by task rather than emotional intelligence, then it is going to take some effort to change that, but we can. It will be uncomfortable, and it will require practice and self-awareness.

Rainmakers are far higher up the vertical axis. Partners are encouraged to do their BD like a rainmaker. That isn't helpful because unless you can see the rainmaker in the room, you just hear about their revenue-generating outcomes. What makes rainmakers successful is not the absolute money they generate, but their behaviors with clients in the room (whether virtual, in-person, or otherwise).

We have carried out research on the different BD styles of partners compared to rainmakers. We have found that rainmakers demonstrate stronger and more natural capability for having the broadest conversation possible. They dial up emotional intelligence, flexibility, adaptability, collaboration, can pivot, and can draw on intuition to be as expansive as possible in their conversations. This enables them to ask any question they need to and to say "I don't know" when they need to. They appreciate the importance of a client feeling heard and they can transform relationships and opportunities.

Nilema Bhakta-Jones, group general counsel at Kantar

What are the attributes of a partner who is a great conversationalist?

A great conversationalist is someone who is an active listener and shows curiosity. They don't bring out a bag of tricks for every GC conversation, including stock answers and attempts to sell, cross-sell, or up-sell the minute the early pleasantries are exchanged.

A good partner works on a relationship and tries to understand the person versus the job title. The relationship must be reciprocal – I believe a good relationship is built on trust and empathy and has to be mutually beneficial, it can't all be one way. I have been a sounding board for partners in the past and many have asked me my thoughts on aspects of their practices, careers, and my views on the next generation. Good partners are also not afraid of having hard or difficult conversations. They don't need to have ready-made solutions – the good ones give themselves time to process and offer creative solutions. Some even make it fun.

The best ones genuinely take an interest in the wider business, have done their homework, and will bring a diverse team to the meeting, enabling them to ask questions. Good partners will also be unafraid to step back and let the team step up and impress. Good partners will be interested in my direct reports and leadership team – they will be interested in meeting them and show as much curiosity about their goals and aspirations. I am always clear that I am not a "gatekeeper" and I prefer the firm and partners to build relationships with my team, independently of me. I have heard many stories where the GC controls all access and every interaction – I am the reverse. I'm keen for my team to build their own networks and relationships.

The questions and conversations that have impressed me have often been from partners I have known for a long time because there is psychological safety there. We have clear boundaries, mutual respect, and often sound friendships based on an investment of time and effort on both sides. For new partners, it's their willingness to show vulnerability and show up and be themselves, as opposed to pretending to be a "know it all". Humor also helps!

About six years ago, I was asked by a senior managing partner, "What's the question people are afraid to ask you?" My response was, "How are you bonused?" Queue laughter and incredulity. Why would any GC tell a partner that? True, you don't need to answer how much, and I agree, not many would answer that question. Some may even be offended. But the real question is why you would ask, and why is it even relevant? It boils down to Maslow's Hierarchy of Needs – how do you structure your offering to match the needs of the client, their business, and team. If you understand what your client is motivated by, you can figure out how to assist them in their goals, objectives, and priorities (so long as those goals are aligned to the business vs for personal gain).

I would ask the GC about vision, purpose, and strategy. I would ask what excites and motivates them? What impresses me about those who listen is that they also remember, and are willing to also share their thoughts, their goals, and plans – it's an even playing field vs one powering over the other.

Expanding the breadth of conversations

Working across the industry and observing the significant impact AI is already having, we realize that the breadth of the conversation between a partner and a GC needs to expand. If you take into account a competitive market, fluctuations in transactional activity, the hybrid vs in-person debate, changing regulation, a range of geo-political issues, and matter management processes, you've got your hands full in preparing for a broader conversation.

The table below breaks down eight of the challenges a partner faces when it comes to BD and how they can address these by adopting the behaviors set out on the right.

Take steps to be a great conversationalist

Think of each of your clients and their situation as their very own iceberg. You can see the tip of it above the water line when you're talking to them.

Stretching into bolder, braver, broader conversations means asking yourself how prepared you are to uncover what is below the waterline, i.e. what you cannot see but you know is important, without knowing what lies there and whether you can help.

One way to identify how effective you might be when it comes to BD conversations is to profile yourself. We work with a six-stage BD cycle and benchmark partners against it.

Table 1: Broadening the client conversation with effective BD behaviors

BD challenge	Effective BD behaviors
Evolving client expectations at pace	Have absolute clarity, without assumptions or unconscious bias, of what clients expect and what is driving those expectations, demonstrating a deep level of intentional listening and challenge where needed.
Intense and increasing competition	Know specifically how to present your firm's capabilities in the best way possible to make it easy for a client to choose your firm, leveraging the complementary technical capabilities of others.
Tough transactional market conditions	Stay relevant and front of mind for when clients' needs change and arise, being agile and astute to keep in touch and ask the right questions at the right time.
Impact of emergent technology on fundamental firm operating model	Be conversant in the latest tech available to clients and comfortable asking questions around client appetite for new delivery models. Partners to be aware of the potential of AI for client delivery and sales.
Remote vs hybrid vs in-person environments	Be equipped to communicate and facilitate effectively whatever the environment so as to engage clients individually and in teams, to achieve the best possible outcome for the client.
Pricing pressures and fee structures	Understand the relative importance of pricing and potential financial constraints of each client uniquely, no matter the simplicity or complexity of a potential matter or tenure of the relationship.
Global matter management with one-firm approach	Have full visibility of all requirements on a matter and have the capacity to build internal teams, all operating with a unified purpose that has been established with the client.
Constant evolution of regulation and compliance	Know what, when, and how to be in contact with clients for both service delivery and relationship building purposes, as and when there are significant changes to the regulatory and compliance environment.

These stages are:

1. Developing market awareness.
2. Prospecting and engaging clients.
3. Understanding needs.
4. Recommending solutions.
5. Getting commitment.
6. Developing institutional relationships.

We can identify where individual partners and teams have natural strengths and potential derailers, so they know what to work on to improve. This is fundamental to the self-awareness you need when you're in the room with a client or preparing to be.

In our research, when comparing the BD behaviors of partners and rainmakers, we have discovered a strong pattern emerging – rainmakers are materially more comfortable when it comes to Understanding needs. Curiously, both rainmakers and partners generally are weakest when it comes to Getting commitment. This in large part can be solved by being more effective at Understanding needs around the decision-making process and therefore likely explains why rainmakers generate more business.

To claim Understanding needs as a natural strength as rainmakers do, correlates to what is cited as a critical skillset for personal and career success. In his world-renowned book, *Seven Habits of Highly Effective People*, Stephen Covey includes as Habit 5: Seek first to understand. He suggests that we can't possibly know what to offer, sell, or deliver until we know with clarity what is needed and why. It's the same as when we go to the doctor – we can't expect a diagnosis or treatment without being asked for information on the symptoms and the impact they are having.

Consider the image below. What do you see?

Is it a vase perhaps? Or candlesticks? Or two faces? Or a trophy? I have heard six different interpretations of this image. You and a client can be looking at the same data and have completely different perspectives. When it comes down to it, you

Jayne Bennett, general counsel at GoCardless

What are the attributes of a partner who is a great conversationalist?

A great conversationalist is a partner who is willing to step outside of their area of law and put themselves into the shoes of the GC. To do this demands an investment of time into a relationship and a willingness to go the extra mile to really understand the pressures the GC faces, the GC's priorities, the business and its objectives. It is much more than simply the business of the law.

Lawyers should ask more about what is actually going on in the business and take a more holistic perspective. They should understand how we operate and what our key concerns are.

I feel that conversations are the most valuable when the relationship has reached a level where there is a true partnership between adviser and GC – openness and frankness are a given and a partner has the humility to admit when they do not know something. I like having very honest conversations with people. Even if they say, "I don't know but can find out," that's great. I don't like waffle or self-importance.

The partners that have impressed me most in my career are those that have shown real creativity when it comes to problem solving – it shows that they have really listened and understood the issues the business faces. They are not just giving a standard lawyer answer but are willing to push boundaries and provide commercially viable solutions. I also admire partners who show real passion and drive.

I do believe that the art of conversation is dying. Partners can be so driven by internal pressures to meet targets that there is no incentive to simply have a conversation without a specific agenda or immediate return. I much prefer to have a conversation than to receive an email – the information and exchange of ideas and thoughts in person are far more valuable than what can be conveyed through email. My experience to date is that not enough partners take the time to really invest in this kind of relationship building, which is definitely a lost opportunity!

need to know and understand theirs, whether you agree or not. Even more importantly, you need to know how they feel about it. This last part is crucial to really empathizing with a client and often gets left out. By stretching to this kind of attentive exploration, you put yourself in the best position possible to overcome the BD challenges and win hearts and minds.

Five essentials for better conversations

There are five essential tools that, if adopted consistently, will lead to broader, bolder, braver conversations for the world we live in today.

1. Being purposeful

This is a mutual agreement as to why you're spending time with each other. It sounds so simple but is often overlooked. Try starting each conversation with "The purpose of our time together is... can I check that's still right and have I forgotten anything?" You have absolute clarity and permission to get stuck in. To determine your purpose, you can consider what you know, what you don't know, what you need to know, and what follow up you want at the end.

2. Choose your mindset

Most people go into meetings on autopilot, thinking about "What are we going to talk about?". Firstly, the mindset should be "What does the client need to hear and experience?" rather than what we want to talk about. Even so, the content is only a proportion of your preparation. Preparing yourself is just as critical. If it's an initial conversation, you will need a different mindset to one where you're negotiating to win a new instruction. When it comes to the mindset for an open, exploratory conversation, the mindsets for success are humility, curiosity, and – as mentioned already – empathy. These are in contrast to mindsets of telling and winning that I have observed partners being distracted by. Being focused on your mindset will influence how you show up and will make you more likely to build trust. I've seen it work. It will work even more effectively if you choose to enjoy it!

Most people go into meetings on autopilot, thinking about "What are we going to talk about?". Firstly, the mindset should be "What does the client need to hear and experience?" rather than what we want to talk about.

3. Asking really good questions

There are many different types of questions that can equip us to really uncover the iceberg. Consider the use of:

- *Open questions:* What's your goal here? Why is it so important?
- *Direct questions:* If we can cover those needs, will you be ready to start next week?
- *Insightful questions:* We're seeing this in the market, to what extent does that resonate with you?
- *Challenging questions:* It's interesting that you're working with those assumptions. We think it can be done more quickly, what's driving your thinking?
- *Checking questions:* I realize we haven't worked together before. I want to check what it will take for you to feel comfortable choosing us?
- *Creative questions:* How far do you want to go with this?
- *Process questions:* What are the timelines, milestones you need to hit, and which stakeholders will be involved and when?

How many questions do you ask in a meeting? When we were toddlers, we used to ask about 300-400 a day. Now, we don't have time as we want results quickly. Make the time to consider what you really want to uncover – scope, scale, decision-making, process, budget etc. If you can think in advance about which questions to use, you'll get a better outcome. If in doubt, you can use the magic question, "What should I be asking you that I haven't asked you yet?"

By the way, you can use ChatGPT to help you craft your questions in a fraction of the time now too!

4. Reflective listening

Sharing back what you have heard to make sure you're really seeing things from the client perspective requires reflective listening. It is very powerful at building engagement and trust. Using statements including those set out below at the right moment can help you significantly in your BD conversations:

"What I am hearing is..."

"Help me to understand..."

"I'm curious, tell me more about that..."

"Let me make sure I have understood this correctly..."

"The main points I have heard you make so far are..."

"I notice you feel strongly / concerned / animated about...."

If you can make it a conscious habit to incorporate these into your conversations, it will pay dividends.

5. Creating space

Patience is a virtue, so they say. Never truer than when it comes to BD. It can take years to build strong relationships. They are borne out of consistent and constructive conversations alongside clients trying you out in different areas. While you might want a specific outcome, giving space and silence in a conversation for a client to process and share is incredibly powerful. It can feel frustrating on the inside, but it's worth the wait, even if it means scheduling a follow up.

Consider which of the above you're proficient at today and which you might need to work on.

Go faster in teams

The premise behind high performance team coaching is that you can achieve stronger optimal results by leverage the diverse strengths of a team in pursuit of a common goal. Consider your practices, sectors, and client teams. Map out where you want to get to strategically. Identify where you don't have the understanding needed to secure the relationships and wins. Work together, leverage your strengths, experience, and differences to be able to uncover the icebergs together. You will create a more compelling offering to clients.

Rupert Hopley, General Counsel at Informa PLC

What are the attributes of a partner who is a great conversationalist?

Every partner should aim to be great communicator, particularly a listener. When you hear them playing back the topics and issues that are important to us then you know they listened.

You need to invest time to understand the business and its risk appetite and culture.

There are enough lawyers who want to prove they are clever and can / will identify all risks without a level of materiality or probability of it crystallizing. This can be too theoretical, which is super frustrating. It needs to be contextualized to our risk appetite and help us prioritize. I've worked with an external partner for ten years and we can be more succinct because he knows us, our business and our appetite for risk.

A constant thirst for knowledge is important because we don't stand still. External partners need to keep pace with how we are evolving and thinking with genuine interest in prospects.

Don't come to me with the law; think of us as a business. Help me apply knowledge of the law to what the business needs so I can filter for decision making.

Getting the skills and personality right for our culture is critical for relatability. 'Humbly confident' is an expression that came up at one of our LT meetings and it is a trait I appreciate from external advisors. You need to create a two-way conversation. Don't be afraid to be proactive and just ask questions you want to ask. Make the effort to meet people, shake hands, and spend time building relationships. If you want to be part of our community, come and see us.

Be brave and enjoy it

Our ability to get better at anything requires us to acknowledge where we are today and where we want to be. That's not the hard part. Choosing to do the things you find uncomfortable is. Experiment with your BD meeting preparation and how you show up in conversations. Step back afterwards and consider what you did well and what you can tweak for next time. Make that reflection a habit, and your relationship development will have unbounded potential.

Michelle Elstein is a seasoned leadership coach and consultant working with in-house legal leaders and their teams as well as private practice leaders and partners. She set up Courageous Co. and built a team to equip clients to tackle the difficult things that matter, the things they haven't done before, or are afraid to do. She brings challenge, courage, creativity, and compassion in supporting leaders to achieve things they don't know are possible yet. Michelle and her team work with legal leaders all around the world and bring a unique approach to get them up and moving to find their way to better and more robust performance that they will be proud of.

Finance

Finance issues facing firms

Brian Dunlop

Brian Dunlop examines the financial pressures facing law firms today, and how the most agile are responding.

The past two decades have been a period of significant growth for many law firms. In addition to domestic growth, a key feature for large law firms has been considerable international expansion. In particular, many US-based firms have expanded into Europe and Asia and many UK-based firms have expanded into the rest of Europe, Asia and the United States. For some, profitability has also grown significantly since the start of this period.

However, following the Global Financial Crisis (GFC), law firms have found that their financial position has been put under increasing pressure. For many firms, this has been exacerbated by significant economic and political events in many jurisdictions across the globe. Some firms have responded well, maintaining or even increasing profitability, but others have not responded so well. It is becoming clear that firms which do not address these pressures are likely to find themselves diminished in terms of profitability, scale, and over time some may even cease to exist.

This article examines what the specific pressures are and how law firms are responding to these pressures. We will examine these pressures under four headings: clients, competitors, costs and cash.

Clients

Following the GFC, almost all industry sectors have been under significant pressure to save costs. For many businesses, much of the low-hanging fruit has been picked years before, starting with commodity items and so they have steadily moved up the value chain, including expenditure on legal services. For law firms this has meant that pressure from clients to reduce fees has increased in recent years and that pressure is likely to continue to increase as general counsel (GCs) are tasked with further reducing legal spend.

As a result of this, many large businesses are now much more sophisticated in the way they manage legal spend and this has had a potentially significant impact on the law firms that service those businesses.

In-house teams

Larger clients have also been intentionally developing and growing their in-house legal teams. The in-house legal teams of some of these organisations now rival many law firms in scale. This allows these organisations to reduce costs, as employing lawyers directly is usually significantly less expensive than engaging the same level of resource from a law firm. These clients are now in a position to handle much of the higher value work themselves and therefore deprive law firms of income streams that they had previously assumed to be theirs.

Another trend that has allowed clients to increase the size of their in-house legal teams is the use of secondees from law firms. Often, these secondees are made available to clients at zero or minimal cost, as part of the relationship 'deal' between law firms and clients. In particular, financial institutions have increasingly made it a condition of being on their legal panels to provide one or more secondees on a rolling basis for the life of the panel. For firms on a large number of legal panels, this can mean a significant investment in staff in relation to whom little or no fee income will be received.

These are, of course, investments with a clear purpose, to secure a place on the legal panel of a client, and therefore have the opportunity to win mandates from that client. In these cases it is often a stark choice between providing the secondees or not being on the legal panel. Once having made this investment, it is important that law firms leverage their position on the client's legal panel to the fullest extent possible. Smarter firms will budget for a number of free secondees that they will then allocate secondees to the clients they feel have the potential to generate significant fees. This will involve matching the firm's capabilities in various practice and geographic areas to the clients' requirements. They will then focus on building relationships with those clients to ensure that they maximise the amount of fees generated.

If the investment in secondees is not generating the expected levels of income from a particular client, firms should be reviewing the situation and looking at whether the secondees could be better deployed with another client. Proactive management of these situations by client relationship partners and BD directors is likely to lead to a better result than those firms that take a passive approach in this area.

The other action that forward-thinking firms are taking is to use their secondees to develop a much better understanding of their clients. The best firms use regular formal reviews with secondees to gather information and help to embed stronger client relationships.

Disaggregation of matters

Another aspect of the growth of in-house legal teams is disaggregation of work on individual matters. This refers to the practice of clients breaking up matters and awarding mandates on different elements of a matter to two or more firms to maximise cost efficiencies.

This practice results in certain types of work being split off to firms which can offer lower-cost solutions, thereby draining that work away from larger, often more expensive firms based in major economic centres. This has often been work traditionally done by trainees or newly qualified lawyers in the larger firms. This is problematic for those larger firms still working with a more traditional model as they have relied on this work to cover the costs of more junior staff as they become more experienced. A drop in client demand for junior staff has required some rebalancing of the new hires taken on each year to ensure that firms continue to operate efficiently. Many large firms subject to these pressures from clients have reduced their intake of trainees and newly qualified lawyers accordingly.

Another way that some larger firms have responded to this is by setting up their own lower-cost offerings, recruiting teams of legal analysts based in lower-cost locations. This has generally been well received by clients, who now have the option to keep all of the elements of a matter within one firm. The challenge for the law firms in setting up such centres is to ensure that the correct balance of traditional associates and legal analysts is maintained and that headcount is not being duplicated.

This means changing the way in which law firms have operated for decades, hiring a relatively large number of trainees or graduates each year and progressively shedding staff from each intake until a much smaller number of senior associates remains. The rise of the new model, which incorporates teams of legal analysts, requires a narrowing of this traditional staff pyramid. The risk of not taking action to narrow the pyramid in these situations is that overall costs will increase and profitability will decline.

Fee arrangements

The other trend that has increased and is unlikely to reverse is that of fixed and capped fees. In the 'good old days', many firms could charge clients on an hourly basis for all of the work that was performed. This put the vast majority of the price risk onto the client. Fast-forward to today, and the majority of clients are looking to move or have already moved that risk back onto law firms.

Even if 'formal' fixed and capped fees might often appear in legal surveys to be a minority of all fee agreements recorded by law firms, the real position is likely to be significantly different for two reasons. One, lawyers are not particularly strong at recording the exact details of fee agreements; and two, many fees may be fixed in the minds of clients once they have been given an estimate for the total amount for a matter. Unfortunately, for many law firms, this perception often becomes a reality. This trend for more fixed or capped fees is likely to continue, while the number of engagements billable on an hours worked basis continues to decline.

The consequence for law firms is that they are now required to manage their matters more efficiently and effectively if they want to avoid cost overruns. Specifically, this means managing internal resources to deliver the original scope and then managing any scope increases with the client.

Some partners and senior associates do this very well.

The best firms use regular formal reviews with secondees to gather information and help to embed stronger client relationships.

However, it does not come naturally to most. In particular, having difficult conversations with clients about scope changes is something that few are skilled at handling and many would rather ignore until the end of a matter. This puts law firms at a disadvantage as it is much easier to agree a fee increase before the additional work is done. In these circumstances, much of the additional work ends up being written off.

By contrast, the large firms of accountants and consultants generally handle these situations very well. They specify the scope of the work very clearly at the outset and ensure that this is enshrined in a signed engagement letter, without which they will not commence an engagement. If scope increases, they are very clear that this will mean further fees will be incurred and have that conversation as soon as the scope change occurs.

Some large law firms have realised that this is an area with potential to increase revenues and therefore profitability. They are starting to give a great deal of focus to the 'leakage' between the agreed fees and the fees actually billed on a matter. With this leakage running into hundreds of millions of potentially lost revenues for very large firms, the more forward-thinking have also been recruiting staff to focus solely on this area.

Use of procurement professionals

Procurement professionals are increasingly being employed by client organisations to reduce costs. Their clear objectives are to achieve cost reductions or 'more for less' across almost all cost categories. While many started with a focus on commodity items like stationery, travel and IT supplies, as these costs have been addressed that focus shifted to costs further up the value chain like consulting and legal costs. This marks a change for many law firms that have traditionally worked on more of a relationship basis and have been used to negotiating price from a position of strength with client staff who were often not highly skilled in price negotiation but more focused on relationships.

For some law firms, the strength of their brand, practices and/or their network in particular markets will have helped to insulate them somewhat from the full force of this trend. However, those firms with less strong brands will have found themselves pitched into intense price competition with their peers. The introduction of procurement professionals into the purchase of legal services has made this more difficult for law firms which may previously have relied solely on good relationships with client GCs to win mandates.

While good relationships (and reputations) may well help firms to continue to win mandates, they are likely to be at keener rates than pre-financial crisis. The final decision is unlikely to rest solely with the procurement professionals but increasingly they now have an important seat at the decision-making table. Many smart GCs will use their procurement professionals as the 'bad cop' to help to drive down fees, enabling them to maintain good relationships with law firms but also to achieve reductions in their legal spend.

Conclusion – clients

Of all the areas being considered, this is the one that can have the most impact on the financial performance of a law firm. Getting client relationships right, and delivering the service in a manner that aligns with clients' expectations, is likely to result in a stronger income position than would otherwise be the case.

Law firms which take a passive stance on their clients' changing expectations are unlikely to prosper. The firms which are likely to prosper are those which have developed and continue to maintain strong relationships with their clients and really take the time to listen and understand what their clients expect, not just today, but more importantly, tomorrow.

Understanding that we are in a time of fairly rapid change in clients' expectations and requirements is the starting point. Developing law firms' offerings to anticipate these changes in clients' expectations and requirements is what will really distinguish the successful law firms of the future.

Competitors

Competition for many law firms has been increasing steadily over the past 20 years as many firms have expanded both domestically and larger firms have expanded globally. This has led to the major cities in many jurisdictions experiencing a significant increase in the number of law firms. With demand for legal services flat in some jurisdictions, or growing at a slower rate than the growth in the number of lawyers in others, this has led to an inevitable downward impact on price.

As noted above, there have been two particular trends in global expansion among large firms, US-based firms expanding into Europe and Asia, and UK-based law firms expanding into the rest of Europe, Asia and the United States.

In addition, there have been a number of new entrants to the sector – traditional law firm start-ups, alternative law firms, or other professional services firms starting up legal practices. With demand for legal services remaining fairly static in many jurisdictions, this has led to increased competition for both work and people.

Competition for work

As a consequence of the factors above, competition for

client instructions has increased among law firms. For incumbent firms in a given jurisdiction this has meant working much harder to win instructions. In order to be successful, firms are often having to give away more on price and provide more in terms of 'value added services' (aka free advice).

New entrants in any given market often use price as a lever to break into the market. This puts pressure on the incumbent firms to reduce their prices, which has a negative impact on profitability. Where new entrants are significantly more profitable than incumbents, they can often afford to compete aggressively on price in the short to medium term in order to gain a position in the market. Firms which carefully select a small number of strategically important jurisdictions to enter are likely to be more willing and able to compete on price than those investing on a broad geographic front.

In these situations, incumbent firms which have developed strong client relationships have an advantage. This provides an opportunity for relationship partners to have a dialogue with the client taking in more than just price and focusing on wider aspects of what the firm can provide. That said, it is likely that in such a situation some hits will be taken on price.

Given this almost inevitable impact on price driven by increased competition, as noted above, smarter firms are starting to look more carefully at the relationship between headline price and what is actually billed. For many firms, this is an area where an eye-watering amount of potential revenue is given away. There are several drivers for this; inefficient staffing of client matters; fee increases for changes to scope not being agreed with the client; and time being written off which perhaps could have been charged to the clients.

In all of these areas, other professional services firms, such as accountants and consultants, are much better at recovering fees from clients. There is significant untapped potential value here for many law firms.

Competition for people

We have also seen an increase in partners leaving one law firm and joining another, as firms 'laterally hire' partners rather than promoting internally. Movement between firms by partners, which was not as common 20 years ago, is now seen as the norm and partners are much more willing to move from one firm to another, as they have seen many of their peers doing so. On any given day, the websites of the legal media regularly report several such movements.

It is increasingly a risk to many law firms that their key partners will leave and join the competition and this is a particular threat to firms with lower levels of profitability, as more profitable firms are able to lure star partners away with the prospect of higher earnings. Due to their generally higher levels of profitability, many US firms are in a particularly strong position to laterally hire partners from other firms in Europe and Asia. If the partner being hired has a strong hold over relationships with key clients, this could lead to a significant loss of revenue for the firm.

Smart firms have been trying to institutionalise client relationships rather than having individual partners control key client relationships. However, many firms have been slow to address this issue with the result that some have seen key client relationships walking out of the door with departing partners. In small or developing offices, this can be catastrophic to the financial health of the office.

Where law firms have long notice periods for partners leaving, this trend for more partners to move to other firms can have an extended destabilising effect as the partner can be required to remain at the firm for anything up to 12 months from resigning. Having partners who have resigned and will be leaving continuing to interact with their peers in the office could spread discontent among other partners who may also decide to leave. Some firms address this by requiring partners to go on gardening leave. However, they are usually required to pay the partner their full profit share while they are doing no work for the firm.

Partner departures can also create a gap in the firm's offering in the relevant office/practice. Sometimes an internal promotion to partner can be made to fill the gap. However, more often, a partner will be laterally hired from another firm. Law firms must judge carefully about how long lateral hires may take to ramp up their business within the firm after a transition. Sometimes, business cases to justify a lateral hire are hopelessly optimistic and this can put the partner under unfair pressure to perform to a level that was never going to be achievable.

Another trend that has helped to fuel the movement of partners between law firms is equity management. Over the past 20 years, the legal trade press has focused on Profit Per Equity Partner (PEP) as the key relative measurement of profitability of law firms. This, combined with a downward pressure of price from clients, has led many law firms to use equity management to improve key external profitability metrics such as PEP.

The result has been many more partners being asked to leave law firms than in the past. Some leave the law altogether, others choose to develop their careers by moving in-house to clients but many choose to join other law firms. This is helpful for firms with lower levels of profitability who might otherwise struggle to attract partners from more profitable firms to join them.

Many law firms have already experienced a negative impact on their business from increased competition. Particularly in Europe and Asia, where the arrival of US firms with significantly higher levels of profitability has led to a loss of both client work and key people for many incumbent firms.

The short-term financial impact of partners leaving and joining firms is therefore often negative. This is particularly true in the cases of less profitable firms which are having their 'star' partners poached by more profitable firms. In addition, there may also be an impact on the firm's culture of large numbers of leavers and joiners. Changes in culture can also unsettle partners who may be tempted to move elsewhere. Either way, this trend for more partner movement between firms can often have a negative impact on the short to medium-term financial health of firms.

Conclusion – competitors

Many law firms have already experienced a negative impact on their business from increased competition.

Particularly in Europe and Asia, where the arrival of US firms with significantly higher levels of profitability has led to a loss of both client work and key people for many incumbent firms.

In some cases, whole areas of expertise are being lost as teams are hired from one firm. The most vulnerable firms are those with lower than average levels of profitability and also without a strong culture and strategy that helps to bind partners together and to the firm.

With partner movements between law firms becoming commonplace in the last decade, smarter firms are taking steps to try to ensure that their key partners stay with the firm. There are several elements to this, including firm profitability, personal remuneration, culture and strategy.

Getting all of these elements right can be tricky in the short to medium term, especially if a firm is starting from a point where they all need some work.

Costs

Up to the end of the 20th century there had generally not been a significant focus on cost control in law firms. Partners are used to having things done in pretty much the same way that they had always been done and law firms were essentially operating as they have done for centuries – lawyers, at desks, giving advice and drafting legal documents. Today, they might be communicating using phones and drafting documents on computers. However, it is still essentially the same model that has been in place for centuries.

A significant number of support staff are generally located in the same office building as the lawyers to ensure that there is always someone on hand to deal with the many tasks required to make a law firm function as a business. In many cases, these office buildings are among the most expensive in the cities in which law firms are located.

In addition to this, the offices are generally occupied in a much less efficient manner than other businesses, with much more space given over to each occupant. At a recent legal industry conference, a partner in a global real estate consultancy explained that when a prime New York office building is being marketed, there are three sample floor plans prepared – for a US law firm, for a non-US law firm and for a corporate. The point being that the density of occupation increases at each stage, with corporates generally having significantly more people in the same space.

It is therefore no surprise that the majority of costs in a law firm are people costs and property costs (ie, the costs of employing lawyers, support staff and the costs of the offices in which they are located). These costs typically make up in excess of 80% of the total costs for a firm.

The remaining costs cover other categories such as IT infrastructure, PI insurance, business development and travel costs. Most of these cost categories vary with the size of the firm rather than the number of chargeable hours worked and billed by its lawyers. As a result, for the majority of law firms most costs are fixed in the short term (ie, there are very few costs that vary directly with each extra hour of legal advice given to clients). For this reason, it is important that firms pitch their costs at the right level, relative to their projected income.

With pressure from clients impacting firms' top line income, there has been much more focus on costs by most firms over the past 10 years, particularly post-financial crisis. Cost is the one area where law firms have most control and, for many, there is still scope to operate in a more efficient manner.

General law firm costs

These are costs that all law firms will incur regardless of size and shape. They can be broken into the cost categories mentioned above – lawyer costs, support staff costs, property costs and other costs.

Lawyer costs

The model for traditional law firms is to take on annual intakes of trainees, and to promote qualified lawyers each year, with commensurate increases in their salaries. In recent years, in many jurisdictions lawyer salaries have increased by more than the general rate of inflation. Without careful management of headcount, the cost of the associate cohort in law firms has the potential to sharply increase. Some firms have been very active in controlling lawyer headcount and ensuring that the 'staff pyramid' stays in shape and does not become inverted, with more senior associates than junior associates. Other firms have not been so good at this.

In the absence of an increase in client demand for legal services and in order to remain efficient, law firms have to manage headcount to ensure that the number of leavers matches the number of joiners each year so that the lawyer staff pyramid remains in shape. To achieve this, many firms have relied on what HR professionals refer to as 'natural attrition', or associates leaving of their own accord.

Associates leave law firms for many reasons but moving to join clients is one of the main reasons. When an economy is booming, there are often significant numbers of opportunities for associates to move in-house with clients, in fact, during particular boom times, some large firms have been unable to retain the numbers of associates they require due to so many leaving to join clients. However, post-financial crisis, the number of opportunities dried up and many firms found that in the absence of proactive management of associate numbers, the number and cost of associates was increasing, as fewer left of their own accord.

Some firms began to more proactively manage their associate headcount, in particular ensuring that annual appraisals were carried out in a robust manner with underperformers being made aware that they would be unlikely to progress in the firm without improving their performance. Clear messages about future prospects are more likely to result in underperforming associates deciding to leave of their own accord.

The problem for many firms is that partners often do not like having these types of direct conversations. The excuse is often "all of our people are good", which can manifest itself as all associates in a particular practice being given the top appraisal rating. This is something that many law firm HR professionals will be familiar with but which simply would not be accepted in most client organisations.

So why is this important? Well, as noted above, the cost of lawyers is the single highest cost category for law firms and lawyer salaries are often subject to increases above inflation. Coupled with a model which generally introduces a new intake of lawyers every year, if not managed, this single largest cost category can easily get out of control.

Perhaps an example is the best way to explain this. Imagine two manufacturing companies (company 1 and company 2), identical in all respects, except company 1 is using three factories of equal size working at full capacity, while company 2 is using four factories of the same size as company 1, but only working at 75% capacity. Clearly, company 1 will be more profitable as it is operating in a more efficient manner by paying for the operation and maintenance of only three factories rather than four. One imagines the shareholders of company 2 might be less than impressed with the management of their company relative to company 1.

Back in the legal world, there is a clear correlation between the efficiency of lawyers, measured by average annual client chargeable hours per lawyer, and profitability. Put simply, those firms where lawyers achieve a higher level of client chargeable (and billed) hours per lawyer than their peers are likely to be more profitable. For some firms, this is the single biggest cost opportunity to improve profitability.

Support staff costs

The other area of cost that has been addressed by many firms is the cost of support staff. There are two ways in which this can be addressed – the number of support staff and the location of those staff. Many firms have cut back on numbers of support staff, especially post-financial crisis. This has impacted many areas of support, including secretarial support, where the ratio of lawyers to secretaries has been steadily increasing in many firms. This has been achievable largely due to generational changes, as younger lawyers are generally much more used to typing than the previous generation.

Often, the reductions in support headcount have been achieved by remaining support staff picking up more work or some tasks simply not being performed by support staff and passed over to lawyers. While this may feel to many partners the right thing to do, it does not often make sense to have senior lawyers and partners engaged in activities that could be performed by staff paid significantly less. Indeed, one could argue that any free time of senior associates and partners should be directed at business development activities, rather than internal administration activities.

The problem for many firms is that partners often look first at support staff numbers whenever cost savings come onto the agenda. This can lead to the efficiency of a firm reducing if, for example, reductions in business development staff result in less support for client pitches or reductions in finance staff result in less support for billing or cash collections. This is, however, an emotive subject. Many managing partners will be keenly aware that they are unlikely to increase their popularity by focusing on reductions in legal headcount rather than support headcount.

Some larger firms have also reduced the cost of support staff by opening near or offshore shared service centres in lower-cost locations. In addition to achieving salary arbitrage by moving support roles from higher-cost locations to lower-cost locations, in situations where significant numbers of roles are moved from one office, there should also be a rental cost arbitrage, assuming space can be sub-let in the original office. Large firms which have taken these steps have saved significant amounts in both salary and property costs.

Property costs

The cost of office accommodation is probably the area where law firms have done the least to reduce costs. In many respects, most firms are still occupying offices in the same manner in which they have done for centuries.

There has been a lot of talk in the legal media about flexible or agile working and open plan. Those two initiatives will undoubtedly have some benefits in relation to key staff retention and collaboration, both of which are very important goals for law firms. They will not, however, have a significant impact on cost. In order to achieve significant reductions in property costs, law firms will either have to move to cheaper areas of the cities in which they operate, or more likely, adopt similar working models to the accountants or consultants and move to a more flexible working model incorporating hot-desking for some or all staff.

An organisation moving to a hot-desking environment could expect to save up to 25% of space relative to a traditional office model where everyone has a dedicated desk. The saving in space will depend on whether everyone moves to hot-desking or whether any dedicated desk/offices are retained. The reduction in office space is achieved by working out how many people are out of the office on an average day and then scaling back the requirement accordingly.

Moving to a hot-desking environment may also require a review of technology hardware with laptops and headsets replacing desktop computers and desk phones. This, combined with improved Wi-Fi networks, would allow partners and staff to work effectively anywhere in the office, on the move, or at home.

As well as saving on property costs, there are significant potential benefits to be achieved in terms of collaborative working. Traditional cellular offices simply do not lend themselves to collaborative working. A hot-desking environment including collaborative space would allow teams working together on client matters to be co-located and so much more effective.

Few law firms have taken the plunge and moved to this model. I predict that will change at some point soon and as soon as a few firms do, others will follow. Cost savings may well be the driver but the change in working environment may well help to attract the top talent of the future who are likely to prefer a more flexible working environment. With the competition for top talent intense, that would be a significant fringe benefit.

Other costs

Over the past 10 years, most firms have addressed the non-people/property cost categories fairly well. Many of the larger firms have employed procurement professionals to ensure that all contracts are properly negotiated in a competitive manner and the best value for money is achieved for every pound, dollar or euro spent. While expenditure policies may not be quite as tight as they are at many of their clients, these areas of cost have generally been controlled fairly well, particularly post-financial crisis.

Law firm costs resulting from strategic decisions

There are two other factors that can make a significant impact on the costs of law firms, both of which are directly correlated to the growth strategy of a firm:

- the size and shape of the firm's network of offices; and
- the number, if any, of fixed share and/or salaried partners.

Office network

The size and shape of firms' networks can have a significant impact on costs. A firm with a small number of well-established offices of reasonable scale is likely to be fairly efficient from a cost perspective. By contrast, a firm that has recently been expanding into multiple jurisdictions by opening new offices is likely to be much less efficient from a cost perspective.

This is because there are certain costs that are incurred, regardless of the size of office. In addition, all the infrastructure for a new office needs to be in place prior to lawyers commencing work, which means hiring all of the relevant support staff. If offices are opened in the anticipation of rapid growth, the office space itself is likely to have room for expansion and therefore be more expensive than is warranted by the current scale of operations.

While the cost (per lawyer) of new offices is likely to be higher than in established offices, the opposite is true of revenue per lawyer which usually takes some time to build up to the same level as established offices. This means is that smaller recently opened offices are not only less cost efficient, but also deliver significantly less profit and, in some cases, will make a loss before paying equity partners.

Depending on the proportion of smaller, new offices to large established offices in a firm, an expansionist strategy can have a negative impact on both cost efficiency and profitability in the short to medium term. This, of course, has to be offset against future opportunities. However, firms need to keep in mind the potential negative impact on short to medium-term profitability.

Ideally, firms would be very focused on which jurisdictions are key for future investment in line with the firm's strategy. In many cases, however, offices are opened on an opportunistic basis, with little regard for priority or scarcity of funds for investment. After a period in which there has been a lot of international expansion, the harsh reality of economics may see this cool off as firms become more focused on key jurisdictions. Indeed, in recent years a number of firms with international networks have closed offices in Asia, Europe and the Middle East, recognising that size (of network) perhaps is not everything. In recent months, two UK-based 'Magic Circle' firms have indicated that, in future, investment will be more focused on a small number of strategically key offices.

Fixed share and salaried partners

Many firms have two broad categories of partners, full equity partners who share the profits of the firm; and fixed share or salaried partners who as the name suggests take a fixed amount or salary. Often, the latter category is the first step to becoming an equity partner, however, many firms have a permanent cohort of fixed share/salaried partners and, increasingly, firms are de-equitising partners to become fixed share/salaried partners.

There is a sense that sometimes de-equitisations are pandering to the legal media's obsession with profit per equity partner (PEP), which has become the industry measure of relative profitability. By taking lower earning equity partners out of the equity, the average PEP of a firm will increase. This may improve external perceptions; however, it can have two unintended consequences.

First, the de-equitised partners are often demotivated by their change in status and this can, in some cases, have a negative effect on wider morale in a partnership. Secondly, while flattering PEP, a de-equitisation increases short-term fixed costs for a law firm. Post-financial crisis, as some firms have seen significant reductions in profitability, some de-equitised partners have taken home more compensation than some of their equity partner peers. Again, this is likely to have a negative impact on equity partnership morale.

This trend seems to be increasing among larger firms but I suspect that not all firms considering this are thinking through all of the consequences. The smarter ones are ensuring that a proportion of remuneration of fixed share/salaried partners does vary with the firm's profitability.

Future law firm costs

For decades, the majority of law firms managed to get

When an economy is booming, there are often significant numbers of opportunities for associates to move in-house with clients, in fact, during particular boom times, some large firms have been unable to retain the numbers of associates they require due to so many leaving to join clients.

In many firms, the more senior partners are those who are closer to retirement and may therefore have strong views on investments being made in their final few years of partnership that will impact on the level of short-term profitability.

by without making significant investments, with the exception of fitting out new offices or implementing new or upgraded practice management IT systems. This has allowed many firms to operate without permanent levels of on-balance sheet debt and also to distribute all annual profits to partners.

This may not be possible in future. We are now in a period where investment in new technologies may be key to the future survival of many firms. The traditional operating model is starting to break down, driven by client demands, and it is those firms which invest in new technologies which are likely to be better able to meet clients' expectations.

In many other sectors, this would be regarded as business as usual. A telecoms business that does not invest heavily in future technology is unlikely to be around for long. A manufacturing business that does not invest in new generation manufacturing machinery is unlikely to remain competitive for long. Law firms, until relatively recently, have enjoyed decades of not really having to invest heavily in new technology or new operating models.

So why might this be a dilemma for law firms? This comes down to the partnership structure of the vast majority of law firms. Unlike corporates, most law firms pay out all of their annual profits to equity partners, which can lead to conflict between short and long-term objectives.

There is also the question of different generations of partners within a firm. In many firms, the more senior partners are those who are closer to retirement and may therefore have strong views on investments being made in their final few years of partnership that will impact on the level of short-term profitability. Those partners, who are unlikely to benefit from the medium or long-term benefits of these investments, may view them as unacceptable.

This is an issue that many firms will be struggling with, particularly those firms which, post-financial crisis, have cut business-as-usual costs to the bone in order to compensate for reduced levels of revenue and therefore profits. In these circumstances, starting to invest significant amounts in new technologies could be a very contentious move, in what may already be a difficult cost climate. However, the decision not to invest could be even more costly in terms of the future viability of the firm.

Conclusion – costs

There is much to consider when it comes to cost in law firms. The danger is that many partners want to focus only on what they might term 'central costs' (ie, support staff and other non-people/property cost). To do so is to ignore the largest cost category in a law firm – lawyer costs – which is where the biggest opportunities for further savings exist for many firms.

Perhaps unsurprisingly, many of the most profitable firms have already addressed their costs in a more holistic manner, with perhaps property costs being the one that most firms have yet to fully address in the manner that other professional services firms have.

In future, cost management will become more complex as costs of investing in future technologies and/or operating models may have to increase if firms are to survive in the medium to long term. This will require careful education to ensure that partners understand why some costs may need to increase while others may decrease.

Cash

The final area where law firms are coming under pressure is their cash position. Due to the ownership structure of traditional law firms, all of the profits from any given year are distributed to partners in most firms as quickly as possible. As a result, many law firm partners had become used to getting a significant proportion of their profit share paid out within the year to which it relates, with the remainder paid out during the following year, in some cases within a few months of the year end.

Post-financial crisis, many organisations have been stretching out payments to suppliers to help to ease their own cash position and many law firms have found themselves on the receiving end of this behaviour. For many law firms, this will have led to a permanent additional funding requirement unless the situation reverses.

At the same time, large client organisations have increasingly turned to electronic billing (eBilling) to control and process legal bills. While in theory eBilling should help to speed up the processing and payment of legal bills, in practice, in the majority of cases, it has had the opposite effect due to the increased complexity it has introduced.

One way to ensure that cash inflows from clients are received in line with, or at least close to, terms of business is to engage cash collection professionals, which some large firms now have in place. However, even in these situations, some partners continue to insist that only they can be responsible for collection of certain client debts. Typically in such situations it takes longer to receive payment than if collections or finance staff are involved in the process.

This trend of clients taking longer to pay their bills has been particularly problematic for law firms that adopt accrual accounting in line with International Financial Reporting Standards. This is because the partnership accounts that determine the annual profit recognise income when the work is performed rather than when clients have paid for the work. As a result, any pushing out of payment times can impact the ability of firms to pay out profits to partners within the expected timeframes. This has become a real issue for some firms in recent years.

There are two immediate options for law firms in such situations: to delay payments to partners or to borrow using the firm's bank facilities to ensure that payments to partners are maintained within the previously expected timeframes. Depending on attitudes to debt, borrowing to pay partners' profit shares may or may not be palatable. If the borrowing is for only a short period, it will certainly be less risky than establishing a long-term tranche of borrowing to fund partner payments. That said, delaying payments to partners can unsettle a partnership and, in extreme cases, lead to partners leaving. This is why it is important to ensure that a firm is adequately funded to ensure that partner expectations are met.

On-balance sheet debt is becoming more popular with law firms, although the majority of firms continue to be funded by partner capital. There are pros and cons to both methods of funding, although the traditional method of partners providing capital to fund their firm gives them more 'skin in the game'. Partner capital is usually funded by a personal 'partner capital injection loan' from a relationship bank of the firm. This is a loan to the partner to enable them to contribute capital to the firm. The loan is therefore on the partner's personal balance sheet rather than the firm's balance sheet.

There is a risk with on-balance sheet debt for law firms that partners can simply walk away leaving their former partners to assume the responsibility of repayment or refinancing of debt. In situations where significant numbers of partners leave a firm, this can also hasten the departure of other partners, who are unwilling to remain as part of a smaller group of partners who are required to assume the responsibility for the debt.

Indeed, most banks providing on-balance sheet debt facilities to law firms will require a covenant relating to a minimum number of equity partners. In extreme cases, where the number of partners falls below this level, the loan becomes repayable immediately. There is at least one large firm currently close to such a situation.

By contrast, funding a firm using the traditional method of partner capital can allow law firms more time to rearrange their funding. Many firms have provisions in place to allow them to delay repayment of capital to departing partners for a number of years

---

It may be obvious that running a firm efficiently to deliver acceptable levels of profit to partners is important. However, it is equally important to ensure that a firm is sufficiently funded to pay those profits out in line with partners' expectations.

---

in certain circumstances. These provisions allow firms to find time to recruit replacement partners who will contribute capital and may even act as a disincentive for partners who might otherwise consider leaving to join another firm.

Conclusion – cash

Pressures on law firms' cash positions are unlikely to ease any time soon. It may be obvious that running a firm efficiently to deliver acceptable levels of profit to partners is important. However, it is equally important to ensure that a firm is sufficiently funded to pay those profits out in line with partners' expectations.

Smarter firms will have funding arrangements in place that allow for a level of headroom to cover unexpected changes in the cycle of cash collections and/or payments. In addition, any significant projects and/or restructuring events should be funded by separate sources of funding so that the partner payment cycle is not interrupted.

Conclusion

The landscape has changed significantly for law firms and that change is unlikely to reverse. As the managing partner of a global law firm put it recently, the "golden decades" have gone. Over the next decade, competition among firms will continue to increase and client expectations will continue to change.

The provision of first-rate legal advice is a given. The ability to anticipate and provide the services that clients want will differentiate firms. Time invested by partners to build close relationships with their clients and really understand them is likely to pay benefits in terms of helping to secure future income streams.

At the same time, running firms as efficiently as possible to maximise profitability will help to retain key partners. A focus on costs alone is unlikely to result in a sustained increase in profitability. However, the most successful firms are likely to be those that address their costs as well as income.

The trickiest part of cost management will be anticipating which investments need to be made in order to be able to meet clients' future expectations and therefore remain competitive in the future. This may mean significantly increasing spend in some areas. A lack of investment in future technologies could result in some firms being left behind in a rapidly changing environment.

Finally, a strong culture that helps to bind partners together and a strategy aligned with that culture is almost as important as the focus on clients. Any significant changes that will have an impact on a firm's culture should be approached with caution. In addition, getting the funding of a firm right so that profits can be paid out in line with partner expectations is also key.

The really successful firms will be those that successfully address all of these issues while being agile, open to change and skilled at implementing new ways of operating.

Brian Dunlop is a big four qualified ACA with experience in several sectors, including real estate development, branded sportswear, and telecoms. He has spent the last 22 years working in the legal sector, initially in various senior finance roles with Allen & Overy and then as CFO of Ashurst. He is currently global director of strategic pricing at White & Case.

Data and dialogue: a relationship redefined

Jaap Bosman

Traditionally clients have focused on the hourly rates in trying to reduce external legal spend. Looking at a decade of fees and spend shows that focusing on price has not brought any gains for clients. Lawyers' fees have gradually risen and clients ended up paying more than they did before.

Fuelled by these poor results, a small group of avant garde clients have started to employ data analysis techniques on external law firms' billing. Focusing on efficiency, backed by data analytics, these companies have achieved remarkable savings of up to 25% on their legal spend. This focus on efficiency might fundamentally transform the legal industry.

In 2007/2008 the world witnessed the financial crisis. This was the beginning of a rough time for many businesses. As demand declined, companies were looking for substantial cost savings to weather the storm. Legal spend was one of them, so it was in 2008 that the Association of Corporate Counsel (ACC) launched The Value Challenge.

In the years leading up to the financial crisis business was good and year after year profits soared. All this ended abruptly in 2008.

The Value Challenge was an initiative by the ACC – the world's largest association of in-house lawyers – to help its members develop ideas and exchange best practices in order to reduce legal spend, improve predictability and achieve better outcomes. With more than 40,000 members employed by over 10,000 organisations in 85 countries, ACC members benefit from a large pool of knowledge.

Over the past decade almost every conference for the legal profession has had General Counsels (GCs) telling the audience that the cost of external legal spend must go down. Clients had experimented with legal panels in the past, but it was only after 2008 that the formation of 'officially appointed' legal panels really took off.

This period also witnessed the start of the initially promising but troublesome relationship between the legal and the procurement departments. When procurement professionals first got involved in the selection process for panel firms, they had little or no experience with the legal market. In those days, even GCs did not favour their involvement due to the perceived lack of understanding of what the GC was looking for. Buying legal services was definitely different from buying office supplies.

Over the following years clients became better at negotiating deals with their external legal suppliers. The panel formation processes got more sophisticated and sometimes even involved online auctions where law firms aspiring to get on to the panel could see their pricing relative to the competition. Law firms were typically also required to offer free secondments and knowledge sharing. Given the macro-economic situation, law firms offered little or no resistance to this changing relationship.

After the financial crisis, clients became more focused on getting a better deal. The Value Challenge provided inspiration and a pool of knowledge and best practice on how to achieve this. However, the relationship between a client and his lawyer remained very much a personal one. One should not forget that clients and lawyers are partners and work together as a team. The consequence is that clients typically prefer to keep the same lawyer once they have built a relationship which they are happy with. This creates a tendency to subjectively favour an existing relationship over a new one even where a new relationship would bring economic benefits while objectively delivering the same quality.

In 2016 TGO Consulting published a report – "The Trend is Clear, the Blow is yet to Come" – on pricing in the legal market. One of the findings was that GCs and their in-house teams are legal insiders. This might seem obvious, but the consequence is that they are used to the high rates and to the way law firms write time and do their billing. What might seem strange to the CFO will probably be totally normal to the GC.

Originally pioneered by Silicon Valley, a new 'big data' industry had emerged. There was (and is) a real enthusiasm for the tremendous insight that data analysis can bring.

Being accustomed to a certain way of working, the vast majority of in-house lawyers preferred to stick to the hourly rate rather than adopt alternative fee arrangements. This has been a typical complaint from law firms. In trying to deliver better value to clients while avoiding plain discounted rates, many law firms started offering alternative fee arrangements only to discover that clients preferred the traditional hourly rate.

What has happened over the last decade is that clients have demanded and got discounted hourly rates. Larger clients also demanded and got further benefits such as secondments. At the same time, once a firm had been appointed to the panel, the relationship and the way of working basically remained the same. The result of 10 years' 'pressure on price' is that clients have ended up paying more instead of less. Revenue and profits of business law firms have steadily grown over the past decade and the clients are paying for this. Clearly, focusing on pricing and the hourly rate is not working.

Efficiency

Around the same time – about 10 years ago – a small number of large corporate legal departments started to analyse their external legal spend. At first they focused on calculating how much budget was spent per law firm, per business unit, per practice area, etc. Initially this data was applied to facilitate the procurement process in selecting panel firms and negotiating discounted rates. In the early days most of this data-gathering had to be done manually and was put into excel spreadsheets. Sometimes the client in part had to rely on data provided by their law firms. Data at that point was not perfect but was usable for the purpose.

Gradually these frontrunners shifted to mandatory e-billing which provided them with easier access and better data. Legal spend analysis became more accurate and was soon adopted in some form by many other legal departments. During that time we witnessed the rise of data analytics as a field in its own right. Originally pioneered by Silicon Valley, a new 'big data' industry had emerged. There was (and is) a real enthusiasm for the tremendous insight that data analysis can bring.

The front-running corporate legal departments soon started riding the wave and gathering even more data in order to do increasingly precise data analytics. The primary aspiration is to be able to do predictive analytics and know the costs before they occur. In order to do this, vast amounts of data are needed. Potentially these large corporate legal departments had the data, it just needed to be found and unlocked – easier said than done.

In 2012 Google famously succeeded in enabling the computer to identify pictures of cats. This achievement generally contributed to the development of artificial intelligence but has in reality more to do with old-fashioned human labour. In order to teach the computer how to identify a cat, millions of pictures first have to be classified manually. Thousands of low-paid people working from home – Amazon Turks – have classified the pictures one by one. This is a cat and this is not a cat. It is no surprise that Google initiated this project as only they had, through Google Drive, access to the millions of cat pictures needed to teach the system.

This example illustrates that in order to do analysis we need vast amounts of data and lots of manual labour. This also applies to analysis of legal spend. The first step would be finding the data. The adoption of e-billing obviously helped but for companies that operate globally and have many semi-independent business units, then huge challenges remain. The second step would be to clean the data. If taken directly from the source, all data will contain errors, inconsistencies and anomalies that, if not removed, will render the analysis useless. Thirdly, after cleaning, an analysis tool needs to be developed that will provide useful insights and will deliver reproducible results.

Let us start with step one – data mining. In order for the data to be usable, it needs to have a uniform format. For legal expenses this would mean that all invoices need to be structured in the same way. This might be more of a challenge than it seems. For instance, in some countries associates are billed per years of experience starting from the first day of employment as a lawyer, while in other countries it is immediately post-qualification, or others merely distinguish junior associates, associates and senior associates. Some law firms have additional ranks such as managing associates. One of the first steps in getting usable data is finding a way to make the input more uniform. This will not only include how the invoice is split-out per level of experience but also a precise description of the activity on which time has been spent and by whom. The billing data should be structured in a way that it generates data for future analysis.

Along with tackling the problem of making the data comparable, is the challenge of cleaning the data. Sometimes a single matter is billed over several invoices. These invoices could even come from different offices of the law firm that might be in different countries. Sometimes more than one law firm is involved. It is important to label all of these invoices correctly and assign all invoices to the correct matter. This problem is, of course, not unique to the legal industry and all CFOs face similar challenges in attributing costs to the right project. Data cleaning is one of the most difficult aspects of big data analysis. All data is 'unclean' by definition. Using uncleaned data for analysis will produce bogus results which cannot be relied upon.

Once we have obtained the right data in the right format and cleaned it, we can start analysing and trying to find meaningful insights. We need to be cautious at this stage not to draw the wrong conclusions. These could, for example, be conclusions based on too few samples. For instance, if last year a car dealership sold one convertible and this year it sold two, technically it doubled its sales. However, the small number makes this information unfit in order to draw meaningful conclusions. This is something that could also easily happen when analysing legal billing data. Even if the whole dataset is large, a subset for a certain legal area could be too small for useful analysis.

A second mistake is mixing up the concept of *causality* and *correlation*. Even if one finds a clear relation between them, it does not necessarily mean there is a meaningful connection. To illustrate this we will use the 'life vest' example. Investigation of data on people who have drowned clearly shows that most people who drowned were wearing a life vest. Knowing this, one could be tempted to advise against wearing a life vest as it seems to increase the chances of drowning. In this case there clearly is a correlation. However, there no causality as most people exposed to perilous situations on the water will more often wear life vests than those who are just swimming in a guarded pool. *Correlation* and *causality* should therefore never be confused.

Even if we do everything described above correctly, we could still end up with a data analysis that is not useful. Let me illustrate this with M&A transactions. Let us say that we have built a database with thousands of M&A transactions and we want to use this data to help predict the price for future M&A transactions – we still would not be able to do this. How come? The reason is that some of the factors that are most detrimental to the complexity (and thus the price) of an M&A transaction are not in the data. For example, the matter may involve multiple jurisdictions, or both parties may be experienced M&A players or one or both of them may be inexperienced. Also, one of the parties may be a family-owned business and there may be intellectual property rights involved or serious competition issues, and so on. These external factors are extremely important in predicting future cost/pricing but will typically initially not be included in the dataset. This means we will have to enrich the data before we can draw any meaningful conclusions.

Despite the fact that data analysis is a minefield, a small avant garde of the large in-house legal departments have achieved remarkable results. Over the years they have overcome most of the hurdles and have built enormous databases containing thousands and thousands of matters classified per law firm, per jurisdiction and per area of legal expertise. After more than five years in the making, many of these in-house departments know precisely how long a certain matter should take an external law firm to complete and what level of experience is required. The availability of this type of data has initiated a shift from focus on hourly rate to focus on efficiency and time spent. For the legal industry this means a fundamental shift in paradigm.

Data and dialogue

Today every single legal matter is littered with inefficiencies. Clients are aware that this is not all the law firm's fault. Sometimes clients want three conference calls where one would suffice. Sometimes, after a period of time clients send the law firm an important document which should have been part of the original file. However, sophisticated in-house legal departments are aware of this and are also hunting down inefficiencies on their own side. Based on analysis of the data, the goal is achieving greater value by finding and dealing with inefficiencies that do not contribute to the final result.

Clients looking to achieve more value out of the relationship with their external law firms is not a new concept – the process started back in 2008 with the launch of The Value Challenge. It is also something that clients want to achieve through a meaningful dialogue with their panel firms. Clients do not want to put law firms out of business, they just want a relationship that works for both parties, and increasing value is a central part of that.

What will be the result if it is no longer the hourly rate, but efficiency which becomes central to the conversations that clients will be having with the law firms handling their business? Just having this conversation consistently and repeatedly will by itself lead to an increase in efficiency. In 2017 the legal department of Shell won The Value Challenge because it had achieved a reduction of 25% on external legal spend over that year. This was the result of a data-based focus on efficiency. Other multinationals have achieved similar results. Through focus on efficiency rather than rates, clients are for the first time actually getting more value and a better deal.

Sharing the data

As illustrated with the example of Google and identifying cats, meaningful analysis will need large amounts of data. The big multinationals are well positioned for this type of data analysis as they spend huge sums of money on external legal counsel each year. Five or more years of data will be a good start for data-based analysis. But what if the data were shared with other in-house departments. Provided the data is formatted correctly and cleaned this would create a super database that would potentially benefit all in-house departments, including those which do not have the capacity to build their own data set for analysis. This is an initiative that I have recently been discussing with the leadership of the ACC. I believe the database should be an open source and should be managed by an independent party that is not looking to monetise the data. The ACC or the CLOC may be well positioned to manage a large database to which all in-house departments contribute and which will be accessible free of charge to every in-house department. Such a database will cause a seismic shift in the relationship between in-house and law firms. It is important to state that all data in such a database needs to be anonymised with no trace to the law firm or the client. It would give only a precise description of the matter, the jurisdiction and the time spent by level of expertise. This open source database would revolutionise the relationship and lead to unprecedented value for clients.

What about law firms?

For law firms, a focus on efficiency would have an enormous impact. The current business model of the leveraged hour is not easily compatible with increased efficiency. Performance measurement in most law firms monitors billable hours. Partners and associates are rewarded for making more billable hours. Not only do the incentives need to be adapted, but a more fundamental change is needed. Most lawyers are primed to do everything possible in order to achieve from a legal perspective the best result for the client. In order to achieve this, every risk is identified and every scenario is taken into consideration. If lawyers were plumbers, they would most likely instal gold plumbing as it would never corrode and never leak. However, the reality is that unless you are building a space station, you do not need gold plumbing – PVC pipes will do. The same goes for clients. In the majority of cases clients will be perfectly served with solutions that bear a certain risk. Clients themselves are used to working with the concept of 'risk appetite'. For a law firm this would mean a complete departure from the present way of working.

Conclusions

Experience has shown that focusing on the hourly rate is not an effective way for clients to get better value. A small number of forward-thinking legal departments of the big multinational companies have been putting a lot of effort into gathering data and making it usable for analysis. They have achieved phenomenal results and for the first time clients are saving on their legal spend. The 25% that Shell managed to achieve is a good example.

In order to make data available for each in-house department we need to create an open source platform that will not be commercially monetised. The ACC might be the ideal party to host this service.

Law firms will increasingly have conversations with their clients about how they can increase their efficiency. This will inevitably lead to more efficiency forcing the law firms to rethink and adapt their present business model from the leveraged hourly rate towards some form of value-based billing.

This shift in paradigm towards greater efficiency will transform the legal sector in an unprecedented way. Time to get ready for legal market 2.0.

Jaap Bosman is a leading strategy consultant and an investor. He is founder and CEO of TGO Consulting, a strategy consulting boutique for the legal sector that operates from New York, The Hague, and Sweden. Jaap is a member of the ABA and has been with various law firms prior to founding TGO Consulting.

His achievements were recognized in 2013 by the Financial Times with the first-ever Innovative Lawyers Award for International Strategy. Jaap is widely considered to be one of the world's thought leaders on the future of the business of law. He is a regular contributor to the ABA Journal and other magazines around the world.

How corporate legal departments can lessen the impact of law firm rate increases

Richard Brzakala

As we begin a new calendar year, buyers and sellers of legal services must find ways to navigate through significant social, economic, and inflationary pressures rarely seen in the legal marketplace.

These pressures have created a new dynamic in pricing structures that in late 2021 and early 2022 resulted in a tectonic pivot, moving pricing leverage away from clients and in favor of law firms and alternative legal service providers (ALSPs). Consequently, many corporate legal departments (CLDs) will remember these past 24 months as the great pricing reset in which law firms required, and received, significantly higher hourly rate increases over and above anything the legal marketplace has seen in decades of legal service delivery.

As many CLDs move into a post-pandemic legal marketplace, both buyers and sellers of legal services are having to grapple with the economic reality of high inflation, increasing labor and infrastructure costs, attrition, labor arbitrage, and dramatic fluctuations in market demand – all of which will in some way or another impact the cost of legal services into the foreseeable future.

If many of these economic factors continue to remain in place, it's no wonder why many CLDs are feeling anxious about the future and the uncertainty of what's to come in terms of continued rate hikes. But it is not necessarily a *fate accompli* for CLDs as there are counter measures that can be deployed to help clients mitigate, control, and even create cost savings in the face of such pricing uncertainty.

Based on my personal 20-year career in the legal operations space, I have outlined 20 strategic options for CLDs to consider in order to help them mitigate the impact of law firm rate hikes.

1. Tiering

Tiering is the practice of moving legal work away from traditionally more expensive firms and professionals to less expensive service providers without having to compromise the quality of one's legal work.

Tiering relies heavily on the utilization of a CLD's law firm billing data and metrics in order to understand which firms on a panel are the most competitively priced. This is then followed by a consideration to move legal work to those firms that are less expensive in order to control costs or to save money.

Tiering activities can also focus on specific timekeepers, a practice area, geographic location, expertise, or years of experience to understand where a CLD can gain leverage and utilize less costly legal service providers. Targeting high areas of legal spend and then understanding which professionals provide work in those practice areas and at what cost provides cost-saving opportunities for CLDs to move work away from expensive to less costly timekeepers.

Another variation of tiering involves leveraging a less expensive firm (Firm A) against a more expensive firm (Firm B) and requiring that Firm B reduce or match a certain level of rates in order for Firm B to continue to be utilized. In this example, Firm B is incentivized to reduce and/or match its rates to Firm A's level in order to stay on a panel and/or continue to be utilized by the CLD.

Lastly, CLDs may want to consider transitioning legal work away from traditional expensive bricks-and-mortar firms to virtual ALSPs or even smaller regional firms, which typically have lower administrative overhead, retention, and infrastructure costs, which all translate into less expensive options than their counterparts.

2. RFPs and competitive bids

Requests for proposals and competitive bids, also known as "going to the market", have grown in popularity to become highly effective tools for clients looking for new market alternatives to existing panel firms. They can proactively incentivize firms and ALSPs to provide competitive pricing options where such may not have existed prior to a competitive bid scenario.

In the face of expected rate increases, conducting an RFP with current panel firms may help reinforce the need for an existing firm to remain competitively priced. From a relationship perspective, utilizing RFPs on an ad hoc basis also helps stop firms becoming too complacent, or worse, feeling entitled to the work and to charge whatever rates they want.

In the face of expected rate increases, conducting an RFP with current panel firms may help reinforce the need for an existing firm to remain competitively priced.

3. Volume discounts

Volume discounts offer up an opportunity to leverage scale in exchange for lower rates across a specific practice area, timekeeper, or project portfolio of legal work. Not all firms will embrace volume discounts based on a certain dollar threshold of billings. But for those that have a significant billing relationship with a firm or group of firms (i.e., scale), requesting volume discounts for specific tiers or volumes of work may result in discounts to existing or newly proposed hourly rates. As CLDs control the sourcing process and levels of engagement they should also control the expectations around what they are prepared to accept in terms of discounts (e.g. five percent discount if billings exceed $1M) for a specific volume of work.

4. Rebates

Similar to volume discounts, most rebates exist with firms that enjoy a large volume of billing with their CLD. Rebates are typically negotiated at the start of a calendar year and are contingent on a firm achieving a certain dollar threshold or tier of billings in that year. An example would be if a firm achieved 500k in billings, it would rebate five percent (or $25,000) back to the CLD at the end of the year.

Rebates are a good tool for CLDs to utilize during any rate negotiation, especially on large matters or a portfolio of work where a CLD is looking to reduce its legal spend, offset the cost of future work, or simply to mitigate the impact of future rate increases.

5. Panel convergence

Paring down the number of legal service providers a CLD utilizes can be accomplished in a variety of ways, but most CLDs utilize either an RFP or other type of evaluation process to make a determination as to which firm stays and which firm goes.

Converging to a panel of fewer service providers creates a lot of efficiency type savings for the typical CLD. However, it also allows CLDs to negotiate more favorable rate discounts if a firm knows it will have exclusivity or be part of a smaller panel of firms in a particular practice area. Being part of a smaller panel of service providers incentivizes firms to look beyond one-sided transactional relationships and develop closer relationships with their clients so that they can survive a convergence process. Surviving for a firm may require that they make greater pricing concessions (e.g. in the form of rate freezes or rate reductions) than they would otherwise be reluctant to give were it not for a CLD convergence process.

As market conditions grow more challenging, so too will the demand on firms to maintain and grow their profitability.

6. Scale and leverage

Many CLDs are now tasked by their general counsels and CEOs to demand more efficient legal services for less money. Consequently, those CLDs that have a large amount of legal spend (i.e., scale) look to utilize their influence (leverage) wherever they can in order to control legal costs. This is especially true during rate negotiations.

2021-2023 was a challenging period for many CLDs and 2024 is shaping up to be no different in terms of leverage as market factors continue to favor firms. Where once CLDs could leverage scale as a negotiating tactic with panel firms, that may still have some sway, but to a lesser extent with larger firms. Despite this, clients should not be dissuaded from trying to utilize scale or leverage as a negotiation tactic. In fact, as market conditions grow more challenging, so too will the demand on firms to maintain and grow their profitability. Despite the great pricing pivot, firms will continue to be under pressure to maintain and not lose existing clients – especially those with sizeable volumes of work.

7. Fee caps

Another opportunity for CLDs to manage their external legal spend is through the utilization of fee caps, whereby a CLD implements a maximum permissible percentage threshold that a law firm is permitted to increase its rates by in a given calendar year. The fee cap may be specific to individual timekeepers, a class of timekeepers, a geographic market, or even a specific practice area. This is an excellent and proactive way for CLDs to try to manage legal costs in an unpredictable marketplace.

However, not all firms may want to comply with fee cap requirements and, depending on the dynamics of their relationship with a CLD, getting a firm to agree to fee caps in today's marketplace may be a formidable challenge. Therefore, CLDs should first ask themselves a few probing questions to understand if a fee cap strategy is worth pursuing (e.g., does the CLD have scale and leverage with the firm? If not, are the fee caps negotiable? Is the law firm of strategic importance to the client? If not, are there alternatives in the marketplace to consider? Finally, is the legal expertise bespoke enough to warrant premium pricing and/or an exception to the fee caps?).

Ultimately, clients should be prepared to negotiate to a middle ground and that negotiation starts with having an unwavering belief in one's data and a mutual agreement that can respect a firm's interest in staying profitable and the CLD's interest in controlling and managing their costs.

8. Communication

Having an open and honest dialogue with a CLD's most strategic law firm on such things as budget constraints, company cost saving targets, or convergence strategies may yield voluntary law firm rate freezes or even reductions, in the interest of building stronger and lasting relationships.

I have always believed that CLDs should treat their panel firms as trusted legal partners beyond merely transactional matters. Having transparent and honest dialogue will go a long way for both a CLD and their law firms.

For example, in exchange for immediate rate reductions or rate freezes, CLDs may offer up a commitment to reward a long-standing firm with more lucrative work in the future in exchange for tactical voluntary price cuts. This was the methodology a GC took years ago with his CLD when he shared his company's goal to slash spending by ten percent with his top 25 most strategic law firms. Each of these firms quickly realized that slashing costs meant reducing the size of the panel and an increased likelihood of losing this client – with significant impact to the firm's profitability. Almost every partner representing each of the 25 firms ultimately committed to reducing their rates in exchange for remaining on the company's panel for at least a three-year period.

Having a candid discussion at an opportune time when a lot of companies are facing financial challenges may remind the firm that the CLD is committed to growing lasting partnerships with firms that understand a client's budgetary pressures and are willing to help the client meet their cost saving targets for the greater good of the relationship.

Not every firm can or will accept this position, but at the very least it will highlight for the CLD those firms that are simply interested in a transactional relationship versus those that are able and can help the client build a more strategic long-term bond.

9. Value added services

Not all clients may be entitled to ancillary benefits with a law firm, aside from the transactional advice and services they provide. Value added services such as free legal advice, secondments, market research, access to proprietary technology, and education and training sessions may need to be negotiated if a CLD does not have scale with a firm.

If a CLD must accept higher rates, then perhaps trying to negotiate or tie some level of complimentary ancillary services to those higher rates may help offset legal costs in other areas that the CLD would have been forced to spend money on.

Having transparent and honest dialogue will go a long way for both a CLD and their law firms.

10. Rate management policy

Having a formalized (i.e. written) billing policy, rather than just "guidelines" that outline specific requirements around billing dos and don'ts, as well as rate management, is a necessity in today's economic cost control environment.

However, while many CLDs have billing guidelines in place with their law firms, far fewer have any language in their guidelines that talks specifically about rate management and prescriptive requirements related to how a law firm is to address any proposed rate increases. Consequently, firms are left to impose their own rate requirements on trusting clients who almost always agree to annual sizeable increases without any pushback.

A proper rate management policy should address such criteria as when a firm can make a request, the frequency of a request (e.g. one increase per year and not two small increases that add up to double digit increases), permissible rate caps for specific professional groups, and the permissible criteria or reasons that qualify for a rate increase (e.g. merit vs market pressures). All these criteria are fundamental to managing expectations up front for both the firm and the CLD and for providing predictability and transparency around rate management.

11. Budgeting and cost estimates

Understanding the scope and legal costs upfront, at the time of an engagement, is critical to the success of any matter. Utilizing such tools as budgeting and cost estimates offers CLDs the opportunity to gain transparency into how a firm staffs and prices its matters. It also confirms the scope and expectations in writing and in advance of a matter. If a CLD must accept higher rates, adding a law firm requirement for mandatory cost estimates helps keep both the client and law firm in check with regards to expectations, variances, and assumptions and mitigates the risk of unchecked and unnecessary expensive legal work.

Finding and hiring the right professional internally offers CLDs an excellent option to control and/or reduce external legal spend and reduce dependence on expensive firms in an unpredictable and volatile market place.

12. Alternative legal service providers (ALSPs)

ALSPs offer CLDs an opportunity to leverage less expensive providers than traditional bricks and mortar law firms. Tiering transactional matters or components of a matter away from expensive firms to ALSPs provides CLDs with cost-saving and convergence opportunities.

There is much written about the ALSP market space and how it has been characterized by being extremely innovative and very competitively priced compared to traditional law firms. The momentum to challenge the traditional law firm model will continue and should be explored as a viable option for any CLD looking to save money and control legal spend.

Contingent worker ALSPs are a good example of legal work that is typically sourced to traditional (more expensive) law firms, but now offers CLDs the option to utilize virtual and less expensive service providers for components of legal matters or ad hoc resource needs.

13. Insourcing

Whenever possible, leveraging in-house legal professionals is almost always less expensive than external law firms. Finding and hiring the right professional internally offers CLDs an excellent option to control and/or reduce external legal spend and reduce dependence on expensive firms in an unpredictable and volatile market place.

However, despite the practice of insourcing offering a significant advantage in terms of cost savings for CLDs, they may be challenged in today's post-COVID marketplace to find and attract the right external legal talent at the right price. As stated earlier, COVID-19 and inflationary pressures have impacted the labor market, creating shortages of available and affordable legal professionals.

If finding the right external resource becomes problematic, CLDs might want to consider exploring opportunities within their existing pool of internal resources. Opportunities may present themselves with administrative staff, paralegals, or clerks that can be optimized better, realigned, or leveraged more effectively and efficiently to create cost savings. Hiring additional clerks or paralegals may be easier and less expensive than hiring experienced associates in order to try to keep as much legal work in-house before engaging external counsel.

Insourcing continues to be atop many GCs' lists of priorities and should continue to be an option for those looking to offset rate increases and control external legal spend. Its popularity may explain why many firms continue to view insourcing as one of the greatest threats to law firm profitability.

14. Billing data and artificial intelligence (AI)

When leveraged correctly, CLD billing data, derived from in-house legal e-billing software, offers CLDs a plethora of opportunities to save money in a runaway market that has pivoted in favor of legal service providers.

For years, CLDs have utilized various e-billing

software tools, which on their own have helped CLDs with their data mining and analysis exercises. However, AI software tools stand to revolutionize data mining and analysis for all CLDs by allowing greater accessibility and analysis of billing data and making it more affordable, expedient, and accessible than ever before.

By measuring and understanding billing patterns and having the ability to perform almost instantaneous benchmarking reports, CLDs can more effectively manage their sourcing strategies, tiering, and RFP initiatives – all for the purpose of creating cost savings and mitigating against rate increases. Furthermore, AI data management tools may help uncover never before realized saving opportunities when comparing billing data between multiple firms and ALSPs.

Over the years, data mining has become much more sophisticated in many CLDs, so much so that some legal operations managers state that the legal billing data "speaks" to them when they have to source legal work.

We have all heard the phrase that data is the new currency and its importance even in the legal industry should not be underestimated. It is, and will continue to be, a powerful factor that can be leveraged in pricing negotiations to help avoid law firm rate increases.

Sharing (anonymized) cross-firm comparisons, staffing ratios, timekeeper comparisons, and benchmark averages with law firms during rate negotiations is an ideal way for CLDs to demonstrate whether a law firm's position, relative to others on a panel, is favorable to the CLD. Linear graphs and visual charts showing one firm as an outlier when compared to their peers speaks volumes in a rate discussion when a firm is looking to retain a client and gain more work.

15. Staffing ratios

Analyzing staffing metrics that are derived from either a CLD's e-billing or AI software is an area of greater focus for many CLDs looking to invert the traditional law firm work pyramid where there is a higher concentration of work being carried out by the most expensive partners.

As part of any rate negotiations, CLDs should consider imposing staffing ratios on firms, requiring them to assign a greater percentage of their work to lower cost mid-level associates, rather than expensive partners, thereby offering up potential cost savings for the CLD.

Depending on the nature of legal work performed by some firms, there may be an opportunity for a CLD to find savings by analyzing the disbursements that are charged by their firms.

16. Disbursements

Depending on the nature of legal work performed by some firms, there may be an opportunity for a CLD to find savings by analyzing the disbursements that are charged by their firms.

Legal e-billing systems are great for implementing quantifiable rules around catching and rejecting non-reimbursable expenses on invoices before they get approved by a CLD. However, there are many charges or billing practices that cannot be quantified and correlated to an automated e-billing rule that rejects the proposed expense. Moreover, there may be other expenses that are subjective in nature and require more powerful AI tools to review and catch non-compliance billing. Diving into law firm disbursement data offers the CLD an opportunity to 1) find questionable patterns of billing behavior that are non-compliant with a CLD's billing guidelines; 2) identify non-compliance gaps to save money; and 3) leverage law firm non-compliance to negotiate rebates or future discounts against historical law firm over-billing.

CLDs should also be aware that increasing numbers of firms are beginning to charge a supplementary fee (as a disbursement) in the form of a percentage multiplied by the sum total of fees

> **Ask any CFO at any big law firm to identify their biggest challenge with managing a law firm and they will probably tell you that it has to do with the challenges they face in collecting their accounts receivables from their clients.**

billed on a client's invoice. Firms position their supplementary fee as a necessary cost of doing business to cover off such things as investments in technology, administrative overhead, leaseholds, premise costs, or insurance. Supplementary fees help the firm recoup its cost of doing business at the expense of the client.

CLDs focused on rate increases typically tend to overlook the impact that a supplementary fee may have on a client's cost savings ability. Whenever possible, CLDs should try to renegotiate any supplementary fee or have it waived altogether as it compounds the impact of any rate increases and diminishes a CLD's ability to generate real cost savings.

17. Quick pay discounts

Ask any CFO at any big law firm to identify their biggest challenge with managing a law firm and they will probably tell you that it has to do with the challenges they face in collecting their accounts receivables (A/R) from their clients. The importance of A/Rs is not lost on a law firm's management team as tracking outstanding A/R balances is instrumental in measuring productivity for its lawyers. These lawyers also view A/R as an important barometer of how efficient and effective they are with their clients. High A/R balances with CLDs may indicate a servicing issue between the lawyer and a CLD so it is in the lawyer's interest to get paid as soon as possible.

CLDs can utilize quick-pay discounts as a solution to a firm's A/R challenges by providing an incentive for the law firm to lower its rates, or give a client a specific (percentage) discount off a bill total, in exchange for the CLD's commitment to process and pay the law firm's invoices within a specific time frame.

Those CLDs with large volumes of matters and legal spend should consider focusing on the firms they bill the most with for opportunities to negotiate quick pay discounts in exchange for helping a firm reduce its financing and carrying costs.

As the global economic environment grows more challenging, so does the pressure on firms to reduce their overhead costs, including the cost of borrowing and carrying receivables for extended periods of time. Consequently, in such economic environments, quick pay discounts become increasingly attractive and may in fact favor CLDs during rate negotiations to help minimize the impact of rate hikes.

18. Alternative fee arrangements (AFAs)

AFAs are often touted as the great pricing panacea to hourly rates. Firms propose AFAs (fixed fees, flat fees, contingency, volume discounts, risk collars etc.) as an alternative to hourly rates, promoting them as cost saving opportunities for CLDs. But unless clients can validate how an AFA saves money, there can be no assurance that the client is actually saving money.

Before accepting any AFA proposal, CLDs should require that the law firm provide quantifiable proof as to the value of the AFA and what if any determination was made to validate that the AFA is a better pricing option for the client. Without any empirical validation, CLDs risk making costly assumptions around cost savings, when in fact it may be the opposite. Asking a firm to provide an empirical explanation of how it arrived on an AFA and how the client is better off with the AFA than an hourly rate should not be a challenging exercise. For those firms looking to create a transparent and lasting relationship, the information and data should be readily available and shared willingly without any hesitation and subjective elements.

19. Proactive negotiation

When it comes to extraordinary matters or large class action law suits, it is understandable that many CLDs initially focus their attention on reacting to the urgency of a matter by ensuring that they line up the right firm and professionals to tackle the legal issue. In such situations, time may be a critical factor and often there is very little in the way of any real rate negotiations as the primary focus almost always is on staffing up the right legal expertise to resolve the legal issue (e.g. regulatory investigation, class action, M&A deal). Negotiating discounts for high priced legal talent may be challenging in the best of times, let alone during an extraordinary event.

CLDs, especially those regularly involved in high priced matters, should consider what I refer to as "proactive negotiations" with a select group of firms in advance of future extraordinary matters. This is especially true in high stakes litigation where CLDs find themselves in highly stressful situations and having to juggle an assortment of legal issues, deadlines, and a cornucopia of internal business issues. What a firm charges for its services in such situations is probably one of the last things a CLD concerns itself with. It's only when a post mortem is carried out that the client realizes they could have gone with another firm or negotiated a better rate. Proactive negotiation allows a CLD to control where pricing will be at any given time in the future and not have to rely on the firm to control that determination.

Moreover, negotiating discounted or fixed pricing on the basis of future commitments provides the CLD with a greater assurance and predictability in terms of resources, budgeting, and forecasting legal costs on significant matters that in the past may have otherwise been previously controlled by market forces or law firms.

Class action matters offer an excellent opportunity for proactive negotiation as many large class actions can be protracted and take years to conclude and result in millions of dollars in legal costs for a CLD. I discussed leverage and scale above, and perhaps there is no better leverage than an opportunity for a law firm to be awarded the next class action lawsuit in exchange for some sort of pricing concessions. Negotiating an arrangement proactively to either reduce and/or freeze rates for a 12- or 24-month period in exchange for a commitment to receive lucrative legal work is advantageous for both the firm and the client.

Proactive negotiations can also be extended to include ALSPs, especially those that a CLD knows it will require during an extraordinary matter. For example, the need for e-discovery services is growing for many companies as the business world is growing to become more regulatory and litigious. Selecting one or two e-discovery providers and proactively negotiating upfront costs and expectations months before their services are required, may save significant costs for a CLD.

Many larger firms rely on market data and pricing consultants to advise them as to where their firm should be in terms of its pricing strategy in order to remain competitive and to ensure the firm stays profitable.

20. Market or rack rates

Many larger firms rely on market data and pricing consultants to advise them as to where their firm should be in terms of its pricing strategy in order to remain competitive and to ensure the firm stays profitable. Built into this methodology is a traditional reliance on market rates (also referred to as "street", "commercial", or "rack rates").

Market rates are typically much higher than the preferred rate discounts many institutional clients receive. The reasons for the discounts vary from client to client, but ultimately firms like to use their market rates as a benchmark against any discounts they give to their clients. The higher the market rates, the bigger the discount appears to the client.

However, as CLDs have matured over the years, many have grown skeptical of these market rates and the continued legal industry practice of benchmarking proposed discounts against market rates. Increasingly, CLDs have come to view law firm market rates as nothing more than an optical illusion where market rates have been artificially inflated to give clients the perception of a large discount.

Consequently, CLDs should approach any rate hikes based on market benchmarks with some level of skepticism, especially when they start to hear generic phrases like "We have given you a sizeable discount compared to our market rates".

There is nothing wrong with challenging a firm on its proposed rate hikes and asking for greater transparency when it comes to a firm's proposal. Just like a client would ask for details on a cost estimate or a budget, CLDs should also have a deeper understanding around a law firm's rate hike request to understand what factors (i.e. direct and indirect costs) and variables were used as the basis for the proposed rate increase.

CLDs should look for things like administrative overhead (i.e. advertisement, leaseholds, training/education, and infrastructure costs), employee retention and promotion, geographic factors, the cost of technology investments, law firm insurance etc., as any one of these will significantly contribute to the size of a rate hike.

Ultimately it's up to the CLD to decide whether they want to absorb a firm's costs of having to do business. If a CLD decides rate increases should be based solely on merit and no other factors, and the client has scale with a firm, there may be an opportunity for the client to negotiate a lower rate increase and save money down the road.

Asking a firm to break down the reasons for a proposed increase is no different than an employer in the corporate world asking an employee to justify why they think they deserve a raise in their hourly rate.

Basing an increase on merit and the value a timekeeper brings to a matter is reasonable and justified. Unfortunately, many CLDs have grown accustomed to being pressured into accepting "across the board" increases without questioning the value or contributions made by individual timekeepers.

Across the board increases or level setting so that a firm can charge its clients one standard rate for a class of professionals is ironic as it contradicts what many firms profess to their clients – i.e. each client is unique and special and as such each deserves to be treated differently from all of the firm's other clients.

Regardless of what approach or strategy a CLD deploys to help avoid rate hikes, clients ultimately need to make a determination as to what price they are willing to pay for the services they receive. If a firm is delivering value, then the CLD needs to determine if the price a firm proposes in terms of a rate increase is worthy and valuable to the client. Price only becomes an issue when the client perceives that the proposed price is overstated, unreasonable, and not in line with what the client perceives as value.

Richard Brzakala has extensive experience in the legal operations field and is based in Toronto. He contributed this article in his personal capacity. The views expressed are his own.

Richard Brzakala is a recognized legal marketplace thought leader and expert in legal operations, sourcing, and cost efficiency strategies. He has been a trusted advisor to many senior executives and general counsels, having worked and consulted for numerous FIs, law firms, and government agencies. Richard is a frequent speaker, panelist, and writer, having published numerous articles on a variety of legal ops topics such as legal sourcing, winning RFPs, convergence practices, and creating corporate cost-saving strategies.

Law departments must become more discerning purchasers of legal tech

Nathan Cemenska and Stephanie Corey

Prior to the 2008 financial crisis, banks made a lot of bad loans. The public blamed them (and maybe it should have), but as explained by billionaire investor Howard Marks in his book *Mastering the Market Cycle*,[1] banks were *forced* to make many of those loans by the politics of big business. The competition profited from bad loans, and any CEO who went against the rest of the industry opened themselves up to charges that they were leaving money on the table. In fact, if a CEO refused to conform in the helter-skelter environment leading up to 2008, he or she would probably have been removed and replaced with somebody willing to go along.

The emergence of Large Language Models (LLMs) put the legal technology marketplace in a position analogous to what we saw with mortgages back in 2008. Facebook, Google, Microsoft, IBM, and many other companies are licensing their LLM capabilities to legal tech providers, and providers are building their own like never before. Just like the banks "had" to put out questionable loans, most legal tech providers are now compelled to put out LLM or other AI-based products, regardless of whether they are ready. If leadership refuses, they can be replaced. They cannot argue that large language models aren't ready yet, that the company isn't ready, that LLMs don't make sense in the context of their current offerings, that they don't see how LLMs are going to

improve the condition of the client, that the licensing and other fees for using LLMs cannot be recouped in the form of increased revenues, or that it is best to take a "wait and see" approach. Those are all "incorrect arguments" in today's heady business climate, even if they happen to be true. Therefore, while we can expect to see many excellent LLM-based products emerge, we can also expect to see many products that should never have been made – just like we saw a lot of loans that should never have been made before 2008.

Indeed, even prior to the advent of LLMs, the legal tech market was already saturated with a dizzying and ever-increasing array of products. According to Stanford Codex,[2] at least 2,278 legal tech products are on the market as of early January 2024; the number was half that a few years ago. In this environment, how can corporate law departments stay abreast of the changing technology horizon and partner only with the best vendors who combine the best technology with the best service?

Simply put, they have to become more discerning. Gone are the days when you could sit through hours of product demos and make a major legal tech purchase with any confidence (if, in fact, those days ever existed). Just as Socrates advised his students to ignore the shadows on the wall and instead focus on what was really going on, corporate law departments must pierce through the smoke and mirrors of the legal tech sales and marketing machine to find the best vendors. Before they do that, they need to get extremely real about what is a true need versus what is a nice-to-have, because imperfect legal technology often forces us to give up things that are merely nice to have.

Thankfully, there are several best practices that law departments can follow. Here are some of them.

Require your law department to be specific about its legal technology needs

Organizations often jump to solutions before defining the problems to be solved, often with dismal results. The company owned by one of the authors of this article, UpLevel Ops, spends much of its time urging GCs and legal teams to slow down and refrain from hastily signing tech contracts. You must step back to get some consensus internally about precisely *why* a new solution is needed in the first place. The reasons may be apparent, at least to you, but other stakeholders in the department likely know about needs you do not. They may also have a different take on the importance, urgency, and exact contours of the needs that other people have identified.

When defining needs, it is important to be clear about what counts. For instance, a CLD that says it wants "a better matter management system" may think it has defined a problem but has not. "Matter management" is a solution category, not an actual use case, *per se*. An explicit use case would be, "As a GC, I need to report to the C-suite on the number and type of new legal matters generated monthly, their status, and to whom they've been assigned, all on a real-time basis".

This use case allows the organization to conclude that the future solution must include at least:

a) A "good enough" way of recording the existence and type of insourced legal matters;
b) a "good enough" way of recording the existence and type of outsourced legal matters; and
c) a "good enough" reporting tool that makes it relatively quick and easy to create a report about the above information.

Failing to generate an explicit use case like the one mentioned above means you are proceeding without your needs being fully defined, and this ambiguity dramatically increases the chances that you will select an inappropriate solution that won't meet your needs.

Rank your legal operations problems by importance, as well as by satisfaction with the current solution

If you are querying enough stakeholders, you should have identified many issues with your current way of doing things, not all of which are equally important. Some issues may be annoying but directly affect only a handful of people, while other issues may not annoy anyone in particular but create systemic issues that can hold back the entire law department. For instance, clunky reporting tools on the back end of many systems can lead to reporting delays and inaccuracies that eventually "train" stakeholders to stop asking for or consulting reports before making decisions. At that point, people stop complaining because they have found a solution to the problem – simply go around the whole idea of reporting altogether and just do the best they can. From a departmental perspective, however, this is not the desired solution. Because no solution will make everyone happy, the law department needs to ensure the issues identified are essential on a departmental level, not just critical in the eyes of a vocal minority.

You can even plot your existing pain points on a "satisfaction/importance" plane, as seen in Figure 1. The volume of the darkened area represents the value captured by the current way of doing things. You will find several areas with high importance but low satisfaction. Those are the differentiators in the new software you want to move into. When you start talking to vendors and other people about solutions, you will want to steer the conversation toward those areas and learn as much as possible.

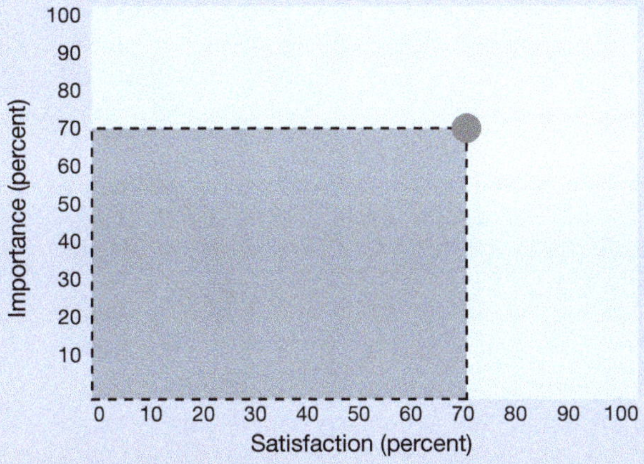

Figure 1: The satisfaction/importance plane. From The Lean Product Playbook, *by Dan Olsen.*

You will also uncover many areas where satisfaction is already relatively high and/or importance is low, so there isn't much room for improvement. The status quo is fine. When you start looking at various solutions, however, you want to make sure the new solution isn't going to cause you to backslide on the areas of high importance and high satisfaction unless you want to risk re-introducing old problems that the status quo had already solved. You will want to deprioritize areas where importance is low, even if the current degree of satisfaction is also very low. This may take some discipline because some low-importance areas may annoy those dealing with them directly. While the needs of this vocal minority are critical and should be considered, it is important to balance them against the interests of the law department.

After defining the problems, make a list of potentially relevant solutions and begin a process of elimination – cutting the most obviously inappropriate solutions first

CLDs should spend tens of hours doing hard, boiler-room detective work before purchasing a system, because changing an important system can generate hundreds of hours of implementation and change management work, can cost tens of thousands if not millions of dollars, and can prove prohibitively difficult to remedy if a poor system is chosen. Some CLDs carry on for years and years with systems that do not meet their needs because the exit costs in time and money – not to mention the opportunity cost in the form of taking resources away from helping the parent corporation solve substantive legal problems – are prohibitive. Economists refer to this phenomenon as "vendor lock-in". Vendor lock-in can exist naturally due to the complexity of the systems involved. However, software vendors are well aware of vendor lock-in, and may intentionally design their products in a way that makes it unnecessarily difficult for customers to leave. This means more subscription revenue for them and more pain for you.

To avoid becoming trapped in such an unhappy situation, consider the following steps:

- *Get to know the players.* This usually isn't hard. The vendors want to be found. There are exhaustive lists online of every vendor category.[3] CLDs can also just Google the name of the product category (e.g., "legal intake software", "workflow software", or "matter management"). Try to list 20 vendors in each category.
- *Separate the wheat from the chaff.* Eliminate companies that don't look like they will have a competitive advantage in "differentiator" categories – the important problems where there is dissatisfaction with the current solution, and where other solutions look like they could do better. For instance, if the problem is the aforementioned "We are unable to timely report on the number and type of new legal matters generated every month, and to whom they've been assigned", disqualify any solution that has a poor or antiquated reporting tool. Working with the IT department, eliminate vendors that do not meet the information security or other IT policies that are beyond law department control. For instance, some IT departments require that most categories of legal software be on-premises solutions, meaning there is no point in speaking with cloud providers.
- *Vet functionality before you demo.* Next, carry out quick calls with the sales teams at the vendors. Be upfront with them about what the most important problems are and see what they say. They may try to steer the conversation to the areas that put them in the best light, but don't let them. When confronted with a buyer who is 100% explicit that they want a quality solution for X, many salespeople will admit right away that X isn't their focus, that they are selling a solution in a different category (e.g., an on-premises solution when the CLD wants a cloud-based one), they are out of the CLD's price range, or are inappropriate for some other reason. Smart salespeople want to focus on prospects who might buy their products, not ones who inevitably won't, and will be happy to "disqualify" CLDs that aren't a good fit for their products.
- *Do extensive demos with your shortlist.* After disqualifying the low-hanging fruit, do hardcore due diligence on the vendors that remain. At this point, by process of elimination, the CLD should have arrived at a short list of three to five vendors. Carry out extensive demos with all these vendors. Demo not just the main user interface of their product, but all the functions likely to be used. Pay particular attention to the reporting tools on the back end of these products. Often, vendors will create what is little more than a mockup of what clients will actually get, populate it with dummy data, and create a few interactive dashboards with "fun" colors intended to wow the audience. Later, after purchasing, the client learns the hard way the difference between a demo environment and reality.

- *Talk to their flagship customers.* The vendors should share a list of "reference clients" – clients who are big fans of theirs, and who have offered to speak to potential customers about their experience with the product. Make a list of ten questions and call those people up. Let them speak in an unguided way for a while (a lot of information is learned this way), then put the questions to them. If they are talking, keep them talking; don't interrupt them. Take extensive notes. Then repeat these interviews for all the reference clients for all the vendors on the shortlist.

- *Really dig into their functionality.* When interviewing, make sure to ask not just about the core functionality of the product, but all the ancillary functionality you expect to use. For instance, in terms of e-billing/outside counsel management, the core functionality includes things like being able to process all invoices[4] and quickly and easily report on how much is being spent on what and with whom. However, with any solution, there will likely be dozens of other ancillary modules with potentially important functionality. For instance, panel management, alternative fee arrangements, diversity, cybersecurity audits, intake/triage, invoice review, quickpay, volume discounts, rate benchmarking/rate management, document management, legal hold, RFP management, law firm score-carding, early case analysis, vendor onboarding, and legal reserves/contingent liabilities are typical modules of e-billing/matter management tools.

  The sad reality is that most buyers rush through their review of these ancillary modules, following a "check-the-box" approach that merely investigates whether the function is present or absent, not whether it is built in a way that will solve the buyer's problem. This is especially common when the IT department, which often doesn't actually have to use the system on a day-to-day basis and doesn't understand the nuances of the problems to be solved, is leading the buying process. Vendors have caught on, and some leading software consultants advise their clients to deliberately craft ancillary modules that offer shallow functionality that is only deep enough to serve as a fig leaf to get past the box-checkers.
- *Be sure to check references.* After speaking with reference clients, start calling "non-reference clients" – people who, unlike reference clients, aren't necessarily "friends" of the vendor and haven't been recommended based on the vendor's estimation that they will provide a rosy picture of the vendor and their offering. Go online and find sales and marketing collateral from vendors that list current and past clients. For instance, vendors create PowerPoints for webinars they occasionally give, listing ten or 20 of their marquee clients on an introductory slide. Go on LinkedIn, identify people working in legal operations at those companies, and shoot them a quick message asking whether they know about the system being evaluated. Would they be willing to chat about it for half an hour? A surprising number will be happy to speak about the good and the bad.

  Also, join industry organizations such as CLOC – the Corporate Legal Operations Consortium – and see what help they have available. Some have a very active community of legal ops veterans with legal technology experience. Some have message boards where users can perform keyword searches and find old discussions between various users about

their experiences. CLDs can also post their own messages, explaining their challenges and asking if anybody has any relevant experiences with the vendors in question. Often users can arrange a private talk with these folks to get the most candid perspective.

CLDs that conduct enough of these interviews will hear horror stories of broken promises, misleading marketing and sales statements, implementations that went years over deadline, finger-pointing between vendor and client, hidden fees, and so on. No vendor is perfect, and most will have more than one very dissatisfied client. However, CLDs that keep hearing negative reports about the same vendor repeatedly should consider that a red flag – the vendor apparently either can't or won't treat their customers in a way that those customers view as fair. No matter how friendly the salespeople are, no matter how good the technology looks in demos, and no matter what story is spun, CLDs that go with a vendor despite widespread customer complaints will probably end up becoming just another one of those complaining customers.

- *Get professional help!* If time and/or expertise are lacking, CLDs can engage a consulting company for the due diligence described above. This has a lot of advantages. However, many consulting companies get kickbacks for recommending specific solutions, and many get "disguised kickbacks" in the form of implementation revenues after recommending vendors with strong relationships. To the extent CLDs engage a consulting company, they should go with one that claims to be vendor-neutral and actually is. Asking around is probably the best way of figuring out who's who. Going with the wrong consulting company can amount to paying for a solution that solves the consulting company's revenue problems and not necessarily the business problems of the CLD.

Conclusion

As the saying goes, haste makes waste, so GCs and law departments need to slow the legal technology selection process down to allow the opportunity for discernment. Those who fail to heed this warning risk winding up in one of two nightmare scenarios.

Nightmare scenario #1 is learning you've just bought tickets for the *Titanic*. There are a lot of "legacy" providers of legal technology with outdated tech stacks, and it would be foolish to make further investments in the products. Those providers will instead invest in their sales and marketing machines to wring the last drops of profitability out of products they know very well they will be forced to sunset. Don't let the sun set on you.

Nightmare scenario #2 is learning you just bought a product that is little more than an idea, aka vaporware. "Early adopter" is often used as a laudatory term, and indeed, there is something

admirable about companies willing to take a risk on a newer provider and help build something great together. However, not all providers will be upfront about the reality of what you're buying into because, if they did, you wouldn't buy into it. It is okay to be a beta tester – it can even be a great way to get in early and inexpensively with promising tech providers, so long as that's a path you've consciously chosen. But this path can be time-consuming and may use up resources that could better be spent solving immediate problems.

By following this advice you can mitigate the risk of the two scenarios and find a product that not only solves your problems today but has the ability to adapt to the new world of large language models and beyond.

Nathan Cemenska, JD/MBA, is the founder of Forthright Consulting, a boutique consultancy focused on legal operations, legal data, legal technology, e-billing, and outside spend management. A former practicing attorney, he got his MBA at night and transitioned into legal operations through his early volunteer work with the Corporate Legal Operations Consortium. He has worked in a consulting capacity for Elevate Services and UpLevel Ops, and most recently served in product management and thought leadership for Wolters Kluwer ELM Solutions, one of the largest legal technology companies in the world.

Stephanie Corey, CEO and founder of UpLevel Ops, is a distinguished legal operations leader with deep expertise spanning IT, finance, and process optimization. She founded and led the professional communities of CLOC (Corporate Legal Operations Consortium) and, most recently, LINK (Legal Innovators Network). Formerly with Flex as senior director of legal operations, her strategic vision has bolstered legal departments globally. Stephanie's academic credentials include an MBA from Lehigh University and a BA in Economics from Wilkes University.

1 *Mastering The Market Cycle: Getting the odds on your side*, Howards Marks, Nicholas Brealey Publishing, 2018.
2 https://techindex.law.stanford.edu/
3 *Ibid.*
4 Clients often expect that any e-billing tool will be able to process any invoice, but that isn't the case. For instance, some cannot process invoices denominated in foreign currencies, some cannot handle invoices with value-added tax issues, and some cannot process PDF invoices. Some of the more mature solutions can handle all of these.

Technology

Legal risk and sound management judgement: can artificial intelligence make us better lawyers?

Jelena Schidzig and Stuart Weinstein

Stuart Weinstein and Jelena Schidzig discuss models of legal risk management and how, without sacrificing qualitative methods, the profession can embrace technology for more efficient analysis of legal risk.

A sound general counsel function in a complex organisation must constantly be scanning the horizon to keep abreast of changes in regulation and law impacting the business and its customers, across the different, specific geographical locations where the businesses and its customers operate, its product lines and where they are distributed, its corporate structures and how they are managed and the impact of the regulatory footprint engendered by these activities and operations.[1] As such, it is essential that businesses employ technology to assist them in developing appropriate systems and structures to manage legal risk in all operations and strategic planning.

Addressing legal risk in a company or an organisation is no easy task, however. While it is true that ownership of the legal risk function typically resides in a legal or compliance department, it is a function that cuts across all lines often with different managers and teams having 'dotted line' responsibility for aspects of legal and/or compliance matters. Moreover, to top this off, it is the board of directors itself that has overall enterprise-wide responsibility for the same. For instance, when a fine is imposed by a regulator on a company for a compliance failure, it will more likely be the result of behavioural failures in an operating department rather than malfeasance in the legal department.

Geoffrey Miller[2] at NYU suggests that attorneys are, in fact, professional risk managers even if they do not think of themselves as such, suggesting they learn to work with enterprise risk management, analysis of inherent risk, controls and mitigation measures, residual risk and the use of quantitative tools such as value at risk. From Enron to Lehman Brothers and SOX 2002 to Dodd Frank in 2010, US regulation of securities law and corporate governance has moved from a period of hands-off retreat and consolidation pre-Enron to a compliance state model where companies face strict liability for risk failures and challenges from law enforcement, private litigators, whistleblowers and gatekeepers and an even greater sanction in the form of reputation risk (eg, BP – Deepwater Horizon). The confluence of reputation risk and compliance can be found in the 21 July 2017 announcement that the US Department of the Treasury's Office of Foreign Assets Control assessed a $2 million civil monetary penalty against ExxonMobil Corporation including some of its US subsidiaries for violations of Section 589.201 of the Ukraine-Related Sanctions Regulations, 31 CFR Part 589 – a strict liability standard compliance violation.[3] In its proper context, it has been reported that financial institutions have paid more than $150 billion in fines in the United States relating to the credit crisis, passing a significant milestone a decade after it became clear that American subprime woes had become a global problem.[4]

Having said this, we should first identify what we mean by legal risk. UCL's Richard Moorhead and Steven Vaughan[5] suggest that corporate understandings of legal risk should encompass both the legal consequences of business risk and business risks with legal origins (such as uncertain law or an unsatisfactory legal work product). Along these lines, they argue that such understandings would ordinarily reflect the organisation of the business and the ability to best influence key drivers of risk. One might say that it is not appropriate that legal and/or compliance impose a 'top down' model of legal risk management but rather work with other teams to have a 'seat at the table' to troubleshoot on approaches to legal risk within and outside the company. Both legal and compliance must have the capacity, motivation and resources to be an important source of advice, support and monitoring of risks with legal origins or consequences.

Lawyers generally take the view that the problem

with using one of the several commercially available data-driven tools that quantify case-law research into 'hard maths' (eg, offering win/loss rates, judge ruling histories, litigation trends over time) is that such legal analysis lacks a necessary qualitative element (eg, weighing different cases in an evaluative manner, such that they can be utilised in the context of a courtroom battle). A common refrain from lawyers is that they can never be replaced by computers because computers cannot 'paint a picture' for a jury to understand or draw appropriate inferences from different case outcomes to be able to predict future trends in judge-made law.

Richard Susskind, President of the Society for Computers and Law, has warned the legal profession that artificial intelligence will move forward at such a pace in the coming years that systems will be able to diagnose and respond to clients' legal problems.[6] The legal profession over the next couple of years will transform itself from using 'gut instinct' or 'seat of the pants' thinking to advise on entity-threatening legal risk questions by employing technologies – systems, processes and solutions – that will change the way lawyers advise on matters. So how will lawyers move from being face-to-face advisers to becoming code-savvy problem solvers adept at using technology and artificial intelligence to keep them at the forefront of the businesses they advise? Best practice in the legal profession will evolve to incorporate legal operations at the heart of every major decision that legal advisers will make (whether they are in-house team members or external law firms). These decisions will not only involve legal matters but will also take into account financial management, knowledge management and IT, systems, tools and internal process improvement and internal consulting.[7]

In recent years, the development of risk management standards at a global level such as ISO 31000:2009,[8] a brief and high-level set of principles and guidelines on how to implement risk management, have inspired the legal profession to look to tools and techniques from enterprise risk management to offer a framework and process for managing risk. Closely aligned with the compliance and risk management functions, ISO 31000 can increase the likelihood of achieving objectives, improve the identification of opportunities and threats and effectively allocate and use resources for risk treatment. The ISO 31000:2009 standards came out of the work in enterprise risk management that arose in the United States to take a risk-based approach to managing an enterprise, integrating concepts of internal control, Sarbanes–Oxley Act of 2002 (SOX) compliance and strategic planning to address the needs of various stakeholders who wanted assurance that the broad spectrum of risks facing complex organisations were addressed in a comprehensive and thought-out manner that is appropriately managed.[9] At the time of writing, ISO is now working on developing appropriate international standards for enterprise legal risk management,[10] a further evolving standard for use in analysing specific legal risk-related matters.

There are a wide variety of computer implemented inventions that incorporate dashboards to collect, process and display data thereby allowing for identification of issues such as complaint resolution processes, corporate reporting, cross-business trending, litigation (either against a business or against other competitors in the area) or other sources of information regarding compliance issues.[11] They can be a useful tool in the process of managing data in order to raise issues or offer a benchmark to measure against in compliance management to ensure that compliance requirements and issues are being appropriately addressed. However, there are limitations to dashboard products in that while they alert and record potential risk exposure, they do not mitigate or remediate the risk factors they monitor.

Moreover, dashboard mechanisms suffer from an inherent confirmation bias in that they only monitor that which they are programmed to monitor. As such, they are ill-equipped to address the 'totally wicked problems' that characterise the behavioural problems

A common refrain from lawyers is that they can never be replaced by computers because computers cannot 'paint a picture' for a jury to understand or draw appropriate inferences from different case outcomes to be able to predict future trends in judge-made law.

Human factors and existing technology can inhibit the ability of companies to manage their legal risk portfolio.

that elude dashboard programme developers (eg, the Société Générale 2008 US $7 billion trading loss).[12]

Human factors and existing technology can inhibit the ability of companies to manage their legal risk portfolio. The issue boils down to the ability of legal counsel and managers to look inside and behind the risk they face – trustworthiness and trustfulness come to the fore. Moreover, the technology is only as good as the people who programme it.[13] In this regard, the divide between lawyers and those who write code for applications that lawyers rely upon to engage in legal risk analysis is not helpful. Neither the lawyers nor the engineers should inhabit separate spheres but they usually do. A collaborative and creative environment between the legal, mathematics and technology driven sciences will produce a much more useful tool than one that is developed by a 'top-down' hierarchical product development strategy or a static approach (eg, the lawyers commission a programming company to develop a product in accord with 'black and white' concrete parameters).

The oversimplification of risk parameters and their approximation by using a static approach to the 'system' problematic may leave estimated risk 'probability' without credible scientific evidence resulting in financial loss. Thus, there is the significant possibility that decision-making processes end up relying upon 'facts' based upon non-objective and non-dynamical valuation (predictability) of risks approach.[14] In short, the applied static patterns do not allow for appropriate risk analysis at the operational and *portfolio specific* levels and fail to account for ongoing changes in the entity and operating environment.

This sort of 'risk myopia' underestimates the synergies between legal risk and associated risk categories of an entity's organisational and administrative procedures. This may lead to a distortion not just among the associated risk categories but could be transformative on a causal basis inside the singular legal risk category itself.

Legal risk is not static by nature and logically other risk categories cannot be assumed and treated as static either. This undermines the 'horizon scanning' capacity of the compliance function of a risk management system to provide an offsetting 'minimalising' mechanism to assist in the making of necessary management actions in a timely manner so that reserves set by management are not exceeded.

The categorisation and valuation of legal risks by default ('the similar portfolio' – mythos)[15] makes the assessment of legal risk management nigh impossible leaving us with an approximated overview rather than a precise management tool.

The current ISO engagement to develop appropriate international enterprise risk management standards must incorporate state-of-the-art approaches to assessing and weighting the dynamic nature of legal risks. This suggests that a departure from a linear approach is necessary in order to effectively enhance legal risk management functions by providing a real-time monitoring capacity.

An artificial intelligence system should not replace lawyer expertise but provide them with a powerful tool which can 'paint the picture' realistically and not just qualitatively in a linear manner.

The accuracy of assembled qualitative information can be dubious due to gaps such as a lack of manpower resources, insufficient data obtained and internal data collection shortcomings. This will result in the inability to precisely quantify and evaluate certain legal risks so as to accurately define the financial and commercial aspects of the same, let alone provide real-time monitoring of these risks on a 'going forward' basis.

To highlight the need for quantification of legal qualitative information, consider the following example:

> *We know that the existing legal risk standards that categorise event probabilities can be divided into four groups as 'low', 'medium', 'high' and 'very high' risk categories. We also know at the outset that we face a 'human factors' and biases problem, since those linguistic variables (low, medium etc.) with their respective ambiguities and inaccuracies do not present the precise information needed to determine attributed values and criterion levels properly to estimate precise business risks. Moreover, the estimated probabilities are not based on complex and multidimensional structures existing between the datasets in dynamic entity and environmental settings.*

What this example shows is that there is a need to apply precise information[16] data into legal risk valuation that is essential to appropriately control the system. For instance, to provide the precise datasets needed, we would need to be able to quantify the qualitative information we would input.

The attributes of 'fuzzy logic'[17] are based on natural

language, that is a base of human communication and legal qualitative information. The precise information determined by using fuzzy logic would map the elements of a set A (eg, medium risk) into the interval values [0,1]. The fuzzy function μA(x) = A —> [0,1] represents the element x affiliation to the respective fuzzy set A. In a classical bivalent logic, the μA(x) would just have two values 0 (wrong) or 1 (right) – 'black or white' – that is often the opposite to a common legal problematic.

In sum, it must be recognised that it is not possible to control or govern any system by using incomplete and inaccurate information, hence a case must be made for the generation of information as a fuzzy function in the sense that respective fuzzy sets are able to control the system.

By using fuzzy functions, the linguistic variables, qualitative legal information within the context of dynamical systems will not be assumed and given fixed values, but rather 'all shades of grey' [0,1] or interval values that we may determine by using fuzzy logic will provide a much more precise and objective valuation of a system condition that is scalable and appropriately granular so that they can be utilised by complex organisations. When lawyers 'paint a picture' by using insufficient and qualitative information setting, this implicates a bivalent logic approach in linear terms resulting in some 'slippery parameters' in decision-making processes.

Thinking in terms of internal and external risk categories, 'big data' and its impact and interaction on dynamic entity and environment, 'scrutinised' data valuation and structured datasets are crucial to provide the distinctive need of a beneficial legal risk valuation necessary for sound decision-making processes.

External legal risk evaluation expertise can also have a long-reaching impact on entities affording them the opportunity to shift financial liability through freedom of contract to the service providers offering such evaluations. Nonetheless, the civil and criminal liability for incorrect and/or misleading signed statements presented to regulatory authorities will remain with the actual individuals who signed them (eg, SOX Section 302). As a result, in-house legal counsel may welcome the opportunity to 'hang their hats' (in part) on such external legal risk evaluations in much the same way as they rely on external legal advisers. While this may create a tension between those who are on-site (in-house counsel) and those who are off-site (the external consultants), an issue will remain as to whose job it is to evaluate and quantify legal risk and whose task it is to implement these evaluations on an operational basis in a dynamic organisation.

The legal community – law firms and in-house counsel – should recognise the potential that legal tech may provide for a prosperous and efficient analysis of legal risk. They should embrace the new technologies and use them to make a more informed analysis of legal risk in the C-level suite and the boardroom. While some resistance to the use of fuzzy logic and other artifical intelligence techniques to assist the legal profession to perform their functions more efficiently and accurately is to be expected, a new mindset is needed to embrace the technology.

This, of course, must not come at the cost of traditional qualitative models of legal scrutiny and methodology. The aim to automate organisational processes is useful, so long as the evidence behind the output provided is trustworthy and reliable. This is essential – otherwise in a couple of years' time we will need to address new problems resulting from an over-reliance on quantitative approaches to legal risk management.

Jelena Schidzig, LLM (Stetson) USA, Master of Laws in German and EU law, BS in Computer Science. An expert in legal risk management and AI, Jelena teaches and advises while developing sophisticated public and customized AI-based work tools for industry partners and future-oriented legal education. Jelena is managing partner and legal compliance and regulatory director in the USA and Germany and a member of the Association for Computing Machinery.

Stuart Weinstein, BA Hons, MBA, JD is Reader in Legal Risk Management at Aston Business School, Birmingham. He is co-consulting editor for the Globe Law and Business series on Legal Risk Management and is qualified as a solicitor in England and Wales and as a lawyer in California, District of Columbia and New York including being general counsel at the multinational Daewoo in both Korea and the United States.

1 Natasha Bernal, "Banking and Finance Report: The Balance between Legal and Compliance", *The Lawyer*, 6 June 2016, comments by Leigh Murrin, GE Capital chief legal operations counsel from panel discussion, https://www.thelawyer.com/issues/ 6-june-2016/banking-and-finance-report-the-balance-between-legal-and-compliance/ (accessed 7 August 2017).

2 Geoffrey Miller, "Compliance and Risk Management: Area for Legal Teaching and Scholarship? ", Harvard Law School Forum on Corporate Governance and Financial Regulation, 22 May 2014, https://corpgov.law.harvard.edu/2014/05/22/compliance-and-risk-management-area-for-legal-teaching-and-scholarship/ (accessed 19 July 2017).

3 US Department of the Treasury, "The U.S. Department of the Treasury's Office of Foreign Assets Control Assesses a Civil Monetary

Penalty Against ExxonMobil Corporation", 20 July 2017, https://www.treasury.gov/resource-center/sanctions/OFAC-Enforcement/Pages/20170720.aspx (accessed 7 August 2017).

4 Kara Scannell, "US haul from credit crisis bank fines hits $150bn: Reckoning continues 10 years after housing downturn became market meltdown", *Financial Times*, 7 August 2017, https://www.ft.com/content/71cee844-7863-11e7-a3e8-60495fe6ca71 (accessed 7 August 2017).

5 Richard Moorhead and Steven Vaughan, UCL Faculty of Laws, Ethics Research Centre, "Executive Report on Legal Risk Definition – Management Ethics" (2013), https://www.ucl.ac.uk/laws/law-ethics/research/papers/erc-executive-report-legal-risk-definition-management-ethics.pdf (accessed 1 July 2017).

6 John Hyde, "Susskind: You have five years to reinvent the legal profession", 27 April 2016, *The Law Gazette*, https://www.lawgazette.co.uk/law/susskind-you-have-five-years-to-reinvent-the-legal-profession/5054990.article (accessed 2 July 2017).

7 Reena SenGupta, "Legal operations – the disruptive ambitions of smooth operators: A new type of executive is set to transform company legal teams", *Financial Times*, 21 June 2017, https://www.ft.com/content/61294270-4567-11e7-8d27-59b4dd6296b8?sharetype=share (accessed 2 July 2017).

8 International Organization for Standardization (2017) (ISO), ISO 31000:2009 – Risk management, https://www.iso.org/iso-31000-risk-management.html (accessed 2 July 2017).

9 The Association of Insurance and Risk Managers, Alarm – The Public Risk Managers Association and the Institute of Risk Management (2010), "A structured approach to Enterprise Risk Management (ERM) and the requirements of ISO 31000", http://www.ferma.eu/app/uploads/2011/10/a-structured-approach-to-erm.pdf (accessed 2 July 2017).

10 ISO, ISO/AWI 31022 (2017), "Guidelines for implementation of Enterprise Legal Risk Management", https://www.iso.org/standard/69295.html (accessed 2 July 2017).

11 US Patent Office (2005), US 6912502 B1 (date of grant: 28 June 2005), System and method for compliance management, James J Buddle et al, Inventor, http://www.google.com/patents/US6912502.

12 Nicola Clark and David Jolly, "Société Générale loses $7 billion in trading fraud", 24 January 20008, *The New York Times*, http://www.nytimes.com/2008/01/24/business/worldbusiness/24iht-socgen.5.9486501.html (accessed 2 July 2017).

13 Peter G Neumann, "Inside Risks", *Communications of the ACM*, June 2017, Vol 60 No 6 (quoting: Risks of believing in computer trustworthiness: "Indeed, computers can be made to lie, cheat, or steal. In such cases, of course, the faults may ordinate with or be amplified by people who commission systems, or design them, or program them, or even just use them, but not with computers themselves"), p27.

14 N Taleb, "Fooled by Randomness" (quoting CP Cavafy (1915): "... ordinary people thinks in present, but the wise perceive things about to happen", 2nd edn, 2007, p67).

15 Michael Stonebraker, "Big Data", *Communication of the ACM*, June 2017, Vol 60 No 6 (quoting: "The trouble with predictive models is that they are built by humans, and humans are by nature prone to bias"), p25.

16 J Schidzig, "Legal – Engineering: Fuzzy Logic in Legal Analysis", MT, 9 March 2017, p93.

17 Lofti A Zadeh, "What is Fuzzy Logic and What Does it Have to Offer?" (quoting: "There are many misconceptions about fuzzy logic. To begin with fuzzy logic is not fuzzy. ... Fuzzy logic is designed to deal with imperfect information that is the norm in a real world rather than the exception"), World Congress on Engineering and Computer Science (WCECS, 2014). See also, Timothy J Ross, *Fuzzy Logic with Engineering Applications*, 3rd edn (John Wiley, 2010).

The lazy lawyer's guide to winning new business
Genuine leads. Less time. Less money. What's not to love about marketing automation?

Rebecca Harding and Andrew Nicholson

As technology and data overtake many areas of our lives, two experienced writers, and digital consultants examine how more sophisticated use of technology combined with analysis of what your clients and potential clients are reading could produce a winning strategy that will be right in line with the ways we now live and work. The article also contains a valuable overview of different marketing automation platforms and their utility.

Getting a grip on technology

With the recent rise of COVID-19 and the implications of social distancing, we have all been forced to embrace technology in a way that we have never done before. Solicitors are experimenting with virtual backgrounds on Zoom for their team meetings and barristers are even using Skype for court hearings!

We will never go back to the way we were before simply because we now have more confidence in our abilities to use technology. We have been forced to make a (some would argue much-needed) step change. Our IT abilities have been stretched further than we imagined. Our firms have put new technologies in place quickly and made it work, because we had to. This current situation will fundamentally change the way we work, the way we use technology in our firms, and will make even the most nervous partner among us embrace technology in a different way.

The technology we've been introducing recently has allowed day-to-day business to be conducted differently. Many partners are seeing the benefits in terms of cost and time savings in using technology solutions rather than being dependent on offices, meetings, seminars etc.

Everyone is producing webinars. Team meetings and training have taken place on Zoom. Even successful pitches for business have taken place over the internet. In fact, two firms have recently commented that they are not sure they need offices any more, having experienced and benefited from this transition.

The problem with networking ...

Historically, professional services firms have relied heavily on face-to-face relationships to deliver new client opportunities, whether that be through word-of-mouth recommendations, golf club connections or the ubiquitous networking events that take place the length and breadth of Britain. Social interaction has always been key to generating new business.

The reality is that these methods are hugely time-consuming and expensive. It is often difficult to identify those targets and clients who are truly interested in what we offer, and those who are just being polite, particularly at networking events or corporate hospitality. They are also non-scalable. In other words, the only way you can increase the number of people that you reach is by throwing more of your people at the problem, which in business terms is very restrictive.

There will always be a place for face-to-face networking, but how do we extend our scope and reach more people quickly? How do we reach people who are genuinely interested in the services that we are offering? Importantly, how do we reach them before somebody else does?

Now, in the face of the COVID-19 pandemic, we are having to find new methods, as the traditional ones have been stopped for us.

Old methods meet new methods

Until now, we have been experiencing a clash of methodology within firms. The old, tried-and-tested, and the new technologies. Younger generation meets older generation. Fundamentally, we know that people buy people. Professional services has always been about developing strong personal relationships and, more importantly, an excellent reputation.

The world is now far more dependent on receiving its information via the internet and through electronic marketing methods. Whether by email or social media, they have become the everyday norm for all of us in our own personal lives.

Even those of us who would say that we are not particularly tech savvy would agree that we are now used to receiving information about suppliers, resources and businesses in this way. COVID-19 has caused an explosion in online activity of this nature. People are even doing online workouts provided by their gyms! But is this really so different to the old methods?

All the messages in the communications are the same, if they are done properly, it is simply the communication channel that has changed. And that's all that digital is – a new communication channel, but one that is clever, responsive and makes our lives much easier. It can also allow us to show very clearly, and to a much larger audience, who we are and what we are about.

However, even though the channels have changed, it is still just as important to write material with an interest hook from the client's point of view rather than from the lawyer's. Poor quality content leads to poor quality response. Lawyers often fall into the trap of being too technical or selling too much and not thinking through their message from their target's point of view.

Building digital relationships

Digital marketing can allow you to develop a much more tailored approach to individuals and a deeper relationship with your target. Not only that, but a large number of people under the age of 35 now see digital information as an integral part of their everyday lives. Digital platforms are where they seek and check out professionals and make decisions as to whether they are credible.

According to Forrester research (forrester.com), for every traditional marketing contact from a firm, B2B buyers will seek out three alternative sources of information. Therefore, a firm can best increase its visibility, strengthen its reputation and build its brand by sharing content, demonstrating thought leadership and clarifying its sales message through digital channels.

Marketing techniques have often been frowned upon, associated as they are with the realm of consumer marketing where spin and hyperbole have sometimes been the name of the game, rather than the serious business of reputation and relationship building. However, the new approach of marketing automation allows law firms to demonstrate their expertise and build a personal relationship with the targets using technology as the primary platform.

Marketing automation versus email marketing

One key point to take on board here is that there is a big difference between marketing automation and simply sending out marketing emails.

Historically, email marketing has been used as a mass media broadcast mechanism. Firms were, and are, guilty of regularly spraying out thousands, if not hundreds of thousands, of emails, in the expectation that a small percentage of those emails would resonate with a tiny number of people. These people might, if the firm is lucky, get in touch about the service. 'Fingers-crossed' marketing.

We justified this with the idea that it might improve our brand reputation in its own right, but with no way of measuring return on our investment. We had no way of knowing whether people were genuinely interested in what we were sending out or not. We didn't even know if we were reaching any relevant people.

Email marketing to this day is still widely acknowledged as one of the top return on investment (ROI) generating marketing channels and so is arguably very successful in comparison to older methods. However, this approach also delivers largely irrelevant communications to the greater percentage of the target audience, most of the time. At best, this can prove an annoying distraction, and at worst, can result in them

Email marketing to this day is still widely acknowledged as one of the top return on investment (ROI) generating marketing channels and so is arguably very successful in comparison to older methods.

Understanding a client's specific requirements or problems, and communicating these back to them in the form of appropriate advice and a relevant service approach is critical to successful client relationships.

unsubscribing from the communications altogether, damaging your contact lists.

Where it goes wrong

To put this into context, let's imagine that you've just had your will written. During the process, you signed up to the firm's family law newsletter. Now, at the time of sign up, your interest in wills was high. You were actively using the will service and over the next few days wills were no doubt high on your agenda, so receiving emails about wills was fine.

The following week, however, your will is finished and signed, and wills are now the last thing on your mind. Not only are emails about wills now completely irrelevant to you, but over time, if sent regularly enough, they may start to become annoying and damage the relationship the family law department has with you. After all, they know you now have a will!

The law firm could, of course, overcome this by only sending out emails at points in time when they know you'll again be interested in family matters. Key dates, such as New Year, or the end of the tax year, are perfectly justifiable trigger events for sending out email communications about various family matters. However, by only using such generic dates, there is a high risk of lost opportunity. There are always personal needs and imminent life changes that could trigger service needs throughout the year.

Bring in the new technology

This is where marketing automation steps in. Marketing automation is a technology that enables you to listen and respond to your audience with relevant, timely and highly targeted communications.

In the 'will' example, marketing automation might be used to trigger promotional emails, not just on key dates, but also when the customer expresses interest in products or services, by, for instance, viewing a specific web page, or downloading a particular brochure/guide that you have sent out as a thought leadership or information piece. This addition of behavioural tracking ensures a dialogue, rather than a monologue, is maintained. In other words, you are not just bombarding them with any email. Instead, the technology is actively monitoring the client's online 'body language' and what they are showing an interest in, and responding with tailored and relevant communications accordingly.

80% see an increase in leads

While this approach ultimately means less emails are being sent than through traditional email marketing, the communications that are dispatched are far more relevant and more appropriately timed. As a result, 80% of marketing automation users see their number of leads increase, and 77% see their number of conversions increase (VB Insight, "Marketing automation, how to make the right buying decision", 2015).

If we can track services the client has been looking at online, monitor the free guides he is downloading, or the content that he is reading for information, then we can offer highly specific services that we know, for a fact, are relevant to that client and are at the top of his or her mind at the current time.

For example, if in the current circumstances a client or target is reading material online about insolvency or options to save their business, then we know the insolvency and restructuring services are the ones that we should be offering them through personalised contact. We know it is relevant for them and timing is crucial when winning a client for these sorts of services. Marketing automation allows us to respond with a speed and accuracy of targeting that we have not been able to achieve before. It also allows us to follow-up with this identified target and engage in relevant conversations. We can establish a human relationship at exactly the right time for them.

Understanding a client's specific requirements or problems, and communicating these back to them in the form of appropriate advice and a relevant service approach is critical to successful client relationships. A high level of personal attention is key when supporting a paying client. However, when prospecting for new clients, providing a high level of one-to-one attention is very hard to achieve, and not at all scalable. You will never be able to reach large numbers.

Marketing automation provides the ability for you to generate and maintain one-to-one communications at scale. Indeed, the top three marketing automation techniques used by all professional services firms are email automation (64%), profiling and targeting (26%), and personalisation using dynamic content (23%) (SmartInsights and Getresponse, "Email marketing and marketing automation excellence 2018", 2018).

One step further

We have already discussed how marketing automation technology tracks a client's behaviour across your digital channels (email marketing, website etc). Well, marketing automation technology enables firms to go a step further. If we know who is reading our web and email content, then we can dynamically adapt that content to best fit the needs of the reader. For example, you can address the content to the Head of Legal and talk about their role and how the issue applies to them personally throughout the content. You are addressing their problem. The automation will adapt the text to different job titles automatically for you, provided you have given it the options and quality, personalised content to use.

For firms with diverse client services, this is of particular benefit. It lets you deliver 'dynamically' generated (generated digitally in a responsive way) and service-specific content to their site visitors. So, each site visitor receives unique content geared towards their own personal requirements.

Saving time and money

If you've ever spent hours, or even days, sorting and processing client data in Excel spreadsheets in order to be able to send out a communication, then the argument for automation is probably already won. Today, 'Middle Man' technology platforms, such as Mulesoft and Zapier, complete this work for you, consolidating data from lots of different sources into your marketing automation system in real time. Setting it all up can be done with just a few clicks of a button. Easy.

Middle Man technology platforms work by having a standard set of 'protocols' (triggers and activity) that all modern communications platforms can adhere to. As long as the communication technology you have chosen has a hook into this Middle Man technology, the Middle Man can pass your data to any other platform within their ecosystem (ie, that they integrate with or partner with) in a fully automated process.

At the last count, the industry leader in Middle Man technology, Zapier.com, had over 2,000 third-party apps contained within their 'ecosystem'. If you're signing up to new software, we would strongly recommend checking to see if your new purchase is on their list of partners and integrating software.

It goes without saying that integration of technology is essential for automation success. Your marketing automation platform cannot, and should not, exist in a bubble. For it to realise its full potential, it must be connected, at the very least, to your customer relationship management (CRM) platforms and website content management system (CMS), and at best, interwoven across all your communication platforms.

The time-saving and efficiency benefits of integrating and automating your data and communications are clear.

Marketing automation platforms are 'always on', therefore constantly synchronising and updating your client, prospect and partner data in the background. This removes the burdensome requirement to cleanse, update, transfer and input data manually. Most of us would cheer at that prospect!

In fact, a 2015 report by Adestra found that 74% of marketers report saving time as the primary benefit of marketing automation (Adestra, "Marketer vs machine", 2015).

Proven leads – hitting the right targets

Modern law firms are already benefiting from marketing automation efficiencies. New client outreach has always been a process fraught with inefficiency. Marketing automation overcomes this by scoring prospective clients using both geo-demographic data (job title, seniority, location, company size etc) and behavioural data (web page views, email engagement, brochure and

If you've ever spent hours, or even days, sorting and processing client data in Excel spreadsheets in order to be able to send out a communication, then the argument for automation is probably already won.

Too often professional services firms fall into the trap of being too technical, too formal or too salesy. If the content that is being sent to clients currently is poor quality, then simply adding marketing automation will not make it any better.

report views etc). The combined total of these scores is known as a 'lead score'.

The lead score provides a 'sales readiness' rating, ie how receptive are they to buying your services. These ratings can be used to concentrate and prioritise your outbound call activity. When combined with the behavioural insight provided by marketing automation's tracking and analytics capabilities, client outreach calls become informed. You know what services and solutions the client is actively looking for now. It is also efficient. You only call people you know are genuinely interested. You are knocking on an open door.

Lead score alerts are triggered by your marketing automation system in real time. They are interested in the time your client communications take place and when the client is most engaged, not when you, or someone in business development, works their way through to that client from an alphabetised, static list.

What are the potential pitfalls?

What are the things to look out for if you are going to introduce marketing automation into your firm?

Many firms suffer from poor quality data, in other words client lists or databases that are fragmented, duplicated, are not standardised and have typing mistakes etc. The introduction of the GDPR legislation did lead to a big clean-up of firm databases and ensured that old data was deleted. However, errors, duplication and different layouts are still common.

Unfortunately, automated marketing is only as good as the data you have and so it can lead to poor targeting. This means your 'reach' will not be as good, ie you won't reach as many people as you want to with the right, relevant information. You will not be able to achieve personalisation in the same way, and personalisation is the primary benefit of marketing automation optimisation.

Despite having access to great digital capabilities, one of most common problems seen is the production of poor content. Too often professional services firms fall into the trap of being too technical, too formal or too salesy. If the content that is being sent to clients currently is poor quality, then simply adding marketing automation will not make it any better. Mastering the art of writing a 'story' with an interest 'hook' from the client's point of view is the key. So often material is written from the lawyer's point of view.

As a result of this oversight, the material does not look interesting when received by the target, does not have an interesting hook, does not educate on an issue that is truly relevant to the target and does not add value. The worst thing is that the author has often spent a long time writing it.

One of the key hurdles for some platforms used for generating marketing automation is the fact that they need to be integrated into the law firm's IT systems. This can often seem like a mountain not worth climbing. Adding in another IT system to an already complex mesh can seem an impossible task. There are so many other internal systems that it will need to integrate with. This in itself leads to crossover with many different areas of the firm, so permissions need to be granted and the required sign-offs can be extensive. There can be a lot of passive resistance and a non-acceptance of change. Sometimes firms don't have the tech capability at the right level to introduce a new platform. One firm recently launched their first CRM system which has taken some nine years to develop and instal. Of course, it is already out of date.

How to choose the right technology for marketing automation

'Marketing automation' is a term that encompasses a huge range of technologies, budgets and approaches. How do you know which solution provides the best fit for your firm?

Often, this comes down to a choice between what is known as 'best of breed', or 'single vendor solution'. The approach you choose is a decision that needs to be taken early on in your journey.

Single vendor solutions, as the name implies, offer a full range of marketing communication technologies within a single IT suite. Going beyond standalone marketing automation, single vendor solutions will often also encompass CRM and CMS technologies (as

	Best of breed	Single vendor solution
Cost	**Low.** A basic single 'stack' solution, encompassing marketing automation, CRM, CMS and Middle Man software can be built and maintained for as little as a few hundred pounds a month.	**High.** Built for enterprise customers with enterprise budgets. Costs can run anywhere from a few thousand per month, to tens of thousands per month.
Commitment	**Short term.** Best of breed SaaS (cloud-based) products often come with rolling monthly commitments, and functionality can be added/removed on demand.	**Long term.** Normally a minimum of one-year commitment, but can be anywhere up to three years.
Support	**Fractured.** Each solution will have its own dedicated support team, and their comprehension of your integrated stack will be limited. Each support team will take responsibility for their own solution, but not others within the stack, which may result in finger-pointing and deferral of responsibility.	**Holistic.** A single point of contact will normally be provided who will deal with all queries, before passing them onto dedicated experts within the supplier business. Single point of contact means the buck stops with the vendor.
Complexity	**Flexible.** In the right hands, a best of breed communications stack can become highly advanced. However, complexity should be avoided wherever possible and building a simple stack solution using tools such as Zapier can be a relatively easy task.	**Complex.** Despite a single point of contact, implementing a single vendor solution is a highly complex project that will cover all areas of the business. It is often necessary to bring in third-party consultants with specialised knowledge to implement the technology and culture changes required.
Time frame	**Days/weeks.** Drag and drop tools and easy integration mean that simple best of breed solutions can be set up very quickly. However, by its nature, best of breed will evolve over time, and should therefore always be considered a work in progress, as technology progresses, new suppliers come into the marketplace and requirements change.	**Months.** Larger integrations involving CRM, marketing automation and web can take between six and 18 months to implement. The larger the organisation, the more complex the requirements, and the longer the project times.
Responsibilities	**Individual.** Can often be implemented by an individual with marketing technology experience and senior support.	**Cross-party.** Will require championing from senior leadership teams across divisions, as well as dedicated resources within the organisation to implement and manage.

mentioned above), and may even go as far as including back office support functions. These large, complex platforms are generally seen as enterprise grade products, and come with correspondingly large price tags, but they do offer a one-stop solution to all your needs. On the flip side of this, just because you have a feature-rich toolset at your disposal, doesn't necessarily mean you will be using all the tools in your toolbox, and customers of single vendor solutions can often find they are paying for lots of tools that they simply don't use.

At the other end of the spectrum, we find the best of breed approach to marketing automation systems. Generally better suited to and used more frequently by smaller firms, the best of breed simply means taking a 'pick-and-mix approach' to marketing automation software. It allows you to cherry-pick the functionality you require from the thousands of individual solutions available, and connect them all together using Middle Man technology platforms. The benefit of using a best of breed solution is that you get exactly the marketing automation 'stack' (combination) that you want. It is also far cheaper than a single vendor solution. The down side to this approach is that you need the resource and skills in house to work out and research the solution in the first place.

To better understand how best of breed and single vendor solutions compare, please see the chart on the next page.

For firms looking for Best of Breed flexibility, functionality and pricing, but without a in-house resource to build their own automated new client outreach programmes, it should be noted that there are a number of professional agencies and consultancies specialising in legal and professional services outreach that can assist with building, supporting and running your communication automations.

Make sure you have a strategy

When choosing your solution, whether best of breed/single vendor, or DIY/third-party led, ensure you define your strategy first. Document your objectives, required tactics and what you need it to do, expected outcomes and responsibilities, and use these as a checklist for selecting your technological partners. Be sure to check for any upfront onboarding fees, as well as ongoing monthly costs, and be sure to review the levels/costs of support on offer.

Red flags to watch out for when buying in to marketing automation technology include:

- The solution doesn't talk to other solutions. If in doubt, go to https://zapier.com/apps/ integrations and search for the technology by name. If it's not featured as a Zapier partner, it's highly suggestive that the technology isn't going to integrate easily with other platforms.
- The solution isn't well received by its users. There are literally thousands of different marketing technology and communications applications available. Keeping track of which ones are fit for purpose is a never-ending task. This is why there are dedicated sites designed for just this purpose. We recommend using G2Crowd to compare notes with others, paying special attention to the set up and ease-of-use scores.
- There are additional non-advertised costs for use. A cheap platform is no use if you then need to employ a dedicated team of expensive consultants to implement your strategy and the platform! Check with the vendor what support is available as part of your subscription, and speak with other customers (or at least check out their reviews – see above) to better understand how intuitive the software is to use.
- Functionality creep. SEO, Instagram posting, Image filtering – the list of available functionality in some solutions is astounding. Before you start looking at solutions, make sure you have a clear list of features/benefits that you need to have, and try not to be distracted by 'shiny' features which you may never use. Even if you don't use them, you will still be paying for them.

Dive in!

With the current sea change in thinking about technology and the willingness to embrace new methods, now is the time to dive in. We have all seen the potential of what we can achieve in the work environment. It is a perfect springboard to improve our client targeting and increase our expectations in terms of generating real leads to new business.

So, let's be lazy about new client generation and get started. There is literally no time like the present.

Rebecca Harding MCIPR, MCIM, FSWWJ is the founder of Saltwhistle and Worldwide Chair of the Society of Women Writers and Journalists. Rebecca's professional services clients have ranged from to Norton Rose Fulbright, DAC Beachcroft, Weightmans and Stephenson Harwood to Deloittes, PWC and WPP, as well as some two-partner firms! Previously, Rebecca was responsible for communications at Andersen. She can be contacted at rebecca@saltwhistle.com or on 07966 459080.

Andrew Nicholson MSc, DipM is CEO and founder of Kulea.ma – marketing automation and founder/owner of The Guku – digital consultancy. Andrew is a Former B2B Marketer of the Year and founder of the UK's Best Emerging B2B Martech platform, Kulea.ma. Andrew's experience in marketing automation specifically, and digital marketing in general, puts him at the forefront of the move towards digitisation. Prior to launching his own consultancy and marketing automation platform, Andrew was head of Online at Sodexo. He can be contatced at andrew@kulea.ma or on 07890 552 441.

The demystification of legal AI

Uwais Iqbal

AI seems to be on the tips of everyone's tongues. With such a complex and new technology, it's easy to get drawn into the hype and hysteria. The sad but unfortunate reality is that not many people really understand what AI is, nor do they know how to speak about it or think about its applications in the legal sector. We want to change that. AI has already started to penetrate our personal lives and it is only a matter of time before it becomes ubiquitous in our professional lives. AI is coming and we should embrace this new technology in a posture of knowledge and transparency instead of ignorance and hype. This article defines what AI is, explores how to think about AI, and shows how it can be applied in the legal industry.

Defining Artificial Intelligence

Let's take a moment to define our terms. There tend to be plenty of buzzwords and jargon floating around with AI. You've probably heard terms like Machine Learning, Deep Learning, and Natural Language Processing being thrown about. Let's actually define what we mean by these terms so we're not just throwing around empty words and adding to the hype and hysteria.

In 1956, one of the founding fathers of AI, John McCarthy, defined artificial intelligence as *'machines that can perform tasks that are characteristic of human intelligence'*. What is meant by *human intelligence* in the definition is a bit opaque.

We can take a crack at the definition and think of artificial intelligence as a *'technique that uses machines to replicate the problem-solving and decision-making capabilities of the human mind'*. The artificial part means that it's pure mimicry and imitation. The intelligence part means that it captures some human ability of problem-solving or decision-making.

The natural question that arises is: *How are machines leveraged to mimic the capabilities of the human mind?* The answer to this question gives rise to two different ways AI can be done:

- **Machine Learning.** One way is through *data*. This gives us Machine Learning. It involves using data to teach machines how to perform specific tasks that a human can do.
- **Rules-based.** Another way is through encoding expected behaviour through a series of rules alongside a system of domain

knowledge. This gives us rules-based AI. Expert systems are an example of a rules-based AI system.

How AI is used in language

There are a few different senses of AI that we can draw out from how AI is normally spoken about and used in everyday language:

- **Technology.** AI tends to get used to refer to the overall technology. It's used in a very general sense to capture various applications of AI. You might hear someone say, *'AI will come to change how we work'*. What they mean by AI here is the general technology. It's kind of like how you might speak about the internet, computers, or smartphones in a general sense.
- **Field of academic study.** AI can be used to refer to a field of academy study and an area of research within computer science. That's the theory part in the definition. You might hear someone say, *'I just completed my master's in AI'*. What they mean by AI here is the field of academic study, just like biology, chemistry, or physics.
- **Machine Learning.** AI can also be loosely used in place of Machine Learning. For now, you can think of Machine Learning as leveraging data to train a computer to perform a particular task without giving it explicit instructions. You might hear someone say, *'We trained an AI model to detect images of dogs'*. When AI is used in this sense, it's synonymous with Machine Learning and is used interchangeably. This is where it gets a bit confusing because if you're not careful you might think AI is just Machine Learning and nothing more. But AI is much more than just Machine Learning.
- **Superintelligence.** AI also gets used in the futuristic sci-fi sense of superintelligence; a sentient being that has developed a level of intelligence superior to human intelligence. You might hear someone say, *'AI will come to control our lives'*. We don't have machines that are super-intelligent and whether we will get there is a question of debate. When AI is used in this sense, it's future looking and purely hypothetical.

The kinds of AI

A common categorisation of the different kinds of AI is based on what the AI system is capable of doing. Researchers usually break AI down into two kinds: Strong AI and Weak AI.

- **Strong AI.** Strong AI refers to an AI system that has reached a level of human intelligence. The system can learn, perceive, understand, and function completely like a human being. At the moment, we haven't developed such systems, so Strong AI is still something purely theoretical. Strong AI is also known as *General AI* or *Artificial General intelligence (AGI)*. Many researchers are still sceptical as to whether Strong AI systems are even possible.
- **Weak AI.** Weak AI refers to an AI system that can perform a specific and precise task, such as extracting a field from a contract or clustering a set of documents. The AI systems we have today are all examples of Weak AI. Weak AI is also known as *Narrow AI.*

What do Machine Learning, Natural Language Processing, and Deep Learning have to do with AI?

We've already seen that Machine Learning (ML) is a branch of AI that *uses data to enable machines to learn how to perform specific tasks as a human would.* ML uses data.

We don't have machines that are super-intelligent and whether we will get there is a question of debate.

Natural Language Processing (NLP) is another branch of AI that *enables computers to understand human language in both written and verbal forms*. NLP looks at language. NLP is of particular relevance to legal because the underlying medium of the legal profession is text.

Deep Learning is a branch of Machine Learning where algorithms are made up of several layers of neurons to mimic the structure of the brain to allow patterns to be learnt from data. Deep Learning uses neural networks with data.

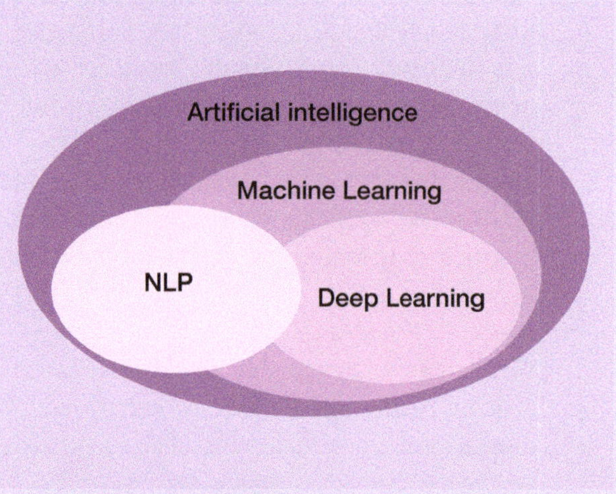

Will AI replace lawyers?

You've probably heard the claim that *'AI will replace lawyers'*. It certainly grabs attention and is great for headlines. But is there any truth to that claim? As we've seen, AI can be used in different senses and there are different kinds of AI. Which sense of AI does this claim use and which kind of AI is this claim referring to? Take a moment to review the different senses and see if you can figure it out.

The claim that *'AI will replace lawyers'* uses AI in the sense of *superintelligence*. It's obvious that if we had AI systems that were as intelligent as humans we could replace lawyers with AI counterparts. The reality is that AI systems aren't that smart. In effect, it's a claim about *Strong AI*. Strong AI systems are still a theoretical estimation – we don't know if we'll ever get to a point where machines are just as intelligent and capable as human beings. Lawyers are still around today despite Weak AI systems being used in the legal sector for a number of years. I don't think we'll ever get to Strong AI, so it's fair to say that lawyers won't be going anywhere!

AI in industry

Now we have developed some grounding in the terms related to AI, we can take a step further to explore how AI is used in industry.

Contexts of doing AI

It's worth noting that there are different contexts for where AI can be done. There are two main contexts that we need to be aware of:

- **A research context.** AI carried out in a research context pushes forward the boundaries of what is possible and steps into the unknown. AI in a research context is usually carried out in university departments and at big tech R&D labs. Much of the work is done through experiments under ideal circumstances with colossal datasets and virtually unlimited budgets and resources.
- **An industry context.** AI in industry is quite different to a research context. Datasets are rarely ever clean and complete, there are stakeholders to manage, and everything has to be done yesterday. Much of the AI work in industry is *applied research*. The goal is not to venture into the unknown and develop something completely new. Rather, the focus is on taking what has already been created in a research context and applying it to new and different problems in an industry context. It usually takes some time, in the order of years, for advances in AI research to trickle down into applications in industry.

Take the recent uproar around Chat-GPT. Chat-GPT is an AI model developed by Open AI that is currently in open beta for testing with the public. Chat-GPT is an example of AI in a research context – there are virtually no restrictions around data privacy or confidentiality and it was trained on a virtually unlimited budget. It will be a while before Chat-GPT makes its way into industry-focused software and applications.

Thinking about applied AI

We are interested in how AI can be used in an

industry context. One intuitive way to think about applied AI in an industry context is to think of it as a way to *capture* and *scale* expertise. There are things that you as a human have to do because they require a level of learned skill or expertise. Take, for example, identifying the termination clause in a contract. You can train an AI system by teaching it what a termination clause looks like so that it *captures* your expertise. Then, since the AI system is a machine, you can scale it to operate at volume and find the termination clause in a massive collection of contracts.

Employing AI for a job

All this talk about AI is great. But how can I tell if AI can be used to help me in my day-to-day legal work? An easy way to answer this question is to think about AI as though it has some sort of agency. Of course, we mean this in a metaphorical sense. Literally speaking, an AI algorithm is just a bunch of numbers. Thinking about AI as though it has agency means you should behave with AI as you would with a person with a particular skill set. You wouldn't randomly employ a complete stranger into your team just because she is popular. So why do we try and do the same with AI?

Before hiring someone into our team, we'd usually sit down and think about what skills, traits, and experience the right person would have. Then we'd interview a bunch of applicants and decide who best fits our requirements. Only then would we hire them into our team and onboard them to make sure they are as effective as possible. We have to undertake a similar process with AI. We have to define a job spec, evaluate potential algorithms and, when we find one that works, we have to work to integrate it within the wider team and organisation.

Legal AI actions

We tend to see AI as this all-encompassing technology that can solve all of our problems. This is far from the truth. We have to think about AI in the same way we think about hiring a new employee who can come into our organisation to carry out a very particular and precise job. So the question that naturally arises is what jobs can AI do? We can characterise an AI solution by what action it can perform, i.e. the job it can do. Within Legal AI there are a small number of relevant actions that AI can perform well.

- **Extract.** Extract involves using AI to extract key pieces of information from a passage of text. A typical use case involves using AI to extract key fields such as the parties and termination date from a contract.
- **Compare.** Compare involves using AI to compare two passages of texts to spot any differences between them. These passages of text could be sentences, clauses, or even entire documents. A typical use case involves using AI to compare a drafted clause against a playbook standard to identify any risky deviations.

You wouldn't randomly employ a complete stranger into your team just because she is popular. So why do we try and do the same with AI?

- **Organise.** Organise involves using AI to organise a collection of texts (clauses or documents) so that similar texts are identified and grouped together. A typical use case involves using AI to organise documents during discovery so related documents are grouped together.
- **Label.** Label involves using AI to provide a label to a passage of text. This passage of text could be a sentence, clause, or document. A typical use case involves using AI to label a document by its document type or a clause by its clause type. Or, labelling a document against a predefined taxonomy for knowledge management purposes.
- **Find.** Find involves using AI to find relevant texts among a large collection of text using a

query. A typical use case involves using AI to find the most relevant cases during legal research.

- **Draft.** Draft involves using AI to draft and generate text. A typical use case involves using AI to draft a clause in a contract.
- **Summarise.** Summarise involves using AI to create a summary from a text. A typical use case involves using AI to summarise a case judgment into a headnote.
- **Forecast.** Forecast involves using AI to forecast a numeric quantity. A typical use case involves using AI to forecast billing or spend for a matter.

Legal AI functions

We've seen that AI can perform particular and precise actions, e.g. to extract information or classify a document. There is also another aspect concerning the approach. In other words, how will AI be used to carry out the particular task at hand? It's a common fallacy to conflate AI with automation. AI can be used to automate an action, but there are other functions AI can perform depending on the circumstance.

To better understand the functions AI can perform, we need to introduce two concepts:

- **Volume** – given a particular task, volume captures the number of times the task is to be performed.

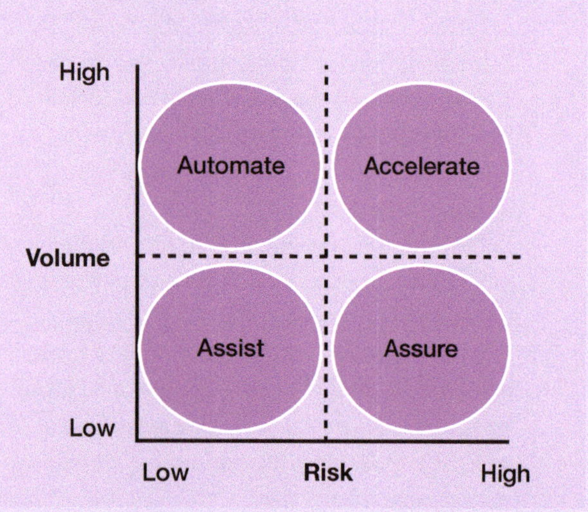

- **Risk** – given a particular task, risk captures the potential cost of a mistake. This can either be in terms of financial cost or cost to reputation.

We can now put together a risk-volume matrix to understand the different approaches of AI. The risk/volume matrix is a framework for determining the function AI can perform under different scenarios with respect to risk and volume.

There are four different AI functions:

- **Automate.** AI can be used in *high-volume, low-risk* scenarios to automate tasks and reduce human capital. High volume means that AI can be leveraged to scale expertise in performing a particular task where otherwise vast resources of human capital would be needed. Low risk means that the penalty or cost of the AI making a mistake is very low. In such circumstances, AI can be trained to scale expertise for a particular task and automate the task, thereby reducing dependency on human capital. A typical use case involves using AI to automate the extraction of fields from a set of contracts.
- **Assure.** AI can be used in *low-volume, high-risk* scenarios to provide assurance in tasks and increase confidence. Low volume means that the human will always be relevant in such tasks. High risk means that making a mistake and getting things wrong is very costly. As a result, AI can play a role to support the human to provide assurance in such tasks. A typical example involves conducting legal research. AI can be used to ensure that no relevant cases have been missed during legal research and help provide peace of mind that all bases have been covered.
- **Accelerate.** AI can be used in *high-volume, high-risk* scenarios to accelerate jobs and improve efficiency. High volume means that AI can be leveraged to scale expertise in performing a particular task where otherwise vast resources of human capital would be needed. High risk means that making a mistake and getting things wrong is very costly. In such circumstances, the human

and machine work in collaboration to reach the desired objective in a shorter time span. AI plays a role to speed up the usual workflow of a legal professional, creating efficiencies and completing tasks quicker. A typical use case of acceleration is during contract review. AI can be used to highlight and surface deviations in wording that may be risky to reduce the time it takes for a lawyer to review the contract and accelerate contract negotiations.

- **Assist.** AI can be used in low-volume, low-risk scenarios to provide assistance in performing certain tasks. Low volume means that these tasks are menial, and the human will always be relevant. Low risk means that there isn't a big penalty if a mistake is made. In these situations, AI can provide support and assist with basic tasks. A typical example would include the use of AI chatbots, much like ChatGPT, to assist in routine administrative and editorial tasks that tend to take up lots of time.

Getting clear on the function AI should perform will inform the choice of model, the extent of user interaction, as well as the data requirements for the AI model.

The *AI action* can be combined with the *AI function* to create an *AI job spec* that captures what the AI should do and how it should do it. The AI job spec should also capture what the minimum acceptable performance is so that the AI, just as every other employee, can be assessed on whether it is succeeding or failing at its job.

Closing thoughts

We tend to fear what we don't understand. Technology is already complex enough and AI shifts how we look at the world. We are all using the same buzzwords but are speaking entirely different languages. The first step to adopting and embracing such a radically novel and revolutionary technology like AI is to develop the language and ideas so we can think about and speak about AI in a meaningful way. Undoubtedly, there are endless applications where AI can be applied in legal but we will never be ready for that revolution if we speak different languages.

"The Revolution will be complete when the language is perfect." 1984, George Orwell

Uwais Iqbal has over half a decade worth of experience designing, building, and delivering Machine Learning and NLP solutions across leading legal tech start-ups and a corporate innovation lab. He has held roles as a Machine Learning engineer at Eigen Technologies, and as a senior NLP data scientist at Thomson Reuters Labs and ThoughtRiver. He is the founder of simplexico, the legal AI consultancy dedicated to serving the AI, ML, and NLP needs of the legal sector.

Data Bites Back

Joanne Brook

Big Data is not about the data

"Big Data is not about the data", Harvard University professor Gary King observed in 2016,[1] and went on to note that data is a largely free-to-use byproduct of the digital economy. Whilst the scale of it is exponential, the key to "Big Data" is new ways with analytics and statistical methods, new computer science methodology, and groundbreaking approaches to application of these to analysis.

As Big Data is not about the data but about the ability to analyse it, as lawyers we can draw parallels with the knowledge bank of precedent and practice we all carry with us in our professional lives – that ability to identify trends and borrow from different disciplines and to use a single fact or observation to turn a case or someone's perspective around.

With Big Data analysis it is as much about the snapshot from accurately observed small data sets as the ability to glean information from the aggregation of these snippets to create a "bigger picture" in large data sets. The complex algorithms that process the snippets, the slosh, and the parsed data are so advanced that they can be used to teach machines to think in human-like ways, or even (if we can believe the AI hype) as well or better than humans. Big Data has paved the way for AI of course, providing the vast banks of training data necessary for machine learning, all taken from the snippets that people and businesses throw into the ether of the internet.

Each piece of data spawns another and each year, the data gets bigger. So how big is Big Data?

Google (other search engines are available)

processes nearly 100,000 searches a second – a second! The are 86,400 seconds in a day or 8,460,000,000, give or take, every day. How do I know that? I asked Google and my question is one of the queries that forms this answer in a symbiotic helical data call and response.

Internet users generate 2.5 quintillion bytes of data every day. It is predicted that, overall, the amount of data generated every day will rise to 181 zettabytes a day by 2025. Figures such as this are not my strong suit, but I can tell you that 181 zettabytes is a whopping 10^{21} (if you prefer long-hand, that's 1,000,000,000,000,000,000,000 bytes, or one sextillion bytes) or a trillion gigabytes (i.e., a million millions, or 1,000,000,000,000 or 10^{21}). That number grows as data spawns data.

In 2021, it would have taken a human around 181,300,000 (181.3 million) years to download all the information on the internet

In 2021, it would have taken a human around 181,300,000 (181.3 million) years to download all the information on the internet[2] and that doesn't include time to read it or to gain perspective on its usefulness. Still, to give some perspective, a 2015 study estimated that 15% of the video content on the internet is cat-related, and that it would take 2,250,000 lifetimes for a human to download everything on the internet.

In the legal profession, we do have a head start in terms of conceptualizing what Big Data actually is as we are a knowledge based communication profession that relies on concepts and the principle of "precedent", which is the original form of Big Data. Precedent requires us to look back at vast tomes of past legal decisions to indicate the likely outcome of further ones and inform arguments in respect of cases. Let's also not forget that, due to the need for social cohesion and societal compliance, we have reduced statutes to writing for centuries. In the legal field then, we "do" Big Data and always have.

As lawyers we know that all the legal knowledge in the world is useless without application. Again, "Big Data is not about the data" – it is about how it is used. Perhaps future academics (be they human or machine) will look on the Anthropocene age and will consider the strangeness of a human race that focused its combined intellect and creativity on memes and gifs and contemplate how things may have been different if we had realized sooner that the real win from Big Data is actually about big application.

In a previous version of this article (chapter four of the 2022 publication *Building the Data-Driven Law Firm*),[3] I considered what Big Data is, how "big" it actually is, how it is aggregated, how bias creeps in, and whether Big Data can be trusted. In this piece, I consider what happens when data users no longer trust the use of Big Data and the output on the internet is no longer considered accurate, reflective of its users, or representative of them; when data is commoditized; and when the environmental cost of processing becomes too high. These bite-size insights propose some themes, but are not exhaustive and the limited space in this article means they are not fully explored and are raised in the context of this work as a thought piece and proposed as "what ifs" for readers to consider.

I then briefly circle back on using Big Data in your firm, what could happen "when data bites back", how legal firms must change, and consider whether lawyers will become the arbitrators of unexpected AI decisions.

Sleeping Beauty and the Beast – the Big Data fairytale

The huge and hairy data beast that is circulated via the internet is all catalogued and stored. Massive repositories of both catalogued and unstructured data exist within data centres. The unstructured data that is not designated for use in a particular manner is held to build knowledge banks in future and in anticipation of not yet known use cases. This type of data is held in storage known as "data lakes". Smaller (much smaller) "data lakes" and knowledge repositories exist in almost all organizations – be they books on a shelf, precedent banks, or bankers' boxes that linger in the corner of a colleague's office long after they should have been archived. Some are more easily accessed than others and all of these seem manageable on a human scale. Big Data differs in that it is never managed by humans, never processed by them, and the vast scale of it is generally not within the bounds of imagination for most people. To try to understand the scale of a single data lake in a data centres, imagine tipping each piece of paper contained in all the books, files, and boxes into a giant recycling bin in your home and your office and, as you do so, watch each letter of every word slip off the page and into the bin, then visualise the blank pages shredding so that each impression left behind by an absent letter is also added to the bin and you will have an snapshot of a one-second flow into a data lake. Now, scale it up again and again and keep going until you think you might have to sit down because you are getting a migraine. By the end of a year of just imagining this, you *might* get a sense of the scale of information in a single data lake and an inkling of how big "Big Data" is.

All this unstructured data can be used, has been used, or might be used in future. Data aggregation is the process of creating some sort of organization from the raw data. To achieve that it is important to ensure the "right" data is chosen. Whether the data used is vast because it is being used to train AI or it is small because the information sought is specialist, to be useful (and therefore represent value for the efforts taken to collect and process it), the data has to be accurate, up to date, and unbiased.

Going back to a legal file analogy, the organized and sub-divided files in marked bankers' boxes, numbered sequentially, organized into pleadings, witness statements, versions of drafts, due diligence reports, disclosure letters, or any other way of organizing a file so that another fee-earner can pick them up if they need to are the analogue equivalent of aggregated data. Again, knowing which facts are relevant is key to understanding and using the data in the file or knowing what data to take from the data lake. The job of identifying the data and what can be gleaned from it is the job of the data analyst – the gate keepers of Big Data.

The enormity of Big Data has facilitated the growth in AI – an area now known to the general public (and even lawyers) through programs such as ChatGPT.

Although data privacy and data protection has been protected by various legislative mechanisms since at least 1998, it is incontrovertible that a good deal of it will have been collected without the data subjects' knowledge or specific consent. Whilst there is no blanket right to process data for "legitimate interests" under GDPR/Data Protection Act 2018, it certainly was the case for a long time that businesses relied on a "social contract" (generally in social media) that the free service offered was predicated on a freely given permission to use the data posted.

The enormity of Big Data has facilitated the growth in AI – an area now known to the general public (and even lawyers) through programs such as ChatGPT. The UK Centre for Data Ethics and Innovation (CDEI) publishes a regular "Attitudes to data and AI" survey[4] that monitors changes in public attitudes to use of AI over time and that supports both the private and public sectors to consider how to facilitate effective use of data and to foster AI ecosystems that engender public trust. The responses to the survey include ones from the 6% of the UK population that Ofcom[5] identifies as being in data or device poverty or who do not participate online due to limits on their ability to access the internet. CDEI concludes that the main concerns that remain in respect of data and use of it for AI are non-secure storage, hacking, data theft, and fear that data will be sold to organisations that profit from its use. Whilst 57% of those surveyed recognized the benefits apparent from using AI, only a third of respondents believed that there is equal benefit across society in use and output.

It is generally recognized that humans have innate bias and so the data that humans record and store will inevitably reflect that bias. That can be as simple as a data search term that becomes embedded in a program or a tick box that is binary in its nature (yes/no, male/female, full-time/part-time). This by its nature creates a problem of ethics in data and therefore credibility for lawyers in the data that they choose to use. How can the outcome ever be "right" if the input was not unbiased and correct? This then begs the question, is Big Data inherently valuable if it is not completely correct?

If people don't believe the data can be trusted at the point of collection, or the custodians of it cannot be trusted, then not only is there a huge trust deficit, but there is also potentially a gulf in what is actual, real, accurate, and honest when it comes to data.

Unfortunately, like history, data is often supplied and stored by the "victor" – the party in control of the equipment to record and store it, the party who believes it may have a future use, or the one who set the parameters of collection in the first place. Data bias is subtle and it is manifested in a million ways and when that is scaled in Big Data, it becomes pernicious. Without vigilance, the bias becomes embedded as a "norm" and goes unnoticed, until the decision output that is based upon it is delivered and is clearly wrong.

There are very valid concerns being raised, as much by the technology community as by leaden-feet Luddites, that if we hand over automated decision-making to AI justice and judges we still may not achieve fairness and consistency because of data bias. Until we can ensure outcomes that are at least as considered, explained, and consistent as those in current human-led courts, "fixing" our justice system by using Big Data and judgment via AI won't be as "smart" as we intend.

If people don't believe the data can be trusted at the point of collection, or the custodians of it cannot be trusted, then not only is there a huge trust deficit, but there is also potentially a gulf in what is actual, real, accurate, and honest when it comes to data. The ethics of data collection, the bias inherent in the data that is used to train AI and that has still not been remedied despite calls to do so for at least the last half-decade are beyond the scope of this short piece, but they are as fundamental to understanding why the best possible outcomes from data use are not yet achievable and will not be until we ensure full, correct, and representative data is available. In this, it is vital to also consider that all Big Data requires analysis to be useful (because "Big Data is not about the data") and there is a huge shortfall in the number of data analysts available compared to the scale of data that could be applied. If there are concerns about the data input and stored and there is a sparsity in the ability to output meaningful data, can the use cases that Big Data is applied to ever really meet or exceed our expectations – particularly in respect of AI? Many will tell you that AI is not as described and the stories about its use and impending dominance are make believe. It may be too that the fairytale for Big Data doesn't have a happy ending either and that "small data" may be the ending we want.

Data Bites

Every person has a right to personal sovereignty, dominion of thought, and protection of their private lives and privacy. If this sounds vaguely familiar, perhaps track back to the United Nations Declaration of Human Rights,[6] a law all lawyers learn about in law school, and every government, state, and individual should strive to align with and protect. Articles 12 and 22 are two I would choose to review as data collection and use encroaches on privacy and personal choice:

Article 12
No one shall be subjected to arbitrary interference with his privacy, family, home, or correspondence, nor to attacks upon his honour and reputation.

Everyone has the right to the protection of the law against such interference or attacks.

Article 22
Everyone, as a member of society, has the right to social security and is entitled to realization, through national effort and international co-operation and in accordance with the organization and resources of each State, of the economic, social, and cultural rights indispensable for his dignity and the free development of his personality.

You may have a different view, but what is clear is that data privacy is often disregarded, devalued, and denigrated as if consent to collection or accuracy are inconvenient obstacles to progress. When we consider data privacy is a civil right and abuse of that is a civil rights breach, we have to ask if we are approaching granting access to data in the right way.

In the UK, if privacy is breached, the Data Commissioner can fine the organization in breach of the Data Protection Act and the data subject can request compensation. There is a call that, coupled with that, there should be a right to privately prosecute data breaches, just as there is with defamation. The obvious disadvantage of this is cost and access to justice. If only those able to afford to bring and prosecute a claim can ever claim compensation for breach, then the right of private prosecution for data breach would fail to achieve its aims of protecting the vulnerable from unauthorized use by others. Worse, if "pay for privacy" schemes gain traction, then only those data subjects who can afford to withhold their data will do so. This segmentation in turn will lead to Big Data being collected only from those who cannot or choose not to pay for privacy, skewing the data sets further. Whilst it can generally be said that all data subjects have a right to opt out of data collection, it would be naïve to think that this means that only "permissioned" data is ever collected and processed. If data is collected without permission, can it ever be "right" and should it be trusted for training AI or used by data scientists?

Data really is everywhere and easy to obtain. More and more data is created every day and the ability to create and to retain data quickly and cheaply has meant that, more often than not, data is considered to have so little intrinsic value that the living individuals (data subjects) to whom it relates literally give it away. If a data subject is prepared to give away their information, surely those snippets have no value?

In the UK, if privacy is breached, the Data Commissioner can fine the organization in breach of the Data Protection Act and the data subject can request compensation.

There is a proposition that data subjects should be able to be paid for the data that is collected and processed by an organization – rather like a recording artist is paid a royalty every time their track is downloaded. Given the scale of data scraping, the sums available for data payments is likely to be miniscule and arguably the usefulness of data from one individual (in the absence of some rarity value) is minute compared to the value of vast data sets from which trends can be identified. This sets a low floor for the price per byte.

Another important issue is to consider how will each byte of data be valued and who will set the price for that? The companies that want to use the data have no incentive to offer a high value for it as it in any economy becomes a cost of business that is passed on to the consumer, likely obviating any gain the data subject will have made from monetizing their data in the first place! Another factor in setting the price arises when differentiating the value of data, particularly if the party purchasing it does not know what it might yield if it is sold on, aggregated and used, or simply warehoused. At the time of purchase it may not be possible to identify if the data is time-bound or evergreen. Either and all of these factors would affect the price and value of it. Data subjects might try to set a price or auction their data, particularly if they believe it is valuable, but without a USP for it, the metrics don't work and there is little chance of one person's data being worth significantly more than another's. If it is the case that an individual's data genuinely is rarer, or more valuable for some particular reason, this could create a whole sub-class of those who suffer "data poverty" by not being able to either sell or auction their data, or having no "premium" to attach to it.

In a scenario where data is treated as a commodity rather than a human or a civil right, regulating use of that commodity in an open market is much more difficult to do at a state or societal level.

In a scenario where data is treated as a commodity rather than a human or a civil right, regulating use of that commodity in an open market is much more difficult to do at a state or societal level. Both developed and emerging economies have a dire record of identifying, pursuing, and prosecuting market abuses and there seems very little chance that the scenario would be different for data. If regulation is imposed at a state level it is difficult to see how that could be policed or monitored for abuse without the obvious intrusions on self and freedom of conscience that would involve. If different societies choose to commoditize data and individuals are able to charge for its use, pernicious self-interest will doubtlessly win the human race to the bottom, which again calls into question issues around whether data that is commoditized can be trusted as true, accurate, complete, or current, where the incentive to supply it is monetary gain.

Could blockchain help to monetise personal data by making it true and trusted? The scandals around loss of electronic currency and the "snake oil" of digital tokens, NFTs, and many other projects have severely impacted trust in a system that uses distributed ledgers to create that which was invented to reboot trust, validation, and immutability. Putting our personal data into the blockchain in any meaningful way would almost certainly compromise it in terms of security (due to the distributed nature of blockchain), and the fact that it cannot be changed might undermine its value. Added to this, the cost of creating an operating blockchain system – both in terms of finance and the environmental and sustainability concerns about blockchain mining and operations – almost certainly indicates that this is not yet the correct repository for data.

Big Data; dark skies

There are 11,000 or so physical internet data centres in the world, with an average size of about 100,000 square metres each. The number of hyperscale centres is growing annually, with the floorspace of such behemoths usually well over 900,000 sqm. As nations that have traditionally encouraged the location of "warehouses" consider the environmental footprint of data centres (such as Singapore's three-year moratorium on new centres) and require operators to demonstrate how land, water, and renewable energy will be used, reused, and sustained, there has been a shift in location of "hyperscale" centres to emerging markets (such as sub-Saharan Africa, south-east Asia, south America, and Australia). Here, operators and construction companies can acquire land and self-build with encouragement and financial incentives offered by local government and telecoms companies that recognize the income available from the knowledge economy and may not have the environmental or regulatory constraints of developed markets.

Every square metre in an internet data centre uses approximately one megawatt of energy per hour to process the data stored in its confines; 60 MWph is 1,440MWpd at 11,000 centres is 15,840,000 megawatts (or 15.8 terrawatts) of energy per day worldwide to feed us with on demand cat videos (other pet-related content is available).

Terrawatts of energy only really have meaning to a few people in the industry and the scale of this might be hard to comprehend, so it is probably easier to note that, annually, energy use by data centres accounted for four percent of global energy consumption in 2023 and for two percent of annual greenhouse gas emissions worldwide. This may feel like a small price to pay for a world of knowledge and entertainment at our fingertips, but given that internet data grows endlessly, as hypercentres move into the realms of processing zettabytes of data daily, we have to ask whether this is sustainable in terms not just of energy use but also the wider spectrum of "consumption". If the answer to this query is no, what happens next?

The main use of power in data centres is for cooling. As summer temperatures soar across the planet, over half of the data centres worldwide have experienced a weather-related outage. Whilst most data centres do not operate at capacity every day, complete equipment failure and a full-scale internet crash is therefore unlikely. As the data processed increases and high-performance computing and AI/ML applications become mainstream, new ways of building data centres with higher heat dissipation standards have to be found.

Whether that will be by building hypercentres under the sea in off-shore centres or applying liquid cooling methods with thousands of times the heat transfer properties of air cooling systems, it is becoming increasingly necessary to insulate data centres against the global warming extremes that the collection, processing, and storage of Big Data has contributed to causing.

Big Data's value-add

The ability to bring together and aggregate data and the use of data-driven AI is huge for the legal profession. Big Data not only brings new opportunities to interrogate data and determine outcomes using it (data scientists call this semantics, which will doubtlessly chime with most lawyers!), but also signals massive change in the profession as data access is wider and predicting outcomes and making determinations are handed over to AI.

In a recent US case I was involved in, US counsel believed there may be inherent bias in the case being heard in the state where the claimant's business had been established and looked for an opportunity to request that the hearing be moved to another state.

In submitting that advice, the US attorney provided the client with details of the outcome of every case determined by the allocated judge in the state where the proceedings were issued and those of the judges who had the necessary specialism and availability in the listings in the state the client indicated they wished to move proceedings to.

The ability to bring together and aggregate data and the use of data-driven AI is huge for the legal profession.

The client was presented with comparable cases, outcomes of cases on similar facts, and on ones with similar facts in dissimilar industries, details of where the judges qualified, their professional life prior to joining the judiciary, where their clerks had studied, and with whom they had worked.

Based on that information, the client chose to apply for a transfer of the case and was successful. The client then secured a listing with a judge whose background they knew and whose industry-specific knowledge they believed would be more aligned with their respondent's case in this claim and who had recommended judge-led mediation in well over half of the cases they had heard. The client then moved for mediation and the matter was settled.

This is a simple example of the use of comparative data to make an informed decision. It wasn't Big Data, but it was smart and helpful, and provided significant value-add to a case where negotiations had stalled.

Overtly or otherwise, lawyers have been doing this sort of research – reading cases and predicting outcomes then packaging it for clients – for years. Lawyers who are considered great are mostly those that can draw on past knowledge to guide future decisions and who seem to be able to "predict" the outcome of a case simply by reading a file. It is, however, a skill that is learned and not simply an inherent and mythic quality of second sight or indicator of vast intellect.

Can a lawyer who has handed over advice to AI avoid responsibility for the output of that program, or shift responsibility onto the technology provider, which provides the means for the advice to be given?

Now, anyone with access to Big Data can make these evaluations and all law firms should be using data in this way. This surely has to be better than relying solely on the partner or associate who seems to have a charmed run in litigation or always seems to be able to predict how a deal will go and swears it's about reading body language.

Are Big Data and smart data a "value add" that lawyers can use to differentiate their practice from other firms? The truth is this is less likely to be a differentiator than how you choose to use it.

Marketing a firm on the basis that it uses Big Data could be one of your least exciting marketing campaigns ever – right there alongside "we are experts" in its bland, self-congratulatory assertions. Marketing your business as "successful in 98% of cases" is an attention seeking, interest grabbing winner though, at least initially. People love the certainty of statistics, even when they don't fully understand them, and if statistics seem inherently trustworthy, a lawyer with good stats is doubly so. That type of assertion and campaign won't last though and the truth will out if the 98% comes from only ever managing two cases!

By virtue of their international reach and scale, as well as the number of transactions and client engagements undertaken, large firms have the jump on smaller ones when it comes to transactional history to create proprietary aggregated Big Data. It is not necessary, however, to draw only on your own firm's data to create value-add for clients. The type of metrics such as "likely outcomes of court cases in this field" and "average awards" from deal logs and blogs, insurance providers, as well as across multiple agencies and sectors, versus negative outcomes including fines and penalties, accident and injury reports, board reports, and published audits are all available, meaning you can present clients with real choices, determine a risk-based preferred outcome, and offer them data-backed choices about their next move.

Expect every sizeable law firm to have data strategists and data scientists as part of their "knowledge" resource by the end of the decade. "Tech support" won't just be for the "Help, I think I've broken it" moment when the DMS goes down – it will include data engineers who provide case support of the type currently undertaken by armies of paralegals, trainees, newly qualified, and associate lawyers. In one act of logging-on, the paper-based research of such teams will seem as arcane as affixing a wax seal on engrossment paper or sewing briefs for counsel.

When data bites back

Can a lawyer who has handed over advice to AI avoid responsibility for the output of that program, or shift responsibility onto the technology provider, which provides the means for the advice to be given? Is providing those means sufficient to make the tech company responsible for the output from its program, particularly if the advice seems "bad"?

This naturally raises the question, what is "bad advice"? Whilst some advice might seem to all reasonable people to be "bad", the subjective nature of advice can often mean that it is hard to tell if, in the circumstances, the advice would have been materially different if it had been given by someone else, or whether the application and timing of the advice and the circumstances in which it was given now make it appear, with even a slight degree of hindsight, to be bad. What is clear is that if clients are to accept advice based on Big Data or judicial decisions based on algorithmic assessment, they are going to want to ensure that they can seek recompense when the data bites back.

This circles us back to how the insurance industry

uses AI and whether it can predict and scope the failings of AI, accept its limitations, and apportion blame to a non-corporeal "thinking" entity such as AI or its supplier. If so, the insurance industry should be able to provide indemnity cover that will allow use of the practical applications of Big Data that the justice system and lawyers need. Whilst this may then seem like a case of "marking its own homework", the insurance industry will need to provide extended or possibly much more specific cover for AI advice or algorithmic decisions when it is not possible to identify the original data source, or even if it is, when the advice output appears to be well-made, but bad advice.

AI and the trusted advisor

In his excellent 2019 book, *Online Courts and the Future of Justice*, Richard Susskind[7] cautions that it is not enough to simply replicate the current judicial system by implementing technology to, in effect, mechanize the current, largely broken, system. He warns that the use of technology must be applied in place of the courts, and even the professionals who advise and profess in them. I agree with the former point but diverge on his latter.

Susskind argues that lawyers are not an inherent or even necessary part of the legal process, and that the role of a "trusted advisor" is not one that needs to be performed by a human. Instead, he anticipates this can be performed by a machine. Yes, it is undoubtedly true that, fed with Big Data, AI is excellent at predicting likely outcomes when applied to legal cases in courts. Such programs can divine strategies and could provide accessible, reliable, consistent, and certain outcomes for applicants, but just as there is mistrust of "fat cat lawyers", there is also suspicion and mistrust of decisions made by algorithms.

Even with planned and in force UK, EU, and US accountability for algorithms acts, we still have a long way to go to enforce standards for transparency in such algorithmic decision-making and, more fundamentally, ensuring that Big Data is unbiased when it is used.

The insurance industry has, perhaps predictably, been an early adopter of Big Data, along with the medical profession. This should not be surprising given that assessing likely outcomes and risk are key in both professions.

In insurance, Big Data and AI are used to analyze and predict trends rather than relying on outdated demographic and social data. It has allowed the industry to use powerful tools that predict customer behaviors, likelihood of claims, and buying engagement, as well as to develop new, more targeted, products.

The insurance industry has, perhaps predictably, been an early adopter of Big Data, along with the medical profession. This should not be surprising given that assessing likely outcomes and risk are key in both professions.

Medtech is massive and segmented, running the gamut of technologies to manage hospitals to those that provide predictive diagnosis, research insights, and lines of enquiry for targeted drug treatment. Wearable medtech already facilitates real-time health tracking and drug administration, all enabled by predictive analysis of Big Data sets.

If we consider the application of Big Data to law, it is easy to see an application for it in "pre-crime", which identifies signaling behaviors and indicates steps that can be taken to prevent a single or multiple signaling individuals from committing a criminal offence or even a breach of contract. Future law practitioners also see applications to the legal system and automated algorithmic justice, not just existing processes "pimped" by AI. Law though, like medicine and insurance, has to deal with life's "what-ifs?" and with those who challenge the status quo. Any AI "pre-crime" model would have to factor that in also. We may feel that a sense of justice cannot be programmed into a machine, but we arrive at that from our own inputs and experiences, just as AI will.

Outliers

At the end, are "outliers". These are the oddities and peculiar outputs from AI programs stuffed full of Big (or little) Data. In statistical analysis, outliers are the upper and lower boundaries of information that sit beyond the usual distribution range of expected results. Often, they arise due to human error, experimental errors or skews in the data, or from lack of clarity in the data sets used. Outliers may be discarded when analysis of them is undertaken but there are instances, particularly in AI, where the outlier is outside of the normal expected results but it remains a valid measurement.

Two notable examples of outliers arise in tactical games played against computers. In the 1997 "Re-Match" of Deep Blue v. Kasparov, Deep Blue played an unexpected move that led to Kasparov resigning the match. Kasparov alleged that the move could not possibly have been suggested by Deep Blue and was in fact a play proposed by a rival Grandmaster working with IBM who had overridden Deep Blue to make the play. Further analysis indicated that the move made by Deep Blue was in fact based on a bug – faced with multiple options for play and no clear choice that would lead to a win, the program chose a random move. If the game had continued, it would have resulted in a perpetual check (adding credibility to the "no clear preference" explanation). It was the AI equivalent of rolling a polyhedron decision-making dice!

In 2017, Google's AlphaGo beat world number one Go player, Ke Jie in all three match games. Ke Jie later commented that he was shocked by a move Alpha-Go made that "would never happen in a human-to-human Go match". That move was another outlier – or was it learnt, if unexpected, "behavior"?

Simply because a result is beyond the normal expectation of a human decision does not mean that it is an unreasonable one to make or that it is not a well-considered, evidence-based one either. In these situations, how to deal with an outlier may

Definitions and interpretation

- **Big Data:** A marketing term that has entered common parlance, meaning unimaginably massive amounts of data from innumerable sources.
- **Data aggregation:** This is not just pooling data, it is the action of compiling data from various sources and preparing it for real world use or summarizing it into an understandable format.
- **Data anonymization:** Scrubbing data so that individuals can't be identified, private information is removed, and location and source data is extinguished (unless that is required).
- **Data bias:** An error in data caused by favoring, selecting, or testing or recording one particular outcome over another.
- **Data lakes:** A storage area where data is pooled to create an information swamp. It may help to consider this as a primordial data swamp, from which Smart Data can "evolve".
- **Developers:** people who work with data and know more about it than any lawyer is ever likely to. The following subsets of Developers are included in this definition, but these are subject to change as the field changes and grows. DevOps engineers generally develop platforms to manage data. Data engineers prepare Big Data for analysis and apply it to use cases. Data scientists measure the value of the Big Data models and analysis undertaken by the data engineers. Data strategists find new uses for the Big Data and smart data. Expect to be baffled by these monikers and for them to be used indiscriminately, but also in practice confuse them at your peril.
- **Outlier:** A piece of data that is detached from the main body of work that may share a source with other data, but that differs significantly from other data and effects a different result or output. Taken from the phrase coined by Malcolm Gladwell in his book *Outliers*, published in 2008, and not about Big Data.
- **Raw data:** Data that has not been structured and is unorganized and generally difficult for humans to read and (crucially) see patterns in.
- **Smart data:** Big Data that is verified, organized, formatted, and contextualized so that it is ready to be applied to a Big Data use case.

come down to human intervention and instinct – the spark of the person who can ask "what if it's right?" of insight or possibly even instinct that makes a synaptic connection in a human that is decisive in a strategy.

Sometimes an outlier is acceptably disruptive and informs a new way of working or changes our perspective on how something should be done and, on closer inspection, its validity is clear. Obviously, the decision about how to deal with outliers depends on the use-case, the context of the output, and it requires knowledge of how it was arrived at. Assessing that and the value of an outlier in that context is simply part of the processing process that a lawyer using AI will need to undertake.

When the outlier, or the "Minority Report", is issued, lawyers will need to step forward and be ready, willing, and able to debate it in the real-world based on really good smart data. In this respect, perhaps the future of the legal profession does lie beyond being a trusted advisor and will move to become one of moderator of advice provided by an AI program?

Now retired from play, Ke Jie commented on AlphaGo's playing capabilities, acknowledging that he had once been its equal but no longer was. He said, "[AlphaGo] sees the whole universe, while what we see is just a pond in front of us". Frankly, I couldn't sum up Big Data and its applications and limitations from a human view point any better.

Joanne Brook works at Lionshead Law, a firm that has been an entirely digital practice for over a decade. She works on complex contracts and advises clients on protecting their innovative technology. One of the first women solicitors in the City to specialize in advising businesses on IT law, Joanne has been through many business cycles with her clients and seen numerous technologies lauded as the "next big thing". From this perspective she considers the future of law, statute, and the legal profession. Joanne is a published authority on law and technology and business development for lawyers.

1 https://gking.harvard.edu/presentations/big-data-not-about-data-12
2 Unicorn Insights and Tech Jury, https://techjury.net/blog/big-data-statistics/#gref
3 *Building the Data-Driven Law Firm*, second edition, 2022, Globe Law and Business, www.globelawandbusiness.com/books/building-the-data-driven-law-firm-second-edition
4 www.gov.uk/government/publications/public-attitudes-to-data-and-ai-tracker-survey
5 www.ofcom.org.uk/research-and-data/multi-sector-research/accessibility-research/access-and-inclusion/exclusion
6 www.un.org/en/about-us/universal-declaration-of-human-rights
7 *Online Courts and the Future of Justice*, Richard Susskind, 2019. Oxford University Press.

Milton Keynes UK
Ingram Content Group UK Ltd.
UKHW051836131124
451109UK00008B/82

9 781837 230556